Truth or Consequences

" When history is wrong,
we have lived a lie,
whether we created it or
we inherited it.

Those who fabricate the lie,
as my generation did, must
fix it or tell our children that
truth doesn't matter.

We must seek to make
history right or we sully
our children's heritage."

- Dave O'Brien, Author
Through the 'Oswald' Window

* Opening Slide of author's
JFK assassination seminar

Through the 'Oswald' Window

Table of Contents

Chapter 4 - The 'Magic' Bullet!

The Bullet They Say Acted Alone
So That History Could Say
Lee Harvey Oswald Acted Alone

- The 'Single Bullet Theory.'
- Magic or Ordinary Bullet?
- The Biggest Possible Problem
- A History Altering Incision
- Quoted Out of Context
- Analysis of Dr. Perry Letter
- Evidence Not Well 'Suited'
- A Bullet's Magical Change in Direction
- Less Magical, But Still Extraordinary
- Historical Mystery or Fact?

Chapter 5 - The Bizarre JFK Autopsy
that Failed History and the Truth

- More Questions Than Answers
- History's Profound Loss
- Military Takeover
- Medical Malfeasance
- Consequences of a 'Military' Autopsy
- The Phone Call That Changed History
- Shocking Disclosure
- New Wound, New Conclusion
- Creation of a 'Magic' Bullet

Chapter 6 - The Zapruder Film:

The Shocking 26-Second Home Movie that Won't Let History Be a Lie!

- The Film That Won't Let Us Forget
- Researchers Do What Media Won't
- Seeing is Disbelieving
- A Frame by Frame Look
- Zapruder Frame 194
- Zapruder Frame 223Zapruder Frame 225
- Zapruder Frame 230
- Zapruder Frame 236
- Zapruder Frame 256
- Zapruder Frame 300
- Zapruder Frame 312
- Zapruder Frame 313
- Zapruder Frame 330
- Zapruder Frame 344
- Zapruder Frame 370
- Zapruder Frame 397
- History Merely Delayed?

Chapter 7 – The Top 8 Indicators That the Fatal Shot Did Come from the Grassy Knoll

- Flash of Light
- Eyewitnesses
- Silent Witnesses or Witnesses Silenced?
- Eyewitnesses
- What History Sounds Like
- The 'Oswald' Window
- Entering a Crossfire
- JFK's Violent Backward Head Movement
- Mrs. Kennedy's Instinctive Reaction

Chapter 10 - The Mysterious Deaths of More than 100 People Linked to the JFK Assassination

Chapter 11 - 12:30 p.m. CST:

What Happened in Those Six Seconds That Changed American History Forever?

- What If?
- Warren Commission's Findings
- Shot #1
- Shot #2
- Shot #3
- The HSCA Findings
- Sequence and Results of FOUR Shots
- Modern Day Perspective
- Supplemental Conclusions – Lee Harvey Oswald
- Not an Assassin
- The Set-Up
- The "Patsy"
- The Murderer
- Enter Jack Ruby
- The Planter
- The Stalker
- The Silencer
- The Association
- CIA Rebels
- Sequence and Results of FOUR Shots Fired from Three Locations
- Shot #1
- Shot #2
- Shot #3
- Shot #4
- Why We May Never Know the Truth

Chapter 12 - Oswald, Ruby and the Robert Kennedy Revenge Alliance that Assassinated JFK

- Two Conspiracies
- A Most Clandestine Alliance
- Comrade Oswaldovich?
- The Oswald-Marcello-Ruby Connection
- Marcello – Kennedy Bad Blood
- 'Goomba' Santo and Sam
- Ultimate Betrayal
- Gamble Doesn't Pay Off
- Change of Target
- Enter Lee Harvey Oswald
- Ponder This
- Another Oswald - Marcello Link
- The Ruby Mob Connection
- Suspicious Phone Calls
- Ruby – Marcello Link
- RFK Jr. Stunner
- Phone Tap Confession
- The Cuba Connection
- CIA Rebels
- The Hidden CIA
- In Search of a Conclusion

Sources and References

Live Links Access

For quick and easy access to links to resources listed in this book, go to:

www.throughtheoswaldwindow.com/resources

Appendices:

  * Dr. Malcolm Perry Letters – 1968 & 1972

  * Donation of Dr. Perry Letters to Sixth Floor Museum at Dealey Plaza

  * The Mississauga News – February 21, 1979 – Black Day in Dallas 15 Years Later

About the Author – More than 50 years as a JFK Assassination researcher, reporter and lecturer to more than 250,000 people.

E-Book Edition – Through The 'Oswald' Window is also available as an e-book for all electronic devices. Available at www.ThroughTheOswaldWindow.com.

Facebook - Please Like us on Facebook - https://www.facebook.com/ThroughTheOswaldWindow/

Through the 'Oswald' Window

Introduction

A History Changing 'Ah-Ha' Moment!

John F. Kennedy - 35th U.S. President

February 11, 1979 was my life-altering 'Ah-Ha' moment.

The moment was so profound, it set me on an exhilarating career path. It changed my belief system. It started what has become more than a 50-year remarkable journey.

My 'Ah-Ha' moment was so astonishing; the JFK assassination became my official personal project as a journalist.

There are JFK assassination researchers who have contributed much more than an 'Ah-Ha' moment to the most controversial crime in American history.

They have slowly, but surely, contributed to truth prevailing over fiction and cover-up.

This book pays homage to the likes of Penn Jones Jr., Mary Ferrell, Mark Lane, Robert J. Groden (see right) and Dr. Cyril Wecht, to name just a few independent researchers.

The truth owes a lot of gratitude to film and photo expert Robert Groden.

These people put careers and reputations on the line back when challengers of the Warren Report were labelled as "nutty conspiracy theorists."

Since age 13, I have been a JFK assassination conspiracy theorist, subject to scorn and ridicule, but nothing like my American colleagues. In Canada, I presented my dissenting views in newspaper articles and seminars mostly to audiences with an open mind.

"UNIQUE PERSPECTIVE"

There are hundreds of books on the JFK assassination either in support of Lee Harvey Oswald acting alone or just about any conspiracy you can fathom, so why another book?

It is precisely this glut of information and misinformation that kept me on the literary sidelines until now.

Time Magazine proclaims Oswald as the lone assassin.

Then my brother Paul pointed out in 2016 that I have a unique perspective that very few people can bring to the discussion, not even most of my esteemed colleagues mentioned above.

On February 11, 1979, I was given rare access to the so-called 'Oswald Window' in the Book Depository Building (next page) when it was vacant, locked and sealed from curiosity seekers. I recount that incredible experience in Chapter 1.

When I stepped into the shoes of the assassin just as if I was looking over his shoulder on November 22, 1963, I was stunned at what I observed. I'll never forget the 'Ah-Ha' moment that overwhelmed me:

> *If I was a lone assassin obsessed with killing the President of the United States, this was a terrible vantage point from which to shoot!*

Correction…

This wasn't just a poor location for an assassin in Dealey Plaza. It wasn't even a smart sniper's perch inside the Book Depository Building where Oswald worked!

A BETTER 'OSWALD' WINDOW

A shooter could have just as easily set up his lair from the '*southwest*' corner window on the sixth floor instead of the southeast corner of the building as Oswald is said to have done.

And this vantage point just a few seconds away from the 'Oswald' window seems to solve some logistical problems for a lone wolf assassin as I detail in Chapter 1.

The author at the 'Oswald' southeast corner window. Can you already see a problem an assassin would have firing from this vantage point?

If I could make these observations in several minutes, plus other disturbing revelations from the 'Oswald window' noted in Chapters 1 and 11, it raises a hypothetical, yet provocative question:

How is it possible that this site was not thoroughly scouted and evaluated by a lone assassin looking for the best place to await JFK's arrival in Dealey Plaza?

Had this 'homework' been done in advance of President Kennedy's visit to Dallas, as you would think it was, it is hard to believe that a 'lone assassin' would have chosen this window as his ideal sniper's perch.

Have you noticed that I have not definitively named Lee Harvey Oswald as the assassin who fired from the 'Oswald' Window?

We know that someone shot President Kennedy from the window at which I stood (page 4). Unlike many of my fellow researchers, I believe that Oswald was involved in the assassination.

However, other observations from my time at this historic site suggest that Oswald could *not* have been the shooter from the window named after him.

Nor could Lee Harvey Oswald have been the *only* shooter in Dealey Plaza that tragic day.

For me, the 'Ah-Ha' moments I experienced in 1979 would come full circle in 1983 when I viewed altered photographic evidence the Warren Commission didn't intend for us to see until 2038.

One of the more alarming examples of the Warren Commission altering evidence is how they edited this picture of JFK under fire. Chapter 11 divulges the cover-up effort.

This photograph (left) brought me back to Dealey Plaza in 1983, where a second 'Ah-Ha' moment changed everything.

As disclosed fully in Chapter 11, it becomes clear why the Warren Commission decided not to publish this version of the photo by AP photographer/reporter James Altgens.

Instead, a severely cropped version of this photo appears in the Warren Report that conceals no less than three different indicators of why shots may have come from as many as two locations in addition to the infamous 'Oswald' window.

Keep in mind that the Commission believed all documents and evidence available to it would be sealed and withheld from the public for 75 years.

In the full photo above, when compared to the altered image in Chapter 11 that the government thought you should see, can you pick out any of the three hidden indicators of other possible shot locations?

Chapter 11 discusses several other blatant attempts by the Commission to disregard, discredit and even alter witness testimony, as well as both medical and ballistics findings that didn't fit its one-assassin agenda.

JFK LINKED DEATH RE-OPENED

More than 50 years ago, celebrity Dorothy Kilgallen was found dead in her Manhattan apartment.

Her death was ruled a suicide from alcohol and barbiturate poisoning. Friends always questioned her death, noting:

- Ms. Kilgallen was not a drug user in any way.

- She was on the verge of breaking what she herself called "an earth-shattering" story.

Why would celebrity/reporter Dorothy Kilgallen take her own life when she was about to become even more famous for her Jack Ruby exclusive?

Dorothy Kilgallen was famous at the time of her death. She was not only a respected newspaper reporter, she was a regular panelist on the popular TV game show 'What's My Line.'

Just before her sudden death, Kilgallen got an exclusive that any journalist would envy – a private interview with Oswald killer Jack Ruby.

As you have probably surmised, Kilgallen never got to publish her major scoop after the Ruby interview. And her notes from that session were never found.

Chapter 10 delves into the Kilgallen-Ruby connection as well as more than 100 deaths linked to the JFK assassination, ranging from natural causes to strange accidents and even unsolved murders.

However, the ill-timed death of Dorothy Kilgallen has resurfaced. In a January 29, 2017 report in the New York Post, New York District Attorney Cyrus Vance Jr. announced that this controversial cold case has been re-opened based on discovered new evidence.

ULTIMATE COLD CASE

With two conflicting government versions about what happened that horrific day in Dallas, the Warren Report (1964) and the House Select Committee on Assassinations (1979), the JFK assassination remains officially unsolved.

Nobody has been brought to justice for the President's murder.

As explored in Chapter 3, it can be argued that Jack Ruby faced justice, but his sordid mafia and police connections leave us with compelling unanswered questions about his silencing of Oswald.

Part of what keeps the JFK assassination so topical despite the passage of time is that it's controversies makes it the ultimate cold case.

Polls by Time Magazine and other news outlets consistently identify the JFK assassination at the top of the list of America's most enduring conspiracy theories.

THE OSWALD ENIGMA

This book breaks ranks with many of my fellow conspiracy theorists.

When Lee Harvey Oswald declared "I'm just a patsy" in the last hours of his life, he was mostly right.

Chapter 2 argues that Oswald was set up as the fall guy, to be forever known as the lone assassin of President Kennedy even though he may not have fired a shot that day.

Oswald bought this Italian weapon that soldiers called "The friendly rifle" because it could "never hurt anyone on purpose."

However, to say that Oswald was a model boy scout who was innocently framed also distorts history. As you will read, Oswald had no trouble with at least trying to take a life even before being accused of killing Dallas police officer J.D. Tippit 46 minutes after JFK was shot.

Oswald came very close to being a serial killer, but in my view, that does not include the President of the United States.

DO YOU BELIEVE IN MAGIC?

Magic is the art of illusion and deception, both of which we find in great abundance as it relates to the JFK assassination.

Chapter 4 attempts to unravel the truth behind one of the greatest deceptions of all time – the flight of The 'Magic' Bullet!

Imagine having to invent an implausible theory in order to make a scenario plausible.

That is what the Warren Commission did when it ignored its own ballistics tests and other scientific data to say that both President Kennedy and Governor Connally's non-fatal wounds were inflicted by a single bullet.

The problem isn't just that this 'Magic Bullet' is required to cause seven wounds on two men, including two major broken bones, and look almost as if it has yet to be fired.

What makes this bullet magical in Chapter 4 is its remarkable flightpath, including two sudden changes of direction in mid-

With Kramer as JFK and Newman as Connally, this Jerry Seinfeld episode parodies the 'Magic Bullet' theory.

air, as well as a pause of nearly a second in mid-air between the two victims.

And yet without this 'Magic Bullet' doing what is ascribed to it by the Commission and the House Select Committee on

Assassinations 15 years later, the entire lone assassin foundation comes crashing down into a pile of make believe history.

ARCANE AUTOPSY

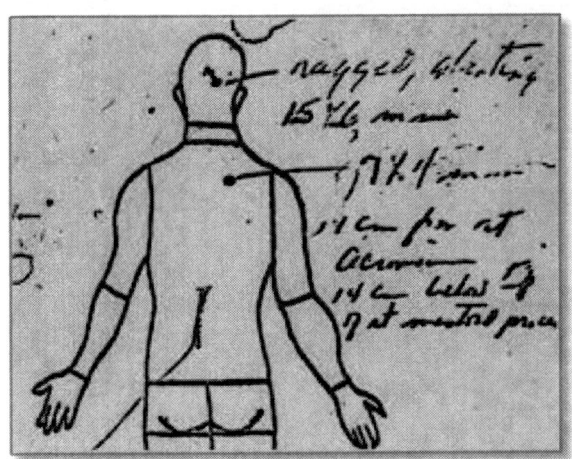

This official autopsy chart shows the measured entry wound in JFK's back, but this wound would mysteriously move up to enable the 'Single Bullet Theory.'

You or I would be entitled to a competent forensic post-mortem examination if our death was by violent means or suspicious in any way.

How are we to explain that the **President of the United States** was not given this same basic right?

Chapter 5 disturbingly conducts a post-mortem on President Kennedy's autopsy. In the interests of truth and fact, the underpinnings of such a procedure, this historic post-mortem fails miserably.

With the help of one of the world's leading forensic pathologists, Dr. Cyril Wecht, who has reviewed the original medical records, this chapter presents a bad ending to a sad day in America.

Before a grieved nation awoke on November 23, 1963, a terribly flawed autopsy would distort the truth and suppress the facts of what happened to it's President.

This chapter will anger you, but don't let your anger be directed at the unqualified surgeons tasked to perform JFK's autopsy.

Dr. Humes, Dr. Boswell and Dr. Finck were put in an impossible situation. Military superiors at the autopsy ordered that routine procedures not be undertaken.

Dr. Finck has testified under oath that military superiors present at the autopsy would not permit him to examine the President's back wound. Given the importance of this wound to the official findings, not to mention the controversy it would generate, this is appalling!

Civilian forensic pathologists, like Dr. Cyril Wecht, could not have been ordered to forgo such standard post-mortem procedures.

Tragically, the President's body was placed in the hands of three men who had never conducted a post-mortem involving death caused by one or more gunshots.

It is hard to imagine that this severely flawed autopsy would have helped to convict Lee Harvey Oswald as the lone assassin had it been presented in a court of law and subject to skilled questioning.

HOW TO BECOME A CONSPIRACY THEORIST

For those of you visiting the JFK assassination for the first time, like many of the people who attended my seminars, this book will help you cut through the maze of information on the Internet.

If you are looking for evidence of Oswald's solitary guilt, you are in the wrong place.

One advancement we have made over these many years is the high probability that Oswald did not act alone. He had confederates.

Starting from this premise, this book makes the case for conspiracy throughout.

In Chapter 12, I endeavor to answer the why, who and how.

Based on the latest information available, the conspiratorial nature of the assassination is presented in the closing chapter, as well as the names of those believed to have been involved.

But do not skip to the end. Each chapter along the way contributes to the alarming scenario proposed.

When all is said and done, you may be left wondering if more than 50 years of secrecy and cover-up was necessary or remains in the best interests of the American people to this very day.

Life Magazine bought the Zapruder film, then decided to show an edited version to the public in support of the Warren Report.

SIX SECONDS OF ENDLESS CONTROVERSY

As Chapter 6 establishes, a mere six seconds of time has morphed into decades of ceaseless mind-numbing debate.

The famous Zapruder film proves that what we see isn't necessarily what we are told. Such is the nature of unsolved conspiracies.

We must remember that the Zapruder film was not shown to the public for a dozen years.

This gave the 'Oswald alone' advocates more than a decade head start in the all-important court of public opinion.

But when the graphic film first aired in 1975 and clearly shows the President's head violently thrust **backward** upon impact, we were doubly shocked by what we saw.

Not only do we see the horrific result of the head shot, we see visual evidence of this shot NOT coming from the 'Oswald' window above and behind the limousine!

From that moment, the Warren Report has continued to lose credibility, as you will discover by the time you get to Chapter 11.

Chapter 6 presents you with an opportunity to view the Zapruder film in full time, as well as slow-motion and enhanced versions of the moments of controversy.

Still frames are also presented and analyzed to further discuss matters of contention. Accordingly, the graphic nature of this chapter is not suitable for persons under the age of 19.

EVIDENCE BE DAMNED!

Thanks to the Zapruder film dissected in Chapter 6, there is need for Chapter 9, which shockingly reveals some of the evidence that demands a shot from the infamous grassy knoll that was covered up by the government.

More alarmingly, it demonstrates that the Commission was not interested from the outset at finding a second gunman in Dealey Plaza.

Some of this conspiracy-suggestive evidence was discredited by the Commission as simply unreliable due to the trauma of the moment. That is easy to do with eyewitnesses, but what about unemotional medical and ballistics evidence?

Even after the purposeful mishandling of the President's autopsy, you will be astounded to learn in Chapter 9 that the Warren Commission had to ignore some of the very tests it directed the FBI to conduct.

And when it encountered physical evidence that did not support the single assassin concept, the Commission either altered the evidence or even tried to suppress it outright for the 75-year ban that was imposed by President Lyndon Johnson.

ON THE GRASSY KNOLL

Every day, people make a pilgrimage to Dealey Plaza and the infamous grassy knoll.

For years, the grassy knoll has become a ridiculing metaphor for anything conspiratorial.

How often have you heard the grassy knoll referenced in jest when someone proposes an alternate theory to consider on any topic?

"Oh sure, just like the grassy knoll," someone will retort to suggest the absurdity of your thought.

After reading Chapter 7, perhaps a grassy knoll reference should be used to prove that myth can be fact.

When we look at the unscripted and instinctive reactions that occurred to several people during the shots in Dealey Plaza, we see distinct evidence of a shot from the right-front of JFK.

These instances come from people who thought they were in the line of fire, as well as people who physically reacted in a way that verifies that the kill shot could only have come from the grassy knoll.

What separates these key witnesses from others in Dealey Plaza is that 'trauma of the moment' excuse the Commission often used to dismiss unwanted testimony cannot be applied here.

These witnesses didn't just react to what they saw or heard in those six seconds of horror, they had a physical reaction just as true as the President did to the bullets that struck him.

And doesn't it make sense that we cannot accept the possibility of a third assassin until we accept the possibility of a second assassin? Herein lies the power of Chapter 7.

UNEXPLAINED ODDITIES

Even if President Kennedy had survived the Dallas attack and went on to serve a full eight years in the White House, we might still be talking about several unexplained occurrences that day.

The Umbrella Man mystery has been solved, but his explanation remains suspicious.

Why would an unidentified police motorcycle cop suddenly leave the motorcade route after initiating the fateful turn onto Houston Street?

Why would one man unfurl a large black umbrella on a rainless day only for the six seconds it took for the shooting sequence?

Why were as many as 11 people arrested in Dealey Plaza after the shooting only to be released without any police records of them being brought in and questioned as witnesses or persons of interest?

At least two of these arrested suspects may be two notorious CIA characters associated with the Watergate break-in nine years later.

Chapter 8 explores several oddities that mostly remain unexplained after several decades.

And although we now know who the mysterious 'Umbrella Man' is, his explanation is highly suspect and does not answer why his actions, as shown on the Zapruder film, happen to correspond with the span of the shots.

Was he a spotter for the assassins in Dealey Plaza? Was his job to give a visual signal that the target had entered the trap for a crossfire or triangulation attack?

Or are we to believe his vague explanation that he was there to heckle JFK because of his father's support of Hitler during the second world war?

The perplexing puzzles described in Chapter 8 leaves us wondering what connection they may have had to the assassination. And why are so many of them yet to be resolved or sensibly explained?

Author Dave O'Brien gives readers a troubling view through the 'Oswald' window.

THROUGH THE 'OSWALD' WINDOW

With no claims of impartiality, I present a compilation of 50 plus years of study, research, investigation and lectures.

Perhaps, for the first time, we would better understand the JFK assassination if we saw it through the eyes of the supposed assassin who made history happen on November 22, 1963.

The time has come for you to look through the 'Oswald' window with me.

Hopefully, my unique perspective, combined with the very latest information at hand, contributes to us getting a step closer to the truth about what happened to President John F. Kennedy.

History, after all, is always a journey in the making. When the ultimate objective is truth, history delayed is way better than history denied.

Whatever your interests be in life, may they one day present you with an 'Ah-Ha' moment. Like me, it may take you on a remarkable adventure.

Welcome to my journey. Enjoy…

Chapter 1

The Day I Discovered that Oswald Nor Anyone Else Could Have Been JFK's Lone Assassin!

Lee Harvey Oswald could not have been the lone assassin of President John F. Kennedy on November 22, 1963.

More specifically, Oswald could not have fired any shots at JFK from the sixth-floor southeast corner window of the Texas School Book Depository Building.

How do I know?

It's certainly not based on more than 50 years of conspiracy theories, two official government investigations, countless independent studies and the hundreds of books that both support and refute the notion that Oswald acted alone.

Lee Harvey Oswald poses with rifle found at the sixth-floor window.

Time has done little to lessen the nearly 75% of Americans who believe that there was a conspiracy to kill the 35th President of the United States.

And during that time, the slow release of classified documents over the years via the Freedom of Information Act tend to side with the probability of a conspiracy to both kill JFK and cover it up.

Even with the Freedom of Information Act of 1967, we might still have to wait until 2038 for the truth when the remaining suppressed JFK files are scheduled for release from the National Archives in Washington.

That will depend on how the Trump administration decides to handle the scheduled release of thousands of classified documents on October 26 of 2017 per the JFK Assassination Records Act of 1992.

Unless President Trump overrules the procedures put in place, the CIA, FBI and military intelligence agency have the right to heavily redact or still withhold documents if they deem them to be more important to the interests of the country than the peoples' right to know.

Read into that what you will, but as this book goes to press, the word 'impeachment' threatens the Trump Presidency after the forced resignation of National Security Adviser Michael Flynn and the firing of FBI director James Comey.

With allegations that Trump asked Comey to halt the FBI's investigation into Flynn's dealings with high level Russians and then lying to Vice President Pence about it, we have no idea how Trump will handle the release of JFK files or if he will even get the chance to help clarify the events of 1963 in Dallas.

Updates on the troubled Trump administration and the scheduled release of JFK assassination documents will be posted on www.ThroughTheOswaldWindow.com.

FROM FACT TO FAIRY TALE

And then Watergate happened, exposing the clandestine, dark side of the highest levels of our own government, including the belief that it could blatantly lie and cover-up its wrongdoings.

By the 1970's, books by Mark Lane, Edward Jay Epstein and Harold Weisberg, as well as researchers the likes of Penn Jones Jr., Mary Ferrell, Robert Groden and forensic pathologist

Dr. Cyril Wecht, began eroding the official government position that both Oswald and his slayer Jack Ruby acted alone.

Mark Lane was a pioneer dissenter of the Warren Report.

And mainly thanks to my fellow JFK assassination researchers, we are much closer to the truth.

So how do I know that Oswald, or any sniper perched at that sixth-floor window, could **not** have fired all the shots that day?

Because I have been there!

I can bring a personal dynamic to the JFK assassination that few other people can.

I have personally stood in Oswald's shoes at that window, or for the sake of historic fact, stood in the shoes of whoever it was that shot the President from that vantage point.

As I crouched at the so-called 'Oswald' window above on February 11, 1979, I could make a number of history-challenging observations that very few people have ever had the opportunity to make.

Prior to my exclusive visit to the Texas School Book Depository Building, only government investigators and very few press people were ever allowed access to the historic sniper's lair.

Famous TV moment when an emotional CBS anchor Walter Cronkite announces that President Kennedy has died.

A 1964 CBS news special by Walter Cronkite, America's most trusted network newscaster, turned out to be nothing more than a 'second-that-motion' expose on the Warren Commission Report.

Cronkite gave America a rare view of the event from the Book Depository sixth floor and affirmed that all the shots came from the 'Oswald' window. Oswald, Cronkite assured America, was the sole sniper.

Oswald may not have lived to stand trial, but for the first critical few years after the assassination, Oswald was unanimously guilty in the court of public opinion.

The American people were fed a summary edition of the Warren Commission findings while the full 26 volumes became very limited to the public.

As a result, the mainstream media were largely restricted to reporting on the summary edition, in essence a rubber-stamping of the Warren Report.

For years, the Book Depository Building was emptied and locked up until February 20, 1989 when the historic site was turned into the Sixth Floor Museum at Dealey Plaza.

Visitors can now view the re-staged 'Oswald' window from behind a glass barricade - courtesy of The Sixth Floor Museum at Dealey Plaza.

Since then, hundreds of thousands have visited the infamous kill site and can view the sixth-floor southeast corner window from behind a glass barricade, re-staged as it appeared in 1963.

It is unlikely that independent researchers will ever again stand at that very spot from which shocking history was made.

As I stood at that window and looked down onto Elm Street, just as the real assassin did 15 years earlier, I could vividly imagine the President's limousine moving away from me. Then it occurred to me.

In literally a matter of seconds, the President's entourage would accelerate out of harm's way onto Stemmons Freeway. He was so close to escaping that fateful day.

This truly was among the last seconds the assassin(s) had that day to kill the 46-year-old President.

UNFORGETTABLE FEELINGS

Before discussing the history-challenging observations I made that day from the assassin's nest, I will never forget the raw emotion, feelings and sense of historic enormity that surged through me at that very moment.

While waiting for a government official to arrive to let me into the vacated building, like all tourists that visit Dealey Plaza, I ventured around the kill site. This included a trek up the grassy knoll and a visit behind the picket fence where so many believe the fatal head shot came from.

Like so many others, I was drawn to that horrific spot on the Elm Street, marked by a simple 'X' to denote the location on the road where the President received his fatal head shot, as graphically shown here in Zapruder film frame #313.

At that time, not many people had seen the full Zapruder film, especially the

The fatal head shot that killed President Kennedy

exploding head shot, but no one came away from that 'X' on the road unaffected. We all knew what happened there.

I was already swept away by tragic history when the Book Depository door opened. I took the freight elevator up six floors with my government host, Bill Smith, Chief of Right-of-Way for Dallas County.

At the window, I was first struck by the immense sense of history, even though the assassin's lair was completely baron accept for a large wooden crate against the wall that I used to rest my camera bag.

As I looked down onto Elm street at the passing cars and tourists mulling about, I made every effort to consciously put myself into the body and soul of the actual assassin.

Bill Smith opened the bottom half of the 'Oswald' window by pulling the lower window pane up to the maximum as you see it open at left.

I then crouched down on one knee as the assassin would have been required to do, pointing to the target below.

The Commission ignored that neither a man standing or sitting had a comfortable shot through the fully open window as shown.

I was stunned to realize that I was tense and my palms were sweaty.

"My goodness," I thought to myself. "How could anyone so calmly point a real rifle and shoot the President of the United States?"

Here, I was just pointing my finger toward an imagined target and I was completely unnerved by merely placing myself where one of history's most notorious moments took place.

Even though I had seen the sixth-floor sniper's nest photos in the Warren Report, the sad and shocking sense of historic reality hit me as I stood at that window.

HISTORY BEGINS TO UNRAVEL

Thankfully, my host was a patient man for it took me a few minutes to stop internalizing the Zapruder film and seeing my target moving along Elm Street below.

When I did manage to mentally go from 1963 to the moment at hand, emotions gave way to the shocking revelations I just observed. Stunned, I did a double-take and a triple-take to be certain.

It hadn't occurred to me, but I was not allowed to bring along a photographer. I was never told I could not take pictures from the infamous window and Mr. Smith didn't object.

But a moment of panic set in. I needed a picture of me at the 'Oswald' window to record my brief step into history.

As you can imagine my plight, cell phones didn't exist at that time and the cumbersome Pentax 35 mm camera I had did not exactly allow for a 'selfie,' so I was distraught at having no evidence of me being there.

It took some coaxing, but Bill Smith finally yielded and took the picture of me crouching at the window.

For the first time since I arrived, I could finally relax, that is until I made some observations that rocked the history books as I knew them.

Before my visit to Dallas in 1979, I was already quite informed about the assassination. I had read all 26 volumes of the Warren Report and found all kinds of discrepancies.

I wrote a 14-part series for The Mississauga Times in 1972, literally performing a journalistic autopsy on the Warren Report's findings. In 1978, I spent a few weeks covering the House Select Committee Hearings on Assassinations in Washington.

Although that committee changed the official government stance on the JFK assassination by asserting that there was a conspiracy of unknown origin, it still left a lot of questions unanswered, especially when it still named Oswald as the assassin from the window at which I was standing.

As I carefully looked about the scene inside and outside the famous building, several observations shook me for the historic untruths they seemed to be suggesting:

A MOST DIFFICULT INSIDE JOB

Perhaps I quickly became unnerved because of the very first observation I made as I approached the infamous 'Oswald' window.

I had seen a photo in the Warren Report of an FBI investigator crouched at the window like I am, pointing the 'Oswald' rifle out the window to the street below.

As you see me pointing in the photo at the start of this chapter, it didn't register on me how problematic this posturing was until I reached the window and my host pulled up the lower pane of glass.

I was startled to discover two things:

1. How little the window could be pulled up. When fully opened, the top of the open window was barely higher than my waist when standing up and I am only 5', 7" tall (see Warren Commission picture on page 28).

2. How low the brick wall is beneath the window, meaning that the window sill was literally no more than 20 inches off the floor (see Warren Commission picture on page 28).

   At that very moment, it became clear that the assassin could not have stood up to fire his rifle at the passing President. He would have had to fire from his hip like Wyatt Earp, which is totally absurd.

To my amazement, the sniper would have had to do exactly as I did, which is crouch down, perhaps resting one knee on the floor for balance.

I tried it, followed by an "*I'll be damned,*" exclamation.

I realized that if this is the position Oswald or anybody assumed to fire three shots at the President, by kneeling or crouching, it is certainly a very unsteady position, thereby making his task even more difficult than what the Warren Commission described.

Even if the shooter could somehow brace his rifle on some boxes he arranged at the window sill, as the Commission asserts, this does not excuse him from having to crouch down or kneel to fire his rifle, making two direct hits out of three shots fired in 5.6 seconds.

This feat is nothing short of astonishing!

A LONER'S MINDSET

The next perplexing observation I made at that window also left me calling recorded history into question, especially given the Commission's primary finding that Oswald was the only assassin, firing all three shots from that window.

From trying to mimic the physical challenges of the gunman at that window, I now found myself dealing with the mindset of a single assassin trying to successfully murder the country's chief executive.

Looking out that window, a bizarre dilemma occurred to me:

JFK limousine turns onto Houston Street and begins to approach the 'Oswald' window.

If I was a lone gunman out to shoot President Kennedy, why did I let the limousine get into a position of escape, thereby making my task all the more difficult?

If you stand at that southeast corner window and look straight out, you are looking at Houston Street. Directly below the window is Elm Street.

As Oswald (or whoever) stood at that window, he watched the presidential motorcade approach him, slowing down to just a few miles per hour to make the sharp left-hand turn onto Elm Street directly beneath him.

The assassin allowed that turn to happen before getting into his awkward position to begin the shooting. Now the president's car is moving away from him, which will prove to be extremely problematic for a lone gunman.

Here's the problem I cannot reconcile to this day:

If Oswald, or the actual assassin, was indeed acting alone and he was hell-bent on killing the President that day, why didn't he take his shots with the limousine directly in front of him on Houston Street as it slowed down to make the left turn onto Elm Street directly below him?

View of Houston Street from the 'Oswald' window. The assassin allowed JFK's car to turn onto Elm Street before shooting. Why?

This is by far a much easier shot.

We cannot possibly predict the mindset of the assassin at that moment, but if the lone gunman scenario is correct, why would he not take the much easier shots at his target?

As we are about to learn, this possibility most likely occurred to the assassin because he was also able to see from his window, as I did, that letting the president's limousine turn left on Elm Street and begin to move away from him was not in his best interests as a solo sniper.

Yet, the gunman chose to ignore his best shooting vantage point, thus decreasing his chances for success and increasing the difficulty of his task.

Why?

Some Warren Report supporters, in trying to discredit alternate vantage points for a sniper at other locations along Main Street and Houston Street, dismiss this notion on the basis that had Oswald fired with the car still on Houston Street, it would have been more obvious as to the origin of the shots, thereby lessening Oswald's chances of escape.

This cannot be discounted, but as it turned out, Dallas police swarmed the Book Depository Building within seconds of the shooting, as evidenced below. The assassin's delay in shooting didn't fool anyone.

However, when the gunman allows the limousine to make its way onto Elm Street before taking the first shot, his decision to take the harder shots may not have been a miscalculation at all.

HOUSTON, WE HAVE A PROBLEM

Even if we concede that Lee Harvey Oswald is the assassin at the sixth-floor nest, the most shocking observation I made from the 'Oswald' window is the challenge he faced with the limousine now on Elm Street.

In allowing the president's dark blue Lincoln to move along Elm Street, a 'lone gunman' Oswald would have been alarmed by what he was looking at through his rifle telescope.

What did he see?

More importantly, it's what he couldn't see that would have scared him. What he couldn't see was his target. Why?

Because the oak tree, pictured here, completely blocked the view of the assassin stationed at the sixth-floor

This photo taken by the author from the 'Oswald' window shows that the sniper had to wait for JFK to clear the foliage of the oak tree before firing three shots in 5.6 seconds...unless...

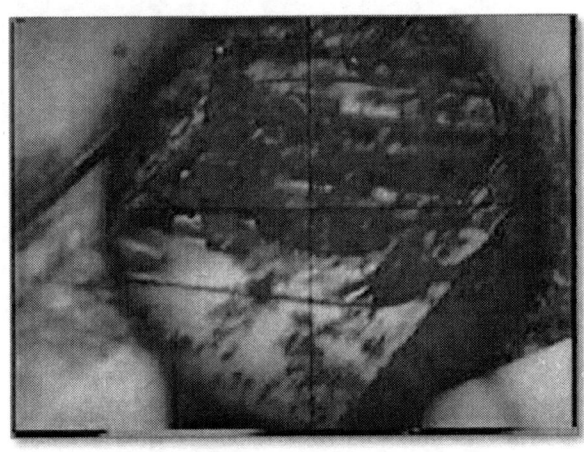

...the assassin was good enough to hit his target through the leaves and branches of the oak tree.

southeast corner window for several critical seconds.

He would have had to wait for the President to clear the foliage before he could fire his first shot (see left).

Otherwise, we are asked to believe he was good enough to hit a moving target with a shot that found its way through leaves and tree branches without being disrupted in flight.

By allowing the limousine to move several yards further down the road before the first shot could occur, he is greatly reducing his timeframe to carry out the assassination.

This delay also gives the limousine a greater chance to escape onto the highway once it disappears under the triple overpass as shown.

Again, from the perspective of a lone gunman, this mistake seems unlikely, given the alternative shot opportunity presented to him on Houston Street.

A top sharpshooter knows to take the best possible shot rather than risk not killing his target.

BETTER OPTION MERE FEET AWAY?

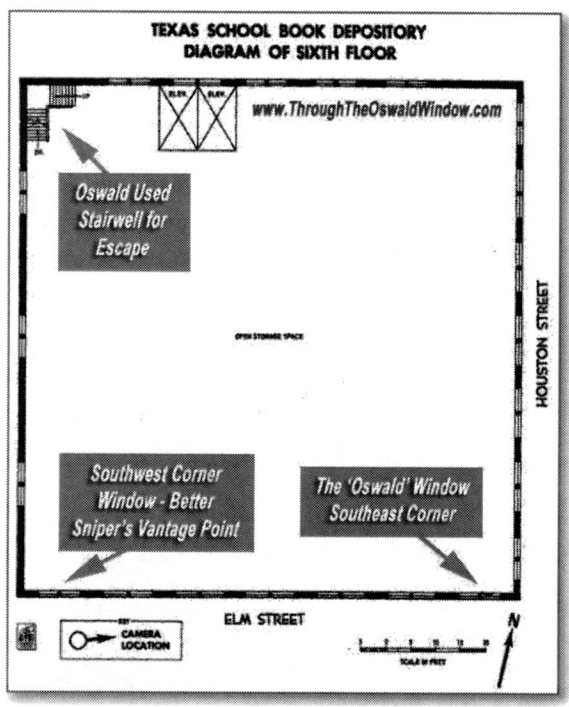

The southwest corner window at left would have solved several previously unknown obstacles for a lone assassin.

Even if we accept that shooting the President on Houston Street was not an option for a single assassin positioned at the 'Oswald' window, yet another 'Ah-Ha' moment struck me as I looked around the empty sixth floor.

My eyes were drawn to the right along Elm Street to the *southwest* corner window on the sixth floor.

In a matter of seconds, I walked over to the *southwest* corner window and was stunned to look down onto Elm Street and see how much more 'shooter-friendly' this location was for a lone assassin.

This alternate firing location would:

1. Remove an obvious obstruction that appears from the southeast corner window at the time of the shots, as explained momentarily.

2. Provide the assassin with easier shots from an easier angle.

3. Provide the assassin a greater timespan to fire three shots, especially if he was the only shooter in Dealey Plaza.

4. Quicken the assassin's escape time by placing him several critical yards closer to the stairwell that he used to exit the building after the shots were fired.

Unquestionably, from either window in the Book Depository Building, Elm Street poses a much more difficult assassination attempt than Houston Street, so why did the actual sniper take that risk?

ENTERING THE TRAP

An astute lone assassin absolutely would have evaluated his sniper vantage point and either decide to boycott his mission or not wait until the JFK car had begun to move away from him.

Further, it is difficult to believe that such a major decision would have been left to the last possible moment, especially if it was Oswald at the window.

Because he worked in the Book Depository, he had ample advance time to scout either window's viability as a sniper perch.

Of all the challenging observations I was able to make as a solo assassin in a few minutes, he had several opportunities to note the same hazards he would face from the 'Oswald' window.

Clearly, Oswald's biggest handicap is that he had to wait for his target to clear the foliage of the large oak tree before firing the first shot.

For instance, he could have fired the first shot much earlier when the limousine was almost directly beneath him on Elm Street, having just made the turn from Houston Street.

However, an earlier shot produces two dilemmas for a single assassin at the 'Oswald' window, as I observed first hand:

1. **That Darn Oak Tree** – The large oak tree still comes into play, meaning that any subsequent shots must wait for the limousine to emerge from the foliage.

2. **Chance of Escape** – An earlier shot gives the Secret Service limousine driver Bill Greer or other trained agents a chance to identify gunfire.

With the Book Depository at back left, 'X' on the road marks JFK's fatal head shot from the grassy knoll. Is this why the shooter couldn't fire at the limousine on Houston Street?

As a result, the President's car could have accelerated earlier while hidden from the assassin's view by the tree, thereby making a second and third shot much more difficult.

However, what if there was a scenario that eliminated the oak tree as a major problem for the assassin at that window?

What if whoever fired a minimum two shots from that historic location was NOT the only assassin present in Dealey Plaza that day?

The Zapruder film and other persuasive evidence places a gunman behind a picket fence atop the grassy knoll to the right front of the President's car.

Therefore, it became necessary for the 'Oswald' window sniper to hold his fire until the President's car had 'entered the trap' on Elm Street, thus giving at least two snipers a clear shot at the President of the United States.

Apart from the evidence in the Warren Report, this is the only viable explanation, given the obvious challenges a single shooter from the Book Depository window faced that day.

Since incriminating her husband Lee before the Warren Commission to avoid possible deportation back to the Soviet Union, wife Marina has since cast doubts about his actions that day in Dallas.

A THIRD SHOOTER?

There is one other option that takes a major challenge out of the equation for the southeast corner shooter.

In 1983, I made a return visit to Dealey Plaza because of a photograph that had been altered by the Warren Commission. The photo it released in 1964 was severely cropped to hide a few things.

As discussed fully in Chapter 11, the full photograph in my possession would produce the biggest 'Ah-Ha' moment yet.

Unbelievably, a single black and white photograph would strongly suggest the possibility of a third assassin at work.

And it would explain why a sniper at the 'Oswald' Window wouldn't have to be concerned with his biggest obstacle – the oak tree.

OSWALD OR NOT?

And finally, while standing there at the southeast corner window, knowing full well that at least two shots came from that location, I could address one final haunting question:

Was Lee Harvey Oswald the sniper at this Window?

Of course, the Warren Commission says that Oswald was the only assassin of the President, but there is ample evidence in its own report to suggest that Oswald was, in fact, in the second-floor lunchroom of the Depository Building at the time of the assassination.

The Commission found that Oswald shot the President and then raced down four flights of stairs in 90 seconds where he encountered a Dallas police officer in the lunchroom.

This required Oswald to stash his rifle carefully behind some boxes to hide it, run to the far opposite corner of the building and descend to the second floor in 90 seconds, all without sweating or losing his breath.

Oswald seemed so calm and collected, officer Marrion Baker verified his employee status and then raced off to look for anyone of suspicious nature.

Could Oswald pull that off like the Commission claims?

While in the building, I decided to put that important Warren Commission finding to the test.

Timing myself, with my host as a back-up timer, I traced Oswald's alleged steps all the way down to the second-floor lunchroom and was yet again astonished at what I discovered.

I was able to get there in 90 seconds, but unlike Oswald, I would not have passed the visual test when confronted by a police officer. Neither would the fitter and trimmer Mr. Smith.

More than likely, we would have been arrested and taken into custody. Oswald, on the other hand, was not regarded as suspicious just 90 seconds after killing the President of the United States!

The astonishing results of this test in the Book Depository Building is fully outlined in Chapter 2.

Footnote: After my history-rethinking experience at the assassin's window, I devoted even more time researching the assassination of President John F. Kennedy.

The results are found here in the remaining chapters. Perhaps they will surprise you…and disturb you as they did me.

Chapter 2

Oswald a Serial Killer?

Does Slain Cop J.D. Tippit and Targeted General Walker Point to Oswald as JFK's Assassin?

Lee Harvey Oswald was not only the lone assassin of President John F. Kennedy, he was a serial killer!

Or so we are asked to believe.

While the Warren Commission claimed that Oswald murdered Dallas policeman J.D. Tippit while trying to escape after assassinating the President, it could not establish clear motivation for Oswald deciding to kill JFK.

In place of any substantive motive, the Commission simply stated that:

"Oswald was a misfit in any society in which he lived," and further declared that *"Oswald desired a place in history."*

Oswald simply did it because he was a loner nut job who wanted to be famous.

Indeed, Oswald did appear to have a troubled past, both in the United States and his brief stay in the Soviet Union.

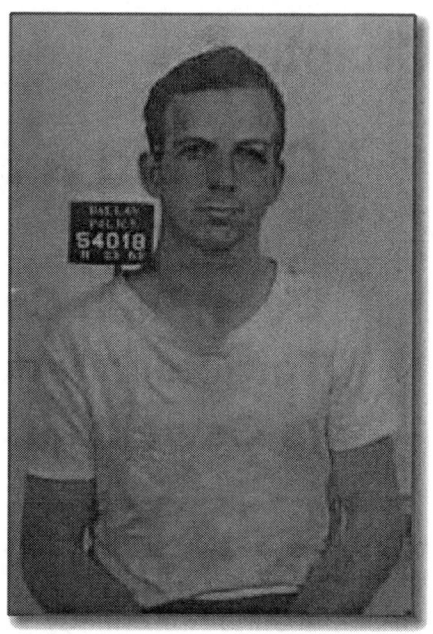

But when given the ideal opportunity to claim his place in the history books, as the Commission postulates, Oswald decided to pass.

So, in the last two days of his life during hours of intense interrogation, as well as several brief appearances before the world press, what did Oswald say?

Lee Harvey Oswald in police custody, booked as a double murderer.

"I didn't shoot anybody!"
And he further declared:
"I'm just a patsy!"

Go to YouTube.com and enter this address -
www.youtube.com/watch?v=IQZ7W6ZeePA

– courtesy of JFK Assassination Forum YouTube Channel

If Oswald was the communist sympathizer and the Fidel Castro supporter attributed to him by the Warren Commission, why didn't the accused assassin use his world stage and limelight to proudly boast "*I did it for Fidel*" or "*Long Live Marxism?*"

At least he could have been a hero to some society!

NEVER CAVED TO POLICE

Instead, despite damaging circumstantial evidence presented to him by Dallas police interrogators, such as his rifle found in the School Book Depository sixth floor where he worked, as well his prints found on the weapon and bag it contained, Oswald steadfastly swore his innocence.

And when it was a press reporter who first informed Oswald that he had been formally charged as the assassin of President Kennedy, he honestly looks surprised (go to video on page 45).

Thankfully, the brief occasions Dallas police paraded Oswald out for the media give us a glimpse into his defiance and proclamation of innocence.

Oswald defiantly defended his innocence before the world press.

Remarkably, Dallas police kept absolutely no notes of the many private hours of questioning of their suspect. And there were also no audio recordings kept, a complete disregard of customary police procedure.

When Dallas police officials appeared before the Warren Commission to talk about Oswald in custody, their recollection of history was purely by memory.

How would that have gone over with jurors or a judge had Oswald lived to stand trial?

Skeptics suggest that the Dallas police knew that notes and testimony would not be needed at a court proceeding.

Otherwise, we are at a loss to explain why this most basic police practice was not exercised, especially involving the death of a President.

Jack Ruby silences Oswald forever.

To his dying breath on November 24, 1963, Oswald denied any guilt. Jack Ruby made sure he could never defend himself in a court of law.

With Oswald silenced forever, the Warren Commission was unchallenged as it crafted its case against Oswald.

In proclaiming Oswald to be the lone assassin, it also named him as the executioner of Dallas police officer J.D. Tippit some 46 minutes after he shot the President.

SETTING THE STAGE

Faced with a troubling lack of motive for Oswald killing Kennedy, the Warren Commission decided it had something far more convincing than a clear-cut motive.

It found that on April 10, 1963, Oswald attempted to assassinate retired Major General Edwin A. Walker, an ultra right-wing activist who was staunchly anti-communist and anti-Castro.

Oswald's first intended victim, Gen. Edwin Walker?

While sitting in his study at home, a single shot shattered a window and whizzed by Walker's head, imbedding itself in a wall.

The recovered bullet, according to FBI ballistic tests, was too damaged to be conclusively linked to Oswald's 6.5 mm Mannlicher-Carcano rifle used in the JFK assassination, but its metallic constitution was identical to the jacketed bullets used to kill the President.

Apparent surveillance photos of Walker's house were found at the Oswald residence after the assassination and were shown to have been taken by a camera owned by Oswald.

Additionally, Oswald's wife Marina told both the Commission and the HSCA hearings that her husband confessed his murder attempt to her on the night it happened.

Here, motive is clearly established. Oswald and Walker were fiercely politically opposed. Walker was loudly calling for a U.S.

military invasion of Cuba and the ouster of Castro, warning of the spread of communism throughout the Americas if it was allowed to start just 50 miles south of the Florida coastline.

Oswald handing out 'Fair Play for Cuba' leaflets in New Orleans.

For his part, while living in New Orleans in early 1963, Oswald was photographed handing out "Fair Play for Cuba" leaflets on the street (see photo left).

He even defended the Castro regime on a radio program and was arrested for a public tussle with anti-Castro militants.

This prompted the Commission to assert: "*The Walker incident proves that Oswald had the tendency toward violence.*"

GUILTY, BUT...

While it is generally agreed that Oswald did try to murder the outspoken Walker, this incident still provides a troublesome dilemma for the Warren Commission.

While this shooting does establish that Oswald had the means, motive and mindset to try to take the life of another man, it does bring into question one vital concern –

Oswald's Ability as a Marksman

As we know, in shooting the President from the sixth-floor window of the Book Depository Building, Oswald is required to pull off a very precise execution by firing three shots with two strikes in no more than 5.6 seconds.

Never mind that FBI ballistic marksmen found this task to be very difficult even though they were under no time pressure to fire the first shot and begin the sequence.

By contrast, in the Walker shooting, Oswald is alleged to have taken up a position some 50 yards across the street from his target, considered an easy shot for a sharpshooter. Walker was seated in a still position, clearly visible through a window.

And yet Oswald **MISSED** his target!

The same man who missed his stationary mark is somehow able to hit a moving target at more than double the distance – twice, with the target moving away from him at 11 miles per hour?

And to boggle the mind even further, how does Oswald hit the moving President twice and yet miss the entire limousine and all its occupants with the middle shot?

In the Presidential assassination, we have an accurate shot to a target about the dimensions of a medium-sized watermelon… preceded by a shot that couldn't even find any section of a large vehicle?

In the Walker assassination attempt, the Commission reasons that the shattered window glass changed the trajectory of the bullet enough for it to miss Walker's head.

This can never be disproved, but expert marksmen will tell you that a thin pane of glass would pose no problem for a skilled sniper.

Isn't it interesting that the Commission would try to explain a slight miss to a still target through a window, but not explain how the same gunman could miss an entire Lincoln sedan?

SURE SHOT?

Oswald's Marine records classify him as an average marksman. Before his discharge, he was barely able to pass the Marine's lowest level of marksmanship.

In the Soviet Union, friends joked that on hunting trips, it was often necessary to provide Oswald with dead game to bring back with him as a face-saver.

NO SWEAT

Marina Oswald linked husband to Walker shooting.

Finally, before moving on to the less than certain Oswald killing of officer Tippit, the Commission made one more foretelling observation in the Walker incident.

To help establish his guilt, the Commission made much of Oswald's physical state after the Walker shooting.

Marina Oswald testified that when he returned home that evening, he was visibly shaken and appeared unnerved and anxious.

51

His voice cracked as he told his wife about what he just did. Keep in mind that this is almost *an hour* after the shooting. Oswald took a bus home from the Walker scene, hid his rifle in the garage and entered the house.

And yet, the Commission would have us believe that the same Oswald, a mere **90 seconds** after shooting the **President of the United States**, having ran down four flights of stairs to the second-floor lunchroom where he was confronted by a work supervisor and Dallas police officer Marrion Baker…and appears perfectly calm, collected and unflustered?

If you just committed a major crime, wouldn't being stopped by a cop just 90 seconds later be a rather uncomfortable position?

Instead of being out of sorts or out of breath from his 90-second rush from the sixth-floor window to the second floor, Oswald seemed so nonchalant that when Book Depository Supervisor Roy Truly identified Oswald as an employee who had a right to be in the building, Truly and officer Baker rushed off to continue their search for anyone of suspicious nature.

We must ask how this contrast would have been interpreted by a jury at an Oswald trial.

Surely, a competent defense team would have put Oswald's alleged actions to the test, just as this reporter

Dallas cop Marrion Baker lets calm-looking Oswald go 90 seconds after shooting.

did in 1979 when I became one of the few people ever allowed access to the sixth-floor sniper's nest (see Chapter 1) before it became a public museum.

After I re-enacted the final shot fired by the assassin from this window, I attempted to rush to the second-floor lunchroom, just as Oswald is alleged to have done.

Like Oswald, or whoever the assassin was, I had two escape options. I could use a freight elevator, which was conveniently waiting for me on the sixth floor.

However, the freight elevator was at that floor because I was the only occupant in the building at the time of my exclusive visit.

At the actual time of the assassination, the freight elevator was in constant use by employees heading off to lunch or departing the building in hopes of seeing the presidential motorcade outside.

It is virtually impossible that the freight elevator would have been conveniently waiting for the assassin at 12:30 p.m. that day at the precise time he fired his third and final shot.

STAIRWAY TO FREEDOM

Option two was a stairwell in the far northwest corner of the building, which is how the Commission says Oswald escaped his sniper perch and raced down to the second-floor lunchroom, to be confronted as described above just 90 seconds later.

Upon feigning my last shot out that infamous window, I carefully discarded my camera bag (in place of Oswald's rifle) behind some boxes to hide it. I then darted to the stairwell. I raced down the stairs as quickly as I could, obviously unimpeded by any other users of the stairs.

Curiously, the Commission could not produce a single witness in the busy building who saw Oswald going down four flights of stairs.

I could get to the second-floor lunchroom in almost precisely 90 seconds, just as confirmed by the Warren Commission's own re-enactments. However, this is where the Commission's version of events become highly unlikely.

When I got to the lunchroom four flights down, I was marginally sweaty, flush of face and clearly short of breath from my sprint.

The Commission makes no mention of the physical state of the investigators who re-enacted the same escape route. They seemed only interested in establishing that it was possible for Oswald to get to the lunchroom from the sixth-floor window in the 90 seconds allotted.

What makes my re-enactment of the so-called Oswald sixth-floor escape problematic for the Warren Commission is testimony from Roy Truly and officer Baker, both of whom said Oswald looked calm, relaxed and natural to the extent that there was nothing suspicious about him, so they let him go and went on their way up the stairs.

Let's pause here to reflect.

I just 'pretended' to shoot the President of the United States, which was unnerving enough to make my palms sweaty even before my race down four flights of stairs.

We are told Oswald really did shoot the President, raced down four flights of stairs and demonstrated absolutely no signs of physical exertion, nervousness or duress mere seconds after reaching the lunchroom and being confronted by a cop?

In the eyes of a jury, that would be called reasonable doubt.

WITNESS AFFIRMATION

A fellow Book Depository employee, Carolyn Arnold, claims to have seen Oswald on the 'first floor' at approximately 12:25, according to an FBI affidavit in March of 1964.

She says she spotted Oswald as she was departing the building to see the President pass by.

Obviously, this is a vexing observation for the Commission since we know someone fired shots from the sixth-floor window at exactly 12:30 p.m.

Arnold's testimony to the FBI casts doubt that it could have been Oswald at the sniper's perch since he was casually mulling about on the lower floors of the building just as the motorcade was nearing Houston and Elm Streets.

How did the Commission handle this conflicting eye-witness account? It ignored the FBI report and did not call Carolyn Arnold as a witness.

COP KILLER

There was a forgotten second murder on the day President John F. Kennedy was assassinated.

That is until it was announced by Dallas police that Lee Harvey Oswald was responsible for both murders on November 22, 1963.

Forty-six minutes after the assassination, Dallas police officer J.D. Tippit was killed instantly when four shots were pumped into his abdomen.

The Commission explains that Oswald successfully escapes the Book Depository after his uneventful confrontation with superintendent Truly and officer Baker.

He gets to his rooming house by taxi, bus and foot, not arousing suspicion of any kind along the way. There, he grabs a jacket and the revolver used to gun down the police officer.

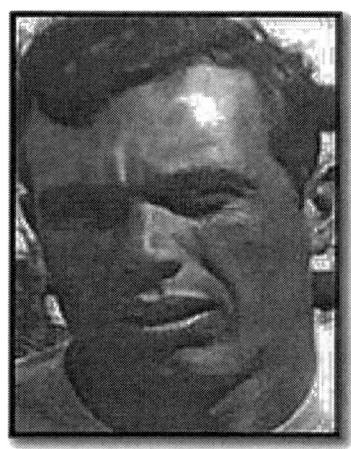

Upon leaving his rooming house, Oswald walks several blocks until a police vehicle approaches him at the intersection of Tenth Street and Patton Avenue.

Oswald allegedly leans into the passenger side of the cop car and has a brief dialogue with patrolman Tippit.

The officer exits his car and as he walks around the front bumper, he begins to draw his weapon, only to be

Slain officer J.D. Tippit.

beaten to the draw by Oswald, who shoots him in the abdomen four times and hurriedly leaves the scene.

A big part of this incident rests on eyewitness testimony, much of which proves to be unreliable. There were a dozen onlookers, but only two could identify Oswald as the cop killer.

And the Commission's star witness in the Tippit murder is Helen Markham, who in fact could not pick out Oswald as the suspect in a police lineup despite more than one attempt.

What follows here is her testimony to the Commission:

Question – *"Did you recognize anyone in the lineup?"*

Markham – *"No sir,"*

Question – *"You did not? Did you see anybody – I have asked you that question before – did you recognize anybody from their face?"*

Markham – *"From their face, no."*

Tippit murder star witness Helen Markham.

Question – *"Did you identify anybody in these four people?"*

Markham – *"I don't know nobody."*

Question – *"I know you didn't know anybody, but did anybody in the lineup look like anybody you had seen before?"*

Markham – *"No, I had never seen none of them, none of these men."*

Question – *"No one of the four?"*

Markham – *"Not one of them."*

Question – *"Not one of all four?"*

Markham – *"No sir."*

It is very strange to note that while Helen Markham could not identify Oswald as the assailant based on facial or physical recognition, she did eventually point out Oswald as someone who stood out to her.

"*Something about this man sent cold chills all over me,*" Mrs. Markham exclaims.

Not to harp on the subject, but how do you suppose multiple failed opportunities to identify Oswald as the man she saw shoot officer Tippit would have played out at trial, especially when the prosecutor asks the jury to accept her picking out Oswald purely based on eerie feelings?

Despite a lack of credible eyewitness accounts, the Commission concludes that Oswald did encounter Tippit and killed him.

MORE BALLISTICS PROBLEMS

Very near the scene of the Tippit murder, a witness found four bullet shell casings neatly grouped together in a small bush and turned them over to police.

The first problem, not surprisingly, is the eyewitnesses, which cannot be relied upon, as often proven in a court of law.

However, it is interesting to note that the revolver confiscated from Oswald after his arrest could not automatically eject cartridges…and if it did, the casings would be strewn over the kill site road rather than neatly stacked together in a bush.

This means that the gunman would have had to manually remove the spent casings and place them as found, but not one witness stated that the shooter they saw ever emptied his weapon.

Secondly, of the four casings found, two were from the Winchester-Western Company and two were from the Remington-Peters Company.

When four bullets were removed from officer Tippit's body, three were manufactured by Winchester and only one was made by Remington.

Officially, we have the shell casings at the scene not totally matching the bullets recovered from the body. This either suggests that the ammunition was somehow compromised to fit a certain scenario or there may have been a fifth shot that remains completely unaccounted for.

Ear witnesses only reported hearing four shots. There was not a fifth wound on Tippit's body and a fifth shell casing was never found.

Despite this conflicting eye, ear and ballistics evidence, the Commission concluded that the bullets recovered came from Oswald's revolver, making him the sole assassin of officer J.D. Tippit.

The Commission asserts officer Tippit had stopped Oswald because he matched a police radio dispatch description of the suspect wanted in the assassination of President Kennedy.

That transmitted description of the Kennedy suspect is as follows:

"Slender white male, about 30, five feet ten, one sixty five, carrying what looked to be a 30.30 or some type of Winchester."

While the 24-year-old Oswald does vaguely fit that description, since he wasn't carrying a rifle with him, what made him stand out to Tippit compared to anyone else he observed?

A court of law would never find out and neither would we.

A LESSER CRIME BRINGS DOWN OSWALD

Even if we accept that Oswald shot and killed Tippit in the aftermath of the JFK assassination, it is nothing less than astonishing how Oswald's flee from justice came to such a bizarre end shortly after the Tippit incident.

Now, police were looking for a cop killer, as well as an unrelated assassin of the President.

According to the Commission, after shooting Tippit to death, Oswald calmly walks away on foot and enters a retail section of the Oak Cliff area.

He stops at an entrance to a shoe store, where he catches the attention of salesman Johnny Brewer.

Johnny Brewer's vague tip leads to Oswald arrest.

Although Brewer had not heard a description of either the cop suspect or assassination suspect, he can't take his eyes off

60

Oswald, who crosses the street and enters the Texas Theater without buying a movie ticket.

Brewer immediately calls the police, never mentioning the murdered cop or President, only reporting that a guy didn't buy a ticket before entering the theater.

Police might normally send a police cruiser to the theater to check it out on a casual day, but on this of all days, when you'd think police would have more on their mind than arresting a petty thief, how did the Dallas police respond to Brewer's call?

By sending multiple police cars and almost 30 officers to the Texas Theater within a couple of minutes!

Police cautiously approached

Oswald is arrested at Texas Theater as Tippit murder suspect?

Oswald in his seat. And it was Oswald who escalated the situation by brandishing a weapon and attempting to resist arrest.

Indeed, Oswald was in the vicinity of the officer Tippit killing, but puzzling questions remain, such as:

- Did officer Tippit approach Oswald to question him, arrest him or possibly even kill him to get Oswald out of the picture?

- While many conspiracy theorists contend that Oswald didn't murder Tippit at all, others suggest that Oswald was supposed to be killed shortly after the assassination to shut him up, but when he was quicker on the draw than Tippit, that necessitated the emergence of Jack Ruby into the picture.

Before you dismiss this possibility as poppycock, film footage of a rare statement by Jack Ruby in Chapter 3 shows him asking perhaps the most important question of all.

Chapter 3

Jack Ruby:

From Goodfella's Kid to Mafia's Most Notorious Hitman?

Jack Ruby shoots Lee Harvey Oswald –
Impulse killing or organized crime hit?

In the movie Goodfellas, the teenage Ray Liotta character, Henry Hill, becomes infatuated with the organized crime lifestyle.

Rather than follow in the innocent, yet boring career path of his father, Henry becomes a trusted errand boy for local crime family thugs.

By the time Henry hits his 20's, even though he can never become a 'Made Man' because he is not of Italian heritage, he is a loyal thug himself, the right-hand man to Mafia lieutenant Jimmy Conway, played by Robert De Niro.

Even local crime boss Paulie Cicero (Paul Sorvino) takes a shine to Henry and the critically-acclaimed movie by Martin Scorsese gives us chilling insights into a powerful crime family.

Jack Ruby - From low-level mobster to famous hitman?

Like Henry Hill, Jacob Leon Rubenstein (Jack Ruby), became a low-level runner for the Capone family in Chicago at age 11 in 1922.

Like Henry Hill, Jack Ruby climbed up the chain and while he never became a crew captain by his 20's, he was well entrenched into the world of organized crime.

Only by now, Ruby had grown more into the Tommy DeVito (Joe Pesci) character - brash, arrogant and short of temper, prone to settling matters with his fists rather than negotiation.

After Ruby became a murder suspect in the Windy City, fellow mobsters Dave Yaras and Lenny Patrick, both of whom were being monitored by FBI wiretaps that showed an upsurge in phone calls to Ruby in the days leading up to the assassination, convinced him to get out of Chicago.

He landed in Dallas and immediately went about the business of establishing relationships with local mafia types like Lewis McWillie, who was a key Marcello player in Texas.

When McWillie moved to Havana in 1958 to work with Florida mob boss Santo Trafficante and Meyer Lansky in their blossoming casino business, it was Ruby who McWillie tapped to help move weapons and cash in and out of the island.

Jack Ruby with two of his 'dancers' in front of his Carousel Club.

But it was the befriending of Dallas police officers that would prove to make Ruby the 'go-to' guy when organized crime needed to take care of a problem immediately after President Kennedy was assassinated on November 22, 1963.

Once in Dallas, Ruby opened the Carousel Club and made it his business to offer up food, drinks and his burlesque dancers to local cops, justice officials and politicians.

This was just good business in those days when the mafia owned or had a significant stake in the nightclub scene.

Although banks weren't exactly lining up to loan cash to open a burlesque establishment, the Commission never asked how

Ruby was able to arrive in Dallas broke, yet able to open his Carousel Club within months of arriving.

FBI files suggest that Ruby personally knew up to 80% of Dallas police officers and most certainly all patrolman who worked his Carousel Club neighborhood.

Dallas Detective James Leavelle watches in horror as a casual acquaintance of his shoots his prisoner on national television.

This might explain how Ruby was arrested eight times, including carrying a concealed weapon (twice) and malicious assaults on people, but charges were always somehow dropped without a court appearance.

There is no greater evidence of Ruby's friendship with Dallas police officials than that provided by detective James Leavelle.

He is famously remembered as the cop in the white cowboy hat handcuffed to Oswald the moment he was gunned down by Jack Ruby in the basement of the police station.

In a local television interview with WFAA reporter Bill Lord soon after Leavelle accompanied Oswald to Parkland Hospital and watched him die, this exchange takes place:

Bill Lord – *"Did you recognize him* (Ruby) *when he came through?"*

James Leavelle – "*Yes. I have known Jack Ruby for a number of years and I recognized him just as soon as he emerged from the crowd.*"

Police connections such as this example would prove to be of historic relevance on November 24, 1963.

RUBY AND THE MOB

The Warren Commission found no connection between Jack Ruby and the mob, which we now know to be utterly ridiculous (see Chapter 11).

To arrive at that conclusion, the Commission gave no relevance to the fact that Joe Campisi visited Jack Ruby in jail less than a week after the Oswald shooting.

Campisi not only owned a restaurant in Dallas as a mob front, it is believed that Campisi may have been Ruby's organized crime handler for top mobster Carlos Marcello. In 1973, Campisi was named head of the Dallas syndicate, proving a long-standing life as a Mafioso.

When Jack Ruby's services were needed after President Kennedy was gunned down on the streets of Dallas, there is absolutely no way that Joe Campisi would have had nothing to do with it.

STALKING OSWALD

A myriad of evidence exists to show that Ruby was stalking Lee Harvey Oswald the moment he was arrested and taken into custody.

Or possibly even beforehand.

Regardless, the Commission found no conspiratorial link between the two.

Photographic evidence suggests that Ruby took a keen interest in the assassination of JFK even as it happened.

As the photo on the next page could indicate, Jack Ruby was possibly in Dealey Plaza as the shots rang out. The Commission says he was in a newspaper office, placing an ad for his club.

Strangely, The Commission made much about Ruby's professed love of President Kennedy, citing his bereavement as the motive for 'spontaneously' killing Oswald 48 hours later.

Yet we are asked to believe that Ruby, who basically had a night job, didn't make an effort to see JFK in the motorcade that morning.

Even more odd, Ruby had made no plans to attend the President's lunch speech at the Dallas Trade Mart even though the who's who of the Dallas business community were waiting for Jack and Jackie to arrive.

Does the circle at right show Jack Ruby was near Book Depository entrance when JFK was shot?

Tragically, the President's limousine did speed past the Dallas Trade Mart on the way to Parkland Hospital.

The photo (left) does not appear in the Warren Report.

Instead, a slightly different angle of this photo appears, coincidentally of course, to not show the image of a man on the right who looks remarkably like Jack Ruby, as revealed on CNN (see below right).

A closer look (above) also seems to show a Dallas cop passing Ruby over his right shoulder. Notice the white round police helmet, suggesting he was one of the motorcycle cops in the presidential motorcade.

Warren Report photo of Book Depository entrance moments after the shots does not show Jack Ruby.

According to Ruby friend and part-time Carousel Club bouncer Reagan Turman's FBI testimony, there would have been up to an 80% chance that Ruby personally knew this unidentified officer.

There are even more alarming examples of 'altered' photographic evidence by the Warren Commission in the chapters to follow.

All of them involve evidence that might cast doubt on the findings that both Oswald and Ruby acted alone.

RUBY AT PARKLAND HOSPITAL?

As well as altering evidence that didn't support the Oswald-lone-assassin or the Ruby-lone-avenger theories, there is disturbing evidence that the Warren Commission choose to

Seth Kantor, reporter and acquaintance of Jack Ruby, gives testimony Warren Commission didn't want to hear.

ignore or disregard eyewitnesses who did not seem to affirm these conclusions.

One example is respected Scripps-Howard wire service reporter Seth Kantor, who was a White House correspondent. The Dallas-based journalist was riding in the motorcade press car that day, which raced off to Parkland Hospital in pursuit of the president's limousine.

It needs to be noted that Seth Kantor personally knew Jack Ruby, so imagine his shock as he watched an acquaintance gun down the President's assassin 48 hours later in the basement of the Dallas police station.

On several occasions, well before the President's visit to Dallas, Kantor had seen Ruby at police precincts handing out coffees and sandwiches. Kantor knew that Ruby owned and operated the Carousel Club.

But there was one Ruby sighting that stood out to Kantor. He told the Warren Commission that at the precise time that the President was pronounced dead at 1 p.m. local time, he and Ruby had a brief chat at Parkland Hospital.

The Commission pushed Kantor on his recollection, saying that it was probably later that night at the police station, but Kantor distinctly remembers it occurring during the tragic pronouncement of death.

Wilma Tice also swore to the FBI and Warren Commission that she saw Ruby at Parkland Hospital shortly after President Kennedy arrived, even noting that "*A man (Kantor?) came up to this man, slapped him on the shoulder and said How are you, Jack?*" She identified that man as Ruby.

When the Warren Report was published, it completely dismissed these eyewitness accounts, calling both Kantor and Tice "confused" by what they saw.

Kantor was so upset by his experience before the Commission, he wrote his own book, titled The Ruby Cover-Up (1978 by Zebra Press).

Was Ruby at Parkland Hospital because he was so emotionally distraught over the President being killed?

The Commission claims that Ruby was not at the motorcade, had no plan to attend the scheduled Presidential luncheon, yet witnesses place him at the hospital minutes after the President arrives mortally wounded.

Kantor, professionally trained to snoop out things that appear unusual, makes no mention to the FBI or Warren Commission of an emotionally overwrought Jack Ruby.

Their brief encounter was uneventful. In fact, Ruby appeared more curious than upset. He made no comments about Jackie Kennedy nor did he express any anger to whoever killed the President.

Ruby's presence at Parkland Hospital becomes troublesome for the Warren Commission because the timing does not support its claim that Ruby was out to avenge the murder for Jackie.

Why was he there if Oswald had not yet been captured or the alleged assassin's name had not yet become public knowledge?

Was there a more sinister reason for Ruby being at the hospital?

EVIDENCE PLANT?

Within minutes of the President's passing, a nearly pristine bullet was found on a floor in a hallway. The Commission says it was a bullet used in the assassination that was traced to Oswald's rifle found in the Book Depository Building.

This bullet, which would become known as the "Magic Bullet" for good reason, was first thought to have come from President Kennedy.

Autopsy surgeons summarized that this bullet struck President Kennedy in the upper back, penetrated only a short distance, then fell out of the point of entry when Mr. Kennedy was administered cardiac massage by emergency room attendants. This accounted for no bullet being found in the President's back.

Perhaps during transfer of the President's body from the operating room table to a stretcher, the bullet fell from the stretcher and was found by a hospital worker.

However, this scenario would become a major headache for the Warren Commission, so the journey of this projectile would dramatically change, hence giving birth to the 'Single Bullet Theory' (see Chapter 4).

In the months to follow, the Commission decided that the autopsy surgeons were mistaken on this one point.

Rather than accept the post-mortem findings, the Commission decided that this bullet did transit the President's body. It continued on to strike Governor John Connally in the back, exited his chest, struck his right wrist and then found the Governor's left thigh, having just enough velocity left to barely penetrate the skin.

The Commission now concluded that during the commotion and transfer of the Governor by stretcher to an operating room, this bullet (Commission Exhibit 399) fell out of the Governor's shallow thigh wound and landed on the stretcher.

Later, when the stretcher was moved, this bullet became dislodged and fell to the floor.

From this startling readjustment, two perplexing questions arise:

CE 399 - The strange journey of this bullet at Parkland Hospital would shape history.

1. Why did the Commission also dismiss the FBI autopsy finding? This report states that the bullet that entered the President's back *"entered a short distance inasmuch as (Dr. Humes) could feel the end of the opening with his finger."*

2. Why would the Commission ignore all medical information pertaining to this bullet to now say the bullet came from another wound on an entirely different victim without providing any evidence whatsoever to support this finding?

In short, the answer is that they had to change this critical conclusion if they had any hope of naming Lee Harvey Oswald as the lone assassin on that fateful day.

Why?

Because all the non-fatal wounds sustained by President Kennedy and Governor Connally had to have been caused by the same bullet...or by a different shot fired within a second of the first shot.

In other words, Kennedy and Connally can both be seen on the Zapruder film (see Chapter 6) reacting to all their non-fatal wounds before the so-called 'Oswald' rifle can be fired twice!

With the Parkland Hospital bullet now shrouded in mystery, but having been traced to the Oswald rifle found near the Book Depository sixth floor, the appearance by Jack Ruby at the hospital presents a mind-boggling possibility.

I'll be the first to admit that the link I am about to make is a long-shot at best, but if we accept the possibility that Ruby and Oswald were both associated with organized crime (see Chapter 11) in Dallas, this bullet may explain his appearance at the hospital so soon after the President was assassinated.

What if Jack Ruby's first assignment in framing Oswald as the sole assassin was to plant this bullet at the hospital?

This ballistic evidence would prove particularly useful if Oswald was killed

Oswald - "I'm just a patsy."

rather than captured alive while trying to escape from Dealey Plaza.

This would give Ruby cause to be at Parkland Hospital within 20 minutes of the President being shot because dead or alive, the circumstantial evidence against Oswald had to be persuasive.

If Oswald was a "patsy" as he proclaimed himself to be before the press in police custody, then Ruby would have been at the hospital already knowing who the assassin would turn out to be before the public knew the gunman's identity.

Did Ruby plant a bullet at the hospital that could be traced back to Oswald's rifle?

This is one aspect of the JFK assassination that we will likely never know.

SCOUTING HIS PREY

There were other Ruby sightings pertaining to Oswald that the Warren Commission could not ignore or sweep under a carpet.

Instead, the Commission used evidence that Ruby was stalking Oswald at the police station as proof that he was emotionally preparing to exact revenge on JFK's assassin for Jackie Kennedy.

The Commission verifies that Ruby was a multiple visitor to the Dallas police station over the two days that Oswald was in custody.

Perhaps the first alarm bell to sound ought to be exactly how Ruby could walk freely among the police and the media hoard at the police station for two days before taking his place in history.

It is mind-numbing to realize that security was so lackadaisical at the police station considering the dozens of death threats received against the suddenly infamous prisoner.

Starting with the hospital visit, we can begin to see how Ruby's cultivation of police contacts may have enabled him to be in places no unauthorized civilians should be.

How else are we to explain Jack Ruby hanging out at the Dallas police station on at least two different occasions as if he were either a detective or a reporter on duty?

Jack Ruby at Dallas police station with Oswald in custody.

Nobody ever questioned his reason for being there or asked him to show credentials of any kind.

Even though Ruby was known to visit the police station with coffee and sandwiches in hand, wouldn't you think that the extraordinary circumstances would dictate that only relevant personnel and accredited media would have free reign of the place?

Also, if Ruby and the cops were well known to each other, can we honestly believe that Ruby's local mob connections were not known?

Would this not be cause for concern when police acquaintances saw him at the cop shop on more than one occasion?

Prior to that famous moment caught on Bob Jackson's camera and on live television, Ruby is photographed at the police precinct more than once.

One such occasion establishes that Jack Ruby was anything but an innocent, heart-broken, curious bystander.

Ruby committed a verbal blunder that suggests he knew quite a bit about the suspect...or perhaps knew Oswald directly.

CORRECTING THE DALLAS DISTRICT ATTORNEY

On the evening of the assassination, Dallas District Attorney Henry Wade gave a press conference which essentially labelled Oswald as the President's assassin.

Less than 12 hours after the assassination, District Attorney Wade revealed much of the incriminating evidence against Oswald.

Dallas District Attorney Henry Wade - Corrected by Ruby at a press conference.

During this proceeding, Wade was discussing Oswald's background and mentioned that he was a member of the *"Free Cuba Committee."*

At a press conference, seen here, Jack Ruby shouts out that Oswald was a member of the Fair Play for Cuba Committee. How did he know before the police?

Suddenly, a voice from the back of the room of media hounds corrects the District Attorney, telling him that Oswald was associated with the *"Fair Play for Cuba Committee."*

Wade is seen accepting the correction as fact before outlining more evidence gathered against Oswald.

Here's what's so fascinating about this exchange:

The correction did not come from an investigative journalist nor a fellow law enforcement official who had some update information to offer.

Instead, the correction came from a most interesting voice in the press gallery – Jack Ruby! (see above).

It was Oswald's eventual killer who stopped DA Wade to clarify that Oswald was a member of the Fair Play for Cuba Committee in New Orleans.

A most obvious question arises:

If Ruby and Oswald were not known to each other, as the Warren Report insists, then how did Ruby know this correct fact about Oswald just hours after the assassination and before the police even had the right information themselves?

Ruby could not have read about it in the newspapers on the same day the assassination occurred. Naturally, initial reports in newspapers and television on Friday, November 22, 1963 centered around the President being assassinated.

Media reports about suspect Lee Harvey Oswald were just beginning to surface when he, himself, was assassinated almost exactly 48 hours after JFK.

EARS OF THE MOB?

Since we know that Jack Ruby was very well connected to Dallas cops, it could be that this relationship went beyond him being given unquestioned access to the police station in the 48 hours before he would act against the accused assassin.

Might Ruby have been at the police station to gather information about what Oswald was saying to cops?

Admittedly, we must jump to some questionable assumptions for this to be possible, such as Dallas police officer J.D. Tippit ruining a plan by the conspirators to kill Oswald while attempting to escape so the assassination could be pinned on him.

Some conspiracy theorists have taken this concept further by suggesting that it was Tippit's job to eliminate Oswald, but was beaten to the draw.

If it was possible that Oswald was supposed to be murdered rather than captured alive, his fellow accomplices would have been deeply concerned about what Oswald might

Did Oswald's denial of guilt prompt his death sentence?

be saying to interrogators, especially when he was using his public platform to declare "*I am a patsy!*"

Cops are just like us. They talk amongst themselves. If Ruby knew as many as 80% of the officers in Dallas at that time, was he trying to gather 'intel' on what Oswald was saying?

Another source for Ruby could have been reporters, who were also trying to find out what Oswald might be saying while in custody. While several reporters said they saw Ruby at the police station, none indicated having talked to him.

Regardless of what Ruby learned from his police and media contacts, it was Oswald's continual public plea of innocence (see above right), widely reported on TV, radio and newspapers, that would necessitate his elimination as soon as possible.

To take his place in history, Jack Ruby needed to know just one thing - exactly when he could get proximity to Lee Harvey Oswald…And that information had to have come from a Dallas police insider.

PERFECT TIMING FOR HISTORY

One of the most perplexing aspects of the Ruby murder of Oswald on national television was the timing of it all.

It has yet to be explained how Ruby knew something that nobody else knew – the exact moment Oswald would be put in position to be attacked.

Oswald being rushed to an ambulance after being shot by the well-timed appearance of Jack Ruby.

Even more remarkable, when the world knew to turn on their TV's at 10 a.m. that Sunday morning to watch Oswald being transferred from the Dallas police station to the County Jail, the world press was told they could witness the transfer take place in the basement at 10 a.m.

Accordingly, the media assembled in that crowded police basement at 10 a.m. as instructed, waiting for the transfer vehicle and the suspect to appear. There was only one problem.

If the transfer had taken place at 10 a.m. as announced, Oswald would have safely been whisked away. Why?

Because Jack Ruby was not there at 10 a.m. to 'impulsively' shoot Lee Harvey Oswald in a moment of vengeful rage.

The media was there. All the TV networks were there with their cameras ready to roll. Millions of Americans were in front of their televisions at 10 a.m., as were millions of others around the world.

But there was no Jack Ruby…and no Lee Harvey Oswald.

Their rendezvous with history would have to wait a bit longer

Of course, it can be argued that it was perfectly normal for the transfer to experience a delay.

Just four minutes before shooting Oswald, Ruby sent dancer Karren Lynn Bennett a $25 money-gram.

A number of things could have caused a delay of 10, 20 or even 30 minutes. But…

- Is a delay of 81 minutes nothing more than innocent happenstance when national TV networks are waiting to broadcast the transfer live?

- Why wasn't Jack Ruby there, waiting 81 minutes like everyone else?

The Warren Report did not attempt to answer these questions. However, it did establish Jack Ruby's actions and whereabouts when Oswald was supposed to be transferred.

Ruby was out running some errands, with two dogs in his car, when Oswald was supposed to be transferred.

We know that at 11:17 a.m. that morning, Ruby received a stamped receipt for a $25 money-gram to one of his dancers, Karren Lynn Bennett of Fort Worth.

From there, we are told that Ruby walked across the street, slipped undetected into the basement of the Dallas police station and arrived in place to 'impulsively' shoot Oswald just four minutes later!

Really? Some troubling dilemmas emerge, such as:

- Are we to believe that Ruby was emotionally distressed and out to seek revenge against President Kennedy's assassin, yet risked this historic moment from happening so he could send off $25 to one of his exotic dancers?

- As Ruby left the Western Union office, how did he know that the transfer of Oswald was about to happen? Could his perfect timing truly be nothing more than a remarkable coincidence?

- How did Ruby avoid police security at every entrance to walk unchecked into his moment of fame?

The Commission could only site a security lapse to explain Ruby getting access to the police basement and did not attempt to explain how Ruby seemed to be the only person on the planet to know, to the minute, when Oswald would make his final public appearance.

Here are the final moments of Oswald's life on film:

Go to YouTube.com and enter this address -
www.youtube.com/watch?v=0xU7Lhd7Wwo

- courtesy of Mr. Kesselring's Videos YouTube Channel

Tragically, for the sake of history, we are asked to believe that:

1. Ruby never knew Oswald.

2. Ruby had no fellow conspirators in his shooting of Oswald.

3. Ruby had no inside help to get inside the police station.

4. Ruby had no inside knowledge of Oswald's transfer time.

5. Jack Ruby's timing that allowed him to shoot President Kennedy's assassin was merely luck!

Of all the questions that arise from Ruby's murder or Oswald, very few were answered by Jack Ruby himself, either in police custody or his trial that resulted in him being sentenced to death.

RUBY ASKS MOST PERTINENT QUESTION?

His own words have only added to the mystery surrounding his place in history.

On June 7, 1964, the Warren Commission finally interviewed Jack Ruby in jail. Rather than clarify any of these matters, Ruby spent much of his time begging Commission chairman Earl Warren and Representative Gerald Ford to get him out of Dallas so he could tell the truth:

Representative Ford – "*Is there anything more you could tell us if you went back (with us) to Washington?*"

Ruby – "*Yes, I want to tell the truth, but I can't tell it here. I can't tell it here. Now maybe something can be saved. It may not be too late. But if I am eliminated, there won't be any way of knowing.*"

When asked why he couldn't say more in Dallas, Ruby responded with perhaps the most pertinent question of his own:

> ***"Maybe certain people don't want to know the truth that may come out of me. Is that plausible?"***

Could those "certain people" (as exposed in Chapter 12) be those who ordered Jack Ruby to use his Dallas connections to silence Lee Harvey Oswald forever?

Chapter 4

The 'Magic' Bullet!

The Bullet They Say Acted Alone
So That History Could Say
Lee Harvey Oswald Acted Alone

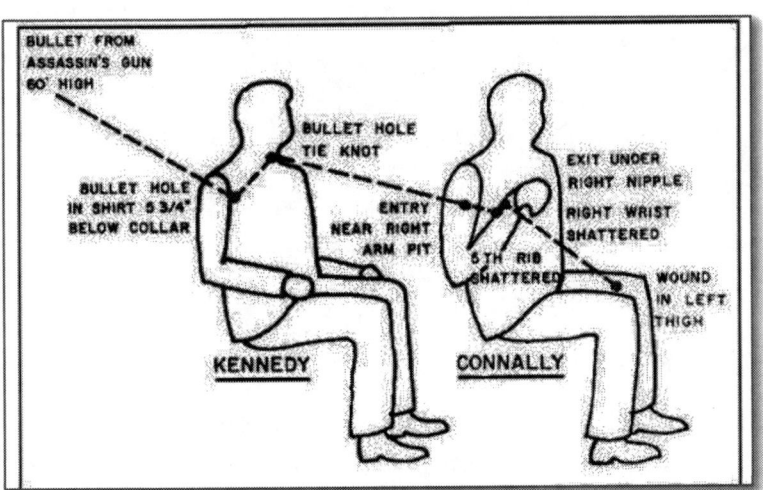

Any forensic pathologist or military surgeon at times of war will tell you that bullets can do remarkable things inside the human body.

Tumbling bullets or fragmenting bullets, for instance, can cause internal unexpected damage that can fool an untrained eye.

Even before a bullet finds its target, it rarely maintains a perfectly straight trajectory unless it is of extreme high velocity.

Wind and gravity, due to distance, can curve a bullet while any type of obstruction can cause a bullet to vibrate or tumble.

These factors are why a qualified forensic pathologist is always required when the death of a victim is by one or more gunshots.

A general hospital pathologist is an expert in death

In Zapruder frame 230, both JFK and Governor Connally must be hit at this point by the 'Magic Bullet' for Oswald to have acted alone.

caused by disease or natural causes.

Despite his medical credentials, he is barely more qualified to conduct a post-mortem examination on a victim who expired at the hands of violence than you or me.

Tragically, you will learn the consequences of unqualified 'general' pathologists being asked to conduct a 'forensic' examination in Chapter 5 when the President of the United States, no less, did not receive a proper autopsy.

A professionally performed forensic post-mortem examination is designed to remove speculation from the equation, leaving us with irrefutable fact about what happened to the deceased.

That did not occur on the evening that President Kennedy was assassinated.

Instead, the highly-flawed post-mortem by unqualified autopsy doctors enabled the Warren Commission to name Lee Harvey Oswald as the lone assassin based on what has become known as:

'THE SINGLE BULLET THEORY!'

Thanks to a theory not supported by scientific, medical or ballistics facts, history as we know it is false.

A thorough *forensic* procedure would have avoided theory and conjecture, thus giving history an accurate accounting of:

- The number of shots fired at President Kennedy's limousine.

- How many shots found a target, namely JFK or Texas Governor John Connally, seated in front of the President.

Warren Commission says this bullet (CE399) caused seven wounds, broke two bones and suffered only nominal damage.

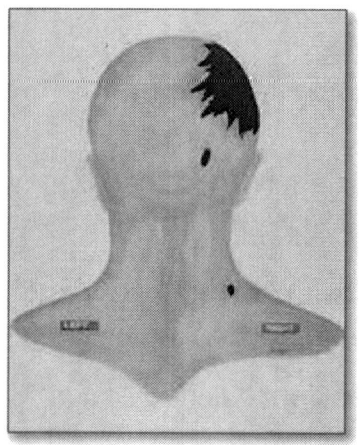

Commission Exhibit 386 showing head entry wound, massive exit wound and entry wound to neck. Evidence suggests all three wounds are not accurately located.

• The non-lethal wounds sustained by **both men**, including points of entry, bullet pathways inside the bodies, exact nature of damage caused by each missile and points of exit from the bodies.

• In the final analysis, since these two men are suspected of being hit by the same bullet, the wounds sustained by Connally should be connectible to the back entry wound and throat 'exit' wound on JFK.

- The exact trajectory and results of all bullets fired at the victims, thereby also establishing the points of origin for all shots fired.

- The official cause of death (gunshot{s} to head). A complete forensic study of the fatal wound should also ascertain the number of shots that struck the President's head, points of entry, pathways of missile(s) inside the skull, damage caused by bullet trajectory or fragmentation and points of exit, if any.

Unfortunately, the autopsy performed on the 35th U.S. President fell well short of its mandate. Consequently, we do not have a precise answer to any of the five relevant points above.

As a result, it can be argued that history was denied the truth about what happened to the youthful popular President.

MAGIC OR ORDINARY BULLET?

You may be wondering how a post-mortem on one person can also answer questions about a second victim.

In this famous instance, a competent post-mortem would have told us the exact trajectory of the so-

Single Bullet Theory demands all non-fatal wounds on JFK and Connally were caused by one bullet (CE399 shown above) – courtesy of Luke and Michael Haag – www.guns.com.

called 'Magic Bullet' that the Warren Commission says did the following:

1. Struck President Kennedy in the upper back.

2. Exited President Kennedy's throat.

3. Entered Governor Connally's back on the right side.

4. Broke off the Governor's right fifth rib.

5. Exited the Governor's chest just below the right nipple.

6. Entered the Governor's right wrist.

7. Caused a compound fracture of the Governor's wrist, blowing a hole clean through the bone.

8. Exited the Governor's wrist.

9. Entered the Governor's left inner thigh, having just enough velocity left to penetrate the thigh a short distance.

After that remarkable journey, the Commission concluded that the bullet fell out of the Governor's thigh wound, where it was found near a stretcher believed to be used to transport Connally to an operating table.

And on top of all that, the Commission says the bullet that caused these seven wounds and two broken bones emerged in nearly pristine condition, suffering only a slight squeeze at the base and lost only 2.4 grains of metal at the nose.

Now you know why this projectile is called 'The Magic Bullet' and how it became the cornerstone of 'The Single Bullet Theory.'

For now, we are going to focus on the autopsy, medical and ballistics evidence to determine if the Single Bullet Theory is fact or fiction.

THE BIGGEST POSSIBLE PROBLEM

Warren Commission council Arlen Specter came up with the 'Single Bullet Theory' to declare Oswald as the lone assassin.

What if I were to tell you that the 'Single Bullet Theory' was not a finding of the autopsy performed on President Kennedy?

In fact, as covered thoroughly in the next chapter, the autopsy findings suggest a 'Single Bullet Theory' is quite impossible. Why?

Because the original autopsy report found that the bullet that struck the President in the upper back *did not* even transit his body!

Therefore, the astounding flightpath of the so-called 'Magic Bullet,' as described by the nine points on page 92, couldn't have happened.

As reported in Chapter 5, what became known as the 'Magic Bullet' is Commission Exhibit (CE)399, the nearly unblemished bullet described above.

The autopsy surgeons did not view this bullet, but when told of it being found at Parkland Hospital, Dr. James J. Humes arrived at what would prove to be a controversial conclusion.

Dr. Humes probed the wound and could feel the end of the path with his finger. He decided the bullet wound in the President's back was a short distance and that, in all probability, the discovered bullet at the hospital worked its way out of the back wound when the President was given external cardiac massage.

How is it that this 13-year-old in 1965 could see a problem that seemed to elude the distinguished Warren Commission members, not to mention the FBI that did most of its investigative work?

There was never a mention of two bullets being found, so how could an autopsy and collaborating FBI report say that CE399 came from a shallow wound in JFK's back only to have the final Warren Report state that CE399 came from a shallow wound in the Governor's thigh?

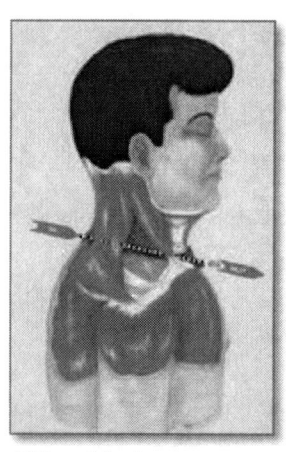

JFK's original autopsy report makes no mention of a throat exit wound and places rear wound 5 inches lower than shown here.

The autopsy/FBI version stood until the Warren Commission realized that if history was to record that Lee Harvey Oswald was the assassin and acted alone, it would have to completely ignore the autopsy/FBI reports (see Chapter 5).

Here, the 'Magic Bullet' is born because instead of it causing only a shallow wound in the President's back, a wound in JFK's throat and all of Governor Connally's wounds are suddenly and mysteriously attributed to it.

And because of this new 'magical' flightpath and all the extra damage being ascribed to CE399, the 'Single Bullet Theory' becomes a necessity for the Warren Commission.

Remarkably, the Commission decided not to accept the only evidence it had that would support a conclusion that CE399 caused the President's back wound only.

Instead, the Commission provided zero evidence in concluding that CE399 did transit President Kennedy's back, then went on to cause all the Governor's wounds.

What happened here?

In a nutshell, when the Commission members viewed the Zapruder film, this harsh reality hit them:

Governor John Connally is seen reacting to his wounds so soon after the President is hit in the back, the Governor is either hit by the same shot that first struck the President or he was hit by a second shot fired almost simultaneously to the first shot.

To put it in the troublesome way the Commission discovered, both men are seen reacting to all their non-fatal wounds less than 1.5 seconds apart.

So, what's the problem?

Oswald's Mannlicher-Carcano rifle had a minimum firing time of 2.3 seconds, meaning that Governor Connally is seen reacting to his wounds before the sniper could get off a second shot!

With the Commission needing to explain the quick reaction of both men, they simply concluded that CE399 did cause all the survivable wounds in both victims.

Zapruder frame 236 shows both men reacting to bullet wounds, but just 1/3rd of a second earlier, only JFK is seen responding to being shot in the upper back.

They did this, despite:

- No evidence of this bullet transiting the President's upper body.
- No evidence of this bullet exiting either JFK or the Governor and falling on a stretcher at Parkland Hospital.
- No physical evidence of this bullet being linked to either man, such as residue tissue or blood on the missile.
- No ballistics evidence linking this bullet to torn clothing, broken bones or fragments either removed or left in either man's body.

THE HISTORY ALTERING INCISION

As far as we can tell, multiple shooters and a conspiracy might be what the history books tell us today about the JFK assassination if it wasn't for an incision performed on the President's throat, just below the Adam's apple.

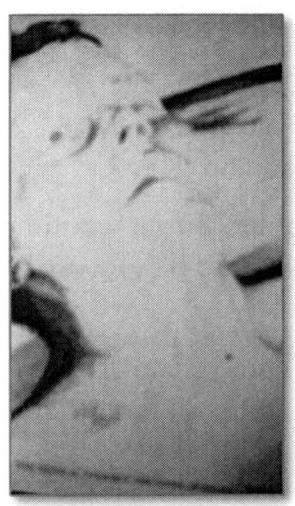

Autopsy surgeons never saw this puncture wound on JFK's throat.

As described in greater detail in Chapter 5, believe it or not, the President's autopsy was completed without the surgeons ever knowing that a wound occurred in the President's throat (see schematic drawing at left, courtesy of Robert Groden's The Killing of a President).

Had Dr. Humes contacted Dr. Malcolm Perry at Parkland Hospital before the autopsy proceeded, as a forensic pathologist would have routinely done, he would have learned that this wound existed.

However, since this throat wound was what Dr. Humes saw when President Kennedy's body arrived at the Bethesda Naval Hospital (see right), he correctly assumed that a tracheotomy incision had been done to aid the patient's breathing.

When Dr. Humes learned of this wound the next day, it would have been horrific news.

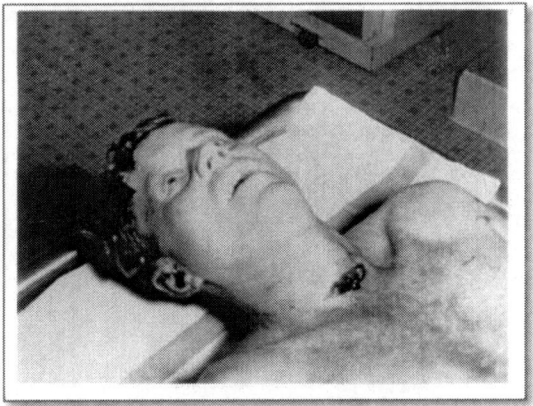

This neck wound is what autopsy surgeons saw. Compare this to original throat wound upper left.

He had just done an autopsy that did not account for all the wounds on the President. Chapter 5 describes the history-altering action he took after talking to Dr. Perry.

Conversely for the Warren Commission, the discovery of the JFK throat wound was nothing less than its savior. Why?

Because now the Commission could say that the throat wound *'must have been'* the point of exit for the bullet that hit Governor Connally and caused all his wounds!

So, why would the Commission invent the 'Single Bullet Theory' and conclude that both men were hit by the first shot fired that day?

With no less than history at stake, and some argue national security, the Commission had little choice for its monumental about-face. Here's the only two choices it had:

A) **Both Men Hit by Separate Shots** – There had to be a second gunman and therefore a conspiracy to kill the President that could have national security implications (see Chapter 12).

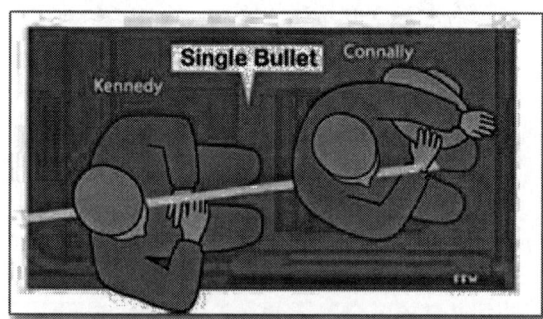

The *'Single Bullet Theory' according to the Warren Report – courtesy of www.frankwarner.typepad.com.*

B) **Both Men Hit by Single Shot (Magic Bullet)** – The conveniently silenced Lee Harvey Oswald could be named as the lone assassin and LBJ would use his Presidential powers to seal thousands of classified documents for 75 years.

Obviously, the Commission chose option 'B' and didn't seem concerned that it had to disregard way more evidence in support of option 'A.'

For instance:

- **The Zapruder Film** – It is not unusual for two people to look at the same thing and see it differently, but the Zapruder Film (dissected and presented in its entirety in Chapter 6) was not supposed to be seen by the public for several years.

  Researchers like Penn Jones Jr. and film expert Robert J. Groden got the film out to pockets of the public by the next decade and more than anything else, this historic home movie started to erode the most essential findings of the Warren Commission.

  Penn Jones gave me a copy of the film and asked me to show Canadians the shocking truth of what happened to President Kennedy that awful day in Dallas.

  He believed that the true Kennedy Assassination story belonged to the world, not just America.

  I kept my promise, showing the narrated Zapruder film to audiences of eight to 1800 at a time.

  As demonstrated in the Chapter 6 study of the Zapruder film, not only does the 'Single Bullet Theory' require CE399 to make a couple of impossible turns in mid air, this bullet earns its 'Magic Bullet' nickname because it must also pause in mid air before striking Governor Connally.

- **Governor Connally's Testimony** – As reported in Chapter 5, the Governor went to his death in 1993 never believing the Single Bullet Theory and presented the Commission with a compelling explanation as to why he was hit by a second shot very soon after JFK was hit by the first shot:

  "Well, in my judgement, it just couldn't conceivably have been the first shot that hit me because I heard the sound of the shot.

  "In the first place, I don't know anything about the velocity of this particular bullet, but any rifle has a velocity that exceeds the speed of sound.

  "And when I heard the sound of that first shot, the bullet had already reached where I was, or it had reached that far.

  "And after I heard that shot, I had the time to turn to my right and start to turn to my left before I felt anything."

  Mrs. Connally's appearance before the Commission seconded her husband's account of what happened:

  "I heard a noise. It was a frightening noise and it came from the right," she said. *"I turned over my right shoulder and looked back and saw the President as he had both hands at his neck.*

  "Then very soon there was a second shot that hit John" (her husband).

- **Autopsy Findings** – In addition to the original autopsy report, as well as a report by two FBI agents present in the room to record the proceedings and secure physical materials, all evidence suggests a bullet did not transit the President's body and therefore did not exit the throat.

So then, how did the President's throat wound occur? All this time later, we can only speculate since an autopsy failed to answer this question. (See Chapter 11 for what stands as the most plausible explanation).

- **No Ballistics Support** – Whereas the Commission could link the 'Magic Bullet' (CE399) to Oswald's rifle found near the sixth-floor window in the Book Depository Building, it saw no need for affirming evidence.

No known tests were conducted to search for minute blood or tissue evidence on the bullet that would prove it passed through JFK, Governor Connally or both men.

And as the X-ray of Governor Connally's wrist on the next page shows, the white dots are bullet fragments never removed from his body. There are additional fragments on the other side of the wrist, which was more extensively damaged.

Fragments also remain in the Governor's chest where a rib was broken off.

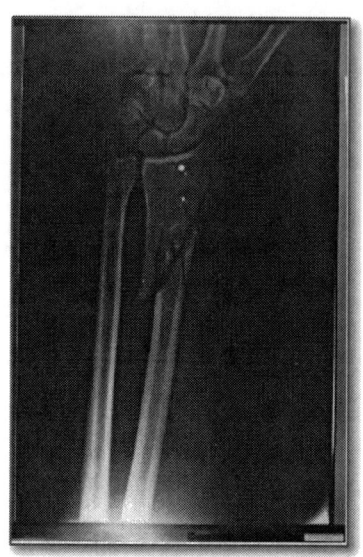

We know that some bullet fragments were recovered from the Governor's body, but no ballistics tests were done to match these fragments to CE399.

Why not? Such tests could have proven that the 'Single Bullet Theory' was fact instead of fiction.

And what about the totality of the fragments removed, as well as left inside the Governor? Some researchers claim that several fragments were never removed because the collective fragments could very well add up to more than the 2.4 grains of metal CE399 is missing.

- **Doctor Malcolm Perry's Critical Role** – When President Kennedy reached Parkland Hospital, he was in obvious respiratory distress. Although the violent head trauma dictated his fate, this was the President of the United States, so all means were carried out to save his life.

Doctor Malcolm Perry's 3-inch incision changed history.

Dr. Malcolm Perry was the first physician to attend to the President. As outlined in Chapter 5, Dr. Perry felt it necessary to obliterate a small wound in JFK's throat for a tracheotomy incision to insert a breathing tube.

Unfortunately for history, this wound was never made aware to the autopsy surgeons with the President's body before them.

They therefore failed to account for all the wounds sustained by the President.

When the existence of this wound was discovered post autopsy, all findings were thrown into chaos. But more troubling, this wound gave licence for the Warren Commission to concoct its 'Single Bullet Theory.'

This led to history becoming a lie, namely that Oswald was the lone assassin.

Here again, how the Warren Commission handled evidence that may not support the 'Single Bullet Theory' is quite alarming.

QUOTED OUT OF CONTEXT

Dr. Perry was the only physician to see President Kennedy before the tracheotomy incision was made, but this was not convenient for the Commission members.

When asked to describe this wound, Dr. Perry said it was a small, neat circular wound, about the diameter of a pencil (see illustration on page 97).

Most ballistic experts will say that Dr. Perry appears to be describing a bullet *entry* wound, but of course, the Warren Commission needs this to be an *exit* wound to support its 'Single Bullet Theory.'

Thus, the Warren Report uses Dr. Perry to declare that the throat wound was, in fact, an exit wound.

The Commission also has Dr. Robert McClelland as describing the throat wound as one of exit, just as it needs it to be.

How are we to question the observations of two medical professionals? Yet, that's exactly what I did at the young age of 16 back in 1968.

As a keen history student fascinated by the JFK assassination, and having just read all 26 volumes of the Warren Report, I decided to write to Dr. Perry about his unwanted role in history.

To my astonishment, Dr. Perry wrote back to me, in his own hand writing. Not only did he not support the Warren Report finding that the throat wound was an exit wound, he denies that Dr. McClelland ever viewed the throat wound "*as I had incised it prior to his arrival.*"

A similar letter was sent to Dr. McClelland, but went unanswered.

Dr. Perry's letter to me is presented here:

For those of you who may not be able to read the doctor's handwriting, the text is reproduced exactly here:

Dear Mr. O'Brien: 7 May '68

I regret that I cannot resolve your problem. As I noted in my testimony (and verified by the transcript of the press conference), I did not know how many bullets struck him and could not state that the neck wound was either entrance or exit. I, unfortunately, in response to questions speculated as to possible trajectory, and this was subsequently reported out of context as my opinion. This speculation was clearly preceded by qualifications indicating my lack of precise knowledge. Dr. McClelland did not see the neck wound, as I had incised it prior to his arrival, and he did not state that it was an entrance wound. He was also quoted out of context in regard to a possible head wound, described to him by an emergency room attendant who only saw Mr. Kennedy being rushed into the operating room. Thus, you can see that many 'facts' have little basis. I hope this will shed some light on your questions.

Sincerely,

MO Perry MD.

ANALYSIS OF DR. PERRY LETTER

Dr. Perry clearly recalls that he could not state that the throat wound was either entrance or exit and says this was *"Reported out of context as my opinion."*

The President's labored breathing did not give Dr. Perry the luxury of time to measure or analyse the throat wound for the benefit of historic accuracy.

As the only man who could shed light on this controversy, Dr. Perry declined this opportunity nearly five years after the event to lend credibility to the 'Single Bullet Theory' by even hinting that the neck wound may have been an exit hole.

To be fair, he cautiously avoids the single bullet debate altogether in his letter to me in 1968, as well as two additional letters in 1972, which are reproduced in the Appendices section at the end of this book.

However, based on Dr. Perry's description of the throat wound to the Commission, a pencil-sized circular puncture, when Oswald's rifle and identical ammunition were test-fired into goat flesh to simulate human flesh, the wound Dr. Perry described matched only entry wounds in the test materials (see Chapter 9).

Exit wounds were consistently larger in size, more jagged and had a 'blow-out' look to them, not at all what Dr. Perry saw on President Kennedy.

After the assassination, Dr. Perry became reclusive and refused almost all press inquiries until his passing at age 80 in 2009. He did not want to fan the fires of conspiracy or defend the Warren Report's findings.

In desperate need of supportive evidence, the Commission went beyond what Dr. Robert McClelland did or did not say about the President's wounds, especially the large hole in the head.

As a neuro surgeon, Dr. McClelland knows the characteristics of bullet wounds and how to accurately describe them and locate them on a human body.

But according to the Warren Commission, Dr. McClelland didn't know his anatomy. In chapter 7, Dr. McClelland is shown pointing to the area of the fatal head wound, which is different than what the Commission represented it to be.

What's the difference?

The Warren Commission needed the JFK massive head wound to be suggestive of a shot from above and behind the limousine where it says Oswald was situated.

But Dr. McClelland's description of the head wound is supportive of a shot fired from the right-front of the limousine.

EVIDENCE NOT WELL 'SUITED'

There was physical evidence at the Commission's disposal that had to be addressed, no matter what that evidence pointed to. Instead, the Commission did the next best thing:

It ignored almost all evidence that did not point to the validity of the 'Single Bullet Theory.' It even sought to suppress that evidence.

There was one piece of evidence that could not be ignored or hidden away. Everyone knew the Governor wore a suit that day.

Governor Connally's suit jacket shows a troubling jagged, elongated entry hole.

What does the Governor's clothing tell us about his wounds, if anything at all?

108

The Governor's suit jacket, according to 'forensic' examiners after the fact, seems contestable to the 'Single Bullet Theory.'

In the photo on page 108, the Governor's suit jacket shows a hole in the right side of his back.

The hole appears to be somewhat elongated and blasted out instead of small and circular, indicating that the bullet was probably tumbling and struck the Governor more sideways than straight on with the bullet nose.

The Governor's shirt shows the same type of damage to the cloth material, indicating it was struck by a tumbling bullet.

In of itself, this does not prove or disprove the 'Single Bullet Theory,' but does pose a bit of a quagmire for the Commission. For instance:

- **Delayed Reaction** - Knowing that CE399 likely did not strike the Governor nose first and therefore at maximum velocity, a variable important to the 'Single Bullet Theory' becomes discredited.

  In essence, this means the Governor was struck as bluntly as possible by CE399 as opposed to the piercing blow of a straight laser-like nose first high velocity bullet.

  It therefore seems highly improbable that the Governor experienced a delayed reaction to his wounds. This was the Commission's way of explaining why Connally was hit by the same bullet as Kennedy, but didn't react promptly.

  A tumbling bullet that severed a large rib bone and ripped a hole through a wrist bone is likely to prompt an immediate physical response because the impact on the bones was blunter compared to a non-tumbling bullet.

- **Bullet Damage** – As clearly shown in the photo of CE399 on page 90, the bullet is nearly pristine in appearance, missing only 2.4 grains of metal at the nose.

  It is almost inconceivable that a tumbling bullet wouldn't show some semblance of damage somewhere along the length of the bullet, especially given the damage attributed to this projectile. Apart from nominal squeezing at the base, the limited metallic loss is restricted to one spot on the nose.

It is also baffling as to why no ballistics evidence exists to link CE399 to the Governor's clothing. This is unthinkable, but rumors persist that the Governor's belongings were laundered before formally being examined by the FBI.

A BULLET'S MAGICAL CHANGE IN DIRECTION

The 'Magic Bullet' gets its nickname because of the sudden changes in direction it is required to make in approximately four feet of space that divided President Kennedy from Governor Connally.

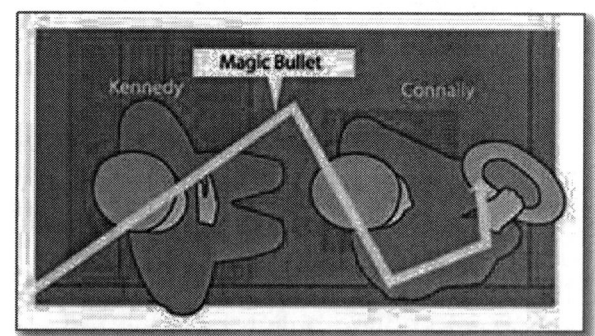

The flightpath of the 'Magic Bullet?' – courtesy of www.frankwarner.typepad.com.

In the schematic drawing to the right, the zig-zag of the

bullet's flightpath between the two men shows it to be quite impossible. No bullet could travel that way.

Additionally, if the Zapruder film accurately depicts the Governor being hit by a bullet slightly more than one second after the President is hit, another impossibility occurs:

If the two men were hit by the same bullet, as decided by the Warren Commission, this bullet would have to 'magically' pause for one second in mid-air before entering the Governor's back.

Even if we eliminate the delay factor from this remarkable trajectory, this bullet must still defy physics to do what the Warren Report claims.

But first, let's dispel a decades-long controversy the conspiracy buffs have wrongly used to debunk the 'Single Bullet Theory.'

As the drawing on page 110 shows, Governor Connally is seated directly in front of the President. This is incorrect.

The Governor was seated in a removable jump seat that positioned him about six inches from the car door.

Governor Connally is seated slightly left of President Kennedy in the jump seat ahead in the ill-fated limousine.

As both men were facing forward, Mr. Connally's upper body was slightly left of JFK's upper body. Why is this important?

This is helpful to the Warren Commission because if the shot came from above and behind the limousine on a slightly right-to-left angle, then the first illustration shown earlier is accurate.

In defense of the Commission, by being seated inches left of President Kennedy, the bullet wouldn't necessarily have to curve to the right after exiting JFK in order to enter the Governor's back on the right side.

LESS MAGICAL, BUT STILL EXTRAORDINARY

Before all you 'Oswald Acted Alone' defenders get excited, the seated positions of the two men simply means that CE399 wasn't as magical as we thought.

Does this make the 'Single Bullet Theory' at least probable?

The answer is 'NO' because this bullet still has some major explaining to do before it loses its moniker 'The Magic Bullet.'

For instance:

Exit JFK's Throat?

All existing evidence establishes that the first shot did not even transit the President's body (see Chapter 5). The Commission never explained how CE399 mysteriously did exit at Kennedy's throat.

There are no X-rays to show the bullet's internal path from JFK's upper back to his throat, which the Commission would have happily published to support its change of mind.

No surgery was performed to track the path of the bullet from the back to the throat because Dr. Humes probed the entry wound in the upper back with his finger and felt the end of its penetration at about the second knuckle.

112

Without a medically proven pathway for this missile to somehow exit JFK's throat, this bullet must be regarded as 'magical.'

Lack of Ballistics

As forensic pathologists will tell you, a bullet will always leave evidence of its journey through a human body. This is usually in the form of missile passageways, bullet fragments or evidence from the victim found on a retrieved bullet.

We know that fragments were removed from Governor Connally and fragments were not removed, but the Commission offers no proof that CE399 is the bullet belonging to any of these metal particles.

Although CE399 bore no evidence of it passing through Connally or Kennedy, the Commission was content to merely establish that it had been fired from Oswald's rifle.

Since there is no definitive proof linking CE399 to the events of November 22, 1963, an alternative possibility for this missile is presented in Chapter 12.

JFK's Mysterious Moving Back Wound

The official autopsy chart on page 114 shows the location of the entry wound in the President's upper back that was probed by Dr. Humes.

It is described in the official autopsy findings as being located 5 ¾ inches below the neckline and slightly to the right of the spinal column. A hole in JFK's shirt and suit jacket verify that location, as does an FBI report.

Unfortunately, that was not good news for the Commission, especially having decided that the bullet which caused this wound inexplicably exited at JFK's throat, just below the Adam's apple.

How did this happen?

According to the Commission, the bullet in question entered the President's back at a downward trajectory of 45 to 60%, having come from behind and above the limousine.

Note bullet entry wound in JFK's back. This wound would mysteriously move up to his neck.

And despite not striking any bony substances in the body or dense organs, this bullet deflects upward so it can exit at the throat.

This is yet another perplexing predicament for the Commission that only magic seems to remedy.

Or as my interview with forensic pathologist Dr. Cyril Wecht in early 2017 puts it:

"*The bullet hole in the back is real,*" says Dr. Wecht, who has studied the medical materials in the National Archives. "*The bullet hole in the front of the neck doesn't match up.*

"*The trajectory inside the body has an 11.5-degree upward angle. So, they have a bullet fired from the sixth-floor window striking Kennedy in the back and moving upward 11.5 degrees.*

114

"So, how did they handle it? Well, what if Kennedy was leaning over? But when you look at the Zapruder film, frame-by-frame, Kennedy is not leaning forward.

"He is sitting up, looking at the crowd, waving his hand as politicians do. He wasn't bending down to tie his shoe or anything."

Amazingly, when the Commission encountered witnesses that did not affirm its 'Single Bullet Theory,' they were simply mistaken about what they saw or heard.

But when the Commission sought to bolster its 'Single Bullet synopsis, it didn't hesitate to propose speculation as fact even when there was no evidence to support it.

Governor Connally, Where Are You?

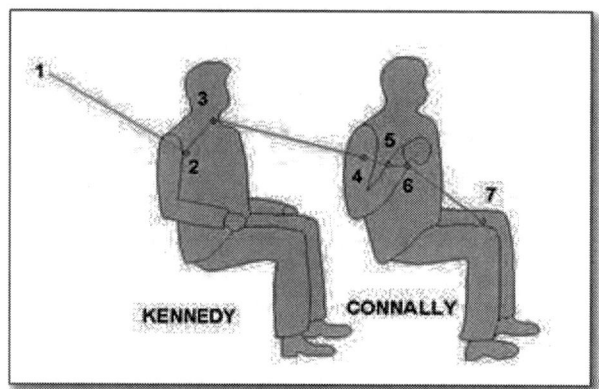

Notice the upward trajectory in position #3 for a bullet that must now travel downward to hit Connally.

Earlier, it was conceded that the 'Magic Bullet' did not have to make a sharp left-to-right turn to find Governor Connally's back, given the seating alignment of the two men.

The pro 'Single Bullet Theory' crowd could be heard shouting a collective "*We told you so!*"

Unfortunately for Warren Report supporters, there is a sudden mid-air turn this bullet still must make before locating the Governor's back.

Having exited the President's throat at an upward trajectory as indicated by the number 3 in the diagram above, CE399 is now required to turn sharply downward to stay in the limousine and find Connally's back (see #4).

Obviously, this was not compatible with the Warren Commission's 'Single Bullet Theory.' So, how did the Commission deal with it?

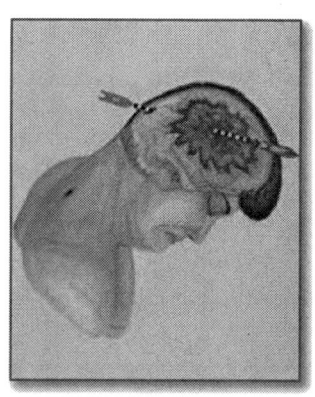

This Warren Commission schematic drawing shows a bullet entry hole in the neck, not the upper back.

Astoundingly, they had the audacity to disregard all the evidence placing the entry wound 5 ¾ inches below the President's neckline.

It is flabbergasting to realize that the Commission simply moved the President's back wound up approximately five inches to the base of the neck.

This way, the Commission could say the entry wound was higher than the exit wound in the throat.

This enabled the Commission to create a fictional downward trajectory from the Oswald window in the sixth floor of the Book Depository Building, through the President's neck and continuing downward to the Governor's back.

Suddenly, we have gone from a 'Magic Bullet' to outright fraud in defense of the 'Single Bullet Theory.'

Connally's Wounds

From a pure trajectory perspective, the rest of the 'Single Bullet Theory' is plausible.

Once the bullet entered Governor Connally's body, all his wounds conceivably line up, but as outlined previously, there are unanswered ballistic questions, as well as his own testimony, that cast doubt on CE399 doing all the non-lethal damage to the two men.

HISTORICAL MYSTERY OR FACT?

Did Lee Harvey Oswald act alone in shooting President John F. Kennedy on November 22, 1963?

For us to believe it to be true, we must first believe that a single 'Magic Bullet' acted alone in causing all the non-life-threatening wounds inflicted on both the President and Governor Connally.

If it was a second bullet that struck the Governor, even the harshest skeptics of conspiracy must admit that history got it wrong.

If the 'Single Bullet Theory' is not correct, the very foundation of the Warren Report comes crashing down in a rubble of deceit and cover-up decades in the making.

Despite what cover-ups are designed to do, all these years later, we not only deserve the truth, we must demand the truth for the betterment of history to come.

Footnote:

A total of three letters from Dr. Malcolm Perry to the author can be found in the Appendices section. These rare public thoughts of Dr. Perry have been donated to the Sixth Floor Museum at Dealey Plaza in Dallas, Texas.

Chapter 5

The Bizarre JFK Autopsy that Failed History and the Truth

Had Lee Harvey Oswald lived to stand trial, it is highly likely that the post-mortem performed on his alleged victim would have proven that he could **NOT** have been the lone assassin of president John F. Kennedy.

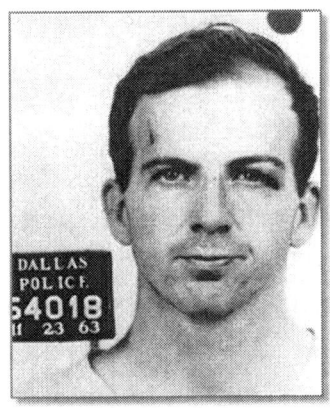
Lee Harvey Oswald - Patsy?

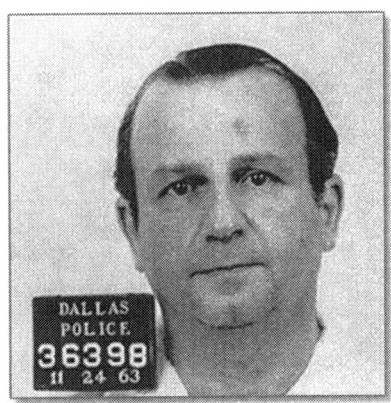
Jack Ruby - Patsy Killer?

Many people believe that would have been the right conclusion, based on the judicial standard that a verdict of innocence must be rendered when 'reasonable doubt' has been established.

Instead, the autopsy findings were used by the Warren Commission to ascertain that they needn't look for accomplices.

Thus, history and the truth were ill served when Oswald, himself, was assassinated by Jack Ruby before a public trial could occur.

A trial of the alleged assassin would have changed everything.

And apart from the Zapruder film itself (discussed in detail in Chapter 6), nothing would have shocked the nation as much as the bungling of the President's autopsy.

A post-mortem examination, especially when death is caused by violent means, is often the most relevant evidence presented in a court of law.

It is intended to cut through any speculation and provide irrefutable medical and scientific evidence of what exactly happened to the victim.

MORE QUESTIONS THAN ANSWERS

The results of a professionally done post-mortem, oftentimes more than any other evidence presented (the science of DNA did not exist at the time), can either exonerate the suspect charged with murder or it can provide proof of guilt beyond a reasonable doubt.

In this historic instance, the post-mortem findings, supported by testimony from the three attending pathologists, as well as the medical witnesses at Parkland Hospital, would have been presented at an Oswald trial to establish the following:

1. The detailed nature of both the non-fatal and fatal wounds sustained by President Kennedy.

2. A thorough accounting of all wounds, including tracking of JFK's back and neck wounds to establish the bullet's pathways, as well as the removal, preservation, sectioning and full examination of what remained of his brain, thereby establishing the exact cause of death rather than rely on mere observation.

3. The trajectory and origin of the shots that struck the President, identifying the location of the shooter or shooters.

Instead of a court of law, where the autopsy findings would have been subject to skilled questioning and counter evidence by defense lawyers and a defense team of 'forensic' pathologists, the uncontested JFK autopsy findings were published in the Warren Report and used prominently to name Oswald as the lone assassin.

HISTORY'S PROFOUND LOSS

It is history's profound loss that a trial never took place for Lee Harvey Oswald. In poll after poll, nearly 75% of Americans still believe that the truth was buried with both the victim and the accused on November 25, 1963.

Even more tragic is how the president's autopsy was handled and how the findings were used by the government to rule out any possibility of a second gunman or a conspiracy.

The flawed findings of the president's death started literally minutes after he was pronounced dead at Parkland Hospital at 1:00 p.m. CST on November 22, 1963.

That moment came when newly sworn-in president Lyndon Johnson refused to order Air Force One back to Washington without the body of his slain predecessor (see below right).

This resulted in a custody battle over the president's body, which by law, was required to remain in the state of Texas and undergo a post-mortem examination before being released to the family.

To be certain, as per normal proceedings, top forensic pathologists in the Dallas Medical Examiner's Office would have been called upon to conduct the president's autopsy.

Tragically, this was not to be.

Following the orders of the new president, Secret

With a shocked and blood-stained Jackie Kennedy at his side, LBJ becomes the 36th U.S. President.

Service agents physically restrained county officials and forcibly removed the president's body, even confiscating a hearse to get it to Love Field Airport.

Let's concede that these were highly unusual circumstances. Even if we agree that laws of the day should not have been adhered to under such extraordinary circumstances, what was to happen later that night cannot be so easily forgiven or excused.

MILITARY TAKEOVER

Once Air Force One landed back in Washington, it can be argued that the official fabrication of events and cover-up began – in the form of a military takeover of sorts!

Iconic photo by Bob Jackson shows Ruby silencing Oswald forever.

In a turn of events that is almost too shocking to comprehend, the President's body was placed in military control rather than the public coroner's office in the District of Columbia.

The consequences of this decision are monumental and when Oswald was murdered two days later, his fate as the lone assassin of President Kennedy was sealed.

Millions of us watched on live television as the President's flag-draped casket was lowered from Air Force One and placed into an awaiting hearse.

Who can forget watching a stunned Attorney General Robert F. Kennedy greeting his deceased brother's coffin or the blood-stained pink outfit of Jackie Kennedy as she was seated in the hearse that drove off.

Most regrettably, the hearse was directed to the Bethesda Naval Medical Centre in Maryland where irreversible consequences were set in motion.

Believe it or not, the first major blunder occurred when qualified 'forensic' pathologists were **NOT** called upon to conduct the president's autopsy.

Instead, the military decided to use in-house 'general hospital' pathologists to execute the president's post-mortem.

None of the autopsy surgeons had ever before conducted an autopsy involving violent death. None had ever worked on a case where death was by multiple gunshots.

Commander James J. Humes was put in an impossible situation.

This is incredulous!

MEDICAL MALFEASANCE

Dr. Cyril Wecht, a professor of law and chief forensic pathologist at Allegheny County in Pittsburgh, is a former director of the Institute of Forensic Sciences.

He notes that forensic pathology and general hospital pathology are very different and distinct sciences.

Dr. Cyril Wecht refutes JFK autopsy findings.

"A hospital pathologist spends much of his time studying organs and tissue slides to establish diagnosis on living patients," Dr. Wecht states.

"A hospital pathologist deals primarily with patients who have died from natural causes. His job usually is to confirm a diagnosis already arrived at, or for research purposes.

"A forensic pathologist, often associated with the medical examiner's office," continues Dr. Wecht, *"must frequently determine the exact cause and manner of death caused by violence."*

Clearly, unqualified military general hospital pathologists were assigned to carry out a complex forensic medical examination because civilian pathologists could not have been ordered to alter or skew their findings in support of a pre-conceived conclusion.

Even when skepticism abounds, the goings on at the autopsy table and the unprecedented editing of the official autopsy findings the next day establish beyond any doubt that the JFK autopsy is filled with fatal flaws, mistakes of procedure, contradictions and glaring omissions, all remarkably in support the lone gunman theory.

CONSEQUENCES OF A 'MILITARY' AUTOPSY

The three military pathologists assigned to the autopsy were Commander James J. Humes, Commander Thornton J. Boswell and Lt. Col. Pierre A. Finck.

These men were always in the presence of military officials who outranked them. As a result, the maligned doctors were handcuffed by the following orders by superiors:

- Dr. Finck was ordered not to examine the President's back wound a second time after word came that a nearly whole bullet was found at Parkland Hospital. This could have changed one of their critical findings.

- The doctors were not permitted to study blood and tissue samples of the brain and other wounds taken at the early stages of the examination.

- The doctors removed what remained of the President's brain, but were not allowed to examine it before it was placed in a formalin solution container and taken away.

  Consequently, they could not establish any sense if the extensive damage was the result of one or more shots, as well as bullet and fragment pathways to establish points of entry or exit.

- Several photographs and x-rays were taken of the President's wounds and such evidence is often processed quickly to help the surgeons arrive at conclusions, such as bullet pathways inside the body.

However, the JFK autopsy surgeons were denied access to any images to help them formulate conclusions.

- The autopsy doctors were not allowed to examine the clothing the President wore that day, which may have alerted them to a mystery wound not evident by observing the body.

JFK's suit jacket and shirt confirm a bullet entry wound nearly six inches below the shoulders and slightly to the right of the spinal column (see next page).

This physical evidence aligns with the wound found on the President's back, as noted in the diagram on page 131 made by Dr. Thornton Boswell.

However, the President's tie (see next page), presents a major problem to the autopsy surgeons and the Warren Commission.

Damage to the front of the President's shirt, just below the buttoned collar, as well as a tiny tear in the knot of his neck tie, cannot be explained by a bullet that did not transit the body.

Entry wound in back, not neck.

What caused this nick?

Hole in JFK shirt below button suggests a
wound never accounted for at autopsy.

Accordingly, for the purposes of the official government report on the assassination of the 35th President of the United States, this evidence was misrepresented to support a theory rather than substantiated facts (more on this later).

THE PHONE CALL THAT CHANGED HISTORY!

Perhaps because of inexperience, a normal procedure was not followed with the President's body still on the autopsy table.

A competent forensic pathologist, knowing that doctors at Parkland Hospital viewed the body and made efforts to save the President's life, would have contacted the attending doctors to gather any evidence or observations they might have.

Dr. Malcolm Perry, first physician to see JFK.

This would normally be done **before** the autopsy proceedings, but because that call was made by Commander James J. Humes the next morning with his autopsy findings already on paper, he received the shock of his life!

Dr. Humes placed a call to Parkland doctor Malcom O. Perry the morning **after** the assassination. Dr. Perry had been the first doctor to attend to the President in Trauma Room One.

He noted that JFK was in respiratory distress and his first action was to perform a tracheotomy (incision) in the throat of his patient to insert a tube to restore normal breathing.

This was not surprising to Dr. Humes at the time of autopsy, who had assumed that this procedure was performed upon viewing the jagged and elongated cut in the President's throat during the autopsy.

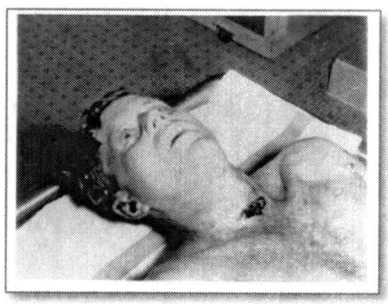

It's what Dr. Perry said next that plunged Dr. Humes' autopsy findings into complete chaos.

Autopsy surgeons didn't know this tracheotomy incision on JFK's throat destroyed a possible bullet wound.

Dr. Perry reported that in making a tracheotomy incision in the throat, just below the Adam's apple, he had obliterated a small, circular wound on the President. He described it as a small, neat, round wound, about the diameter of a pencil.

SHOCKING DISCLOSURE

We don't know if Dr. Humes dropped the phone in shock or fainted, but we do know that what he did after hearing this news altered his autopsy findings completely, thereby altering history.

This may be the moment that gave birth to conspiracy theorists around the world.

Upon realizing that he just oversaw an autopsy of historic nature, and in fact, reached conclusions without accounting for **all** the wounds sustained by the President, Dr. Humes tossed his official autopsy notes into his home fireplace.

He then reconstructed a secondary set of autopsy notes that would allow investigators to conclude that Oswald fired all the shots from above and behind the Presidential motorcade.

Here's how this historic about-face happened:

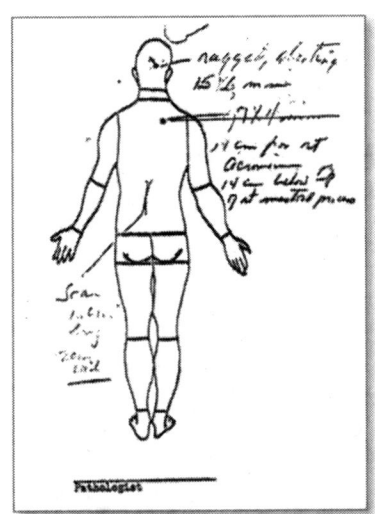

Dr. Boswell drawing shows bullet hole in JFK's back, a major problem for the Warren Commission.

Dr. Humes originally concluded that a non-fatal wound appeared on President Kennedy's back. He measured it to be 5 ¾" below the collar line and 2 inches to the right of the spinal column (see diagram by Dr. Thornton Boswell left).

Commander Humes further concludes that the bullet that caused this wound did not transit the body.

This important discovery was reported by FBI special agents James Sibert and Francis O'Neill, who were present in the autopsy room to record and retrieve evidence. Their report states:

"During the later stages of this autopsy, Dr. Humes located an opening, which appeared to be a bullet hole, which was below the shoulders and two inches to the right of the middle line of the spinal column.

"This opening was probed by Dr. Humes with the finger, at which time it was determined that the trajectory of the missile entering at this point entered at a downward position of 45 to 60 degrees.

"Further probing (by Dr. Humes) determined that the distance traveled by this missile was a short distance inasmuch as the end of the opening could be felt with the finger."

A short time later, word came to the autopsy room that a nearly whole bullet was found on a stretcher at Parkland Hospital. This news, plus his own examination of the shallow wound, prompted Dr. Humes to write this conclusion:

Dr. Humes – "*The bullet that entered the Presidents back entered a short distance and worked its way out of the body during external cardiac massage at the hospital.*"

This statement, as well as the location of the entry wound in the back, would become historically significant.

Supportive evidence comes from Secret Service agent Clint Hill, who is the agent you see on the Zapruder film jump onto the trunk of the limousine, push Mrs. Kennedy back into her seat and climb on top of the fatally wounded President:

Secret Service agent Clint Hill with JFK and Jackie shortly before assassination.

Warren Commission Member Hale Boggs –

"*When the President's body was being prepared for placement in a casket, did you see the whole body?*"

Agent Hill – "*Yes, sir*"

Mr. Boggs – *Did you see any wound other than the head wound*?"

Agent Hill – "*Yes, sir. I saw an opening in the back, about six inches below the neckline, to the right-hand side of the spinal column.*"

NEW WOUND, NEW CONCLUSION

While the well documented location of the back entry wound on the President would also soon mysteriously change, so did the conclusion that the bullet entered a short distance and fell out of the body during external cardiac massage at the hospital.

After his phone conversation with Dr. Perry, Dr. Humes stunningly amended his final autopsy report to conclude that the non-fatal first shot that struck JFK in the back, in fact, *did* transit the body!

Dr. Humes decided, based solely on the eyewitness account of Dr. Perry, and contrary to his own documented probing of this wound, that this front throat wound was now the point of exit for the bullet that hit JFK in the upper back.

What? So, the bullet that hit the president in the back DID transit the body?

Can you imagine how defense attorneys and medical experts such as Dr. Cyril Wecht would have destroyed this finding at an Oswald trial?

The integrity of the post-mortem examination would have been thrown into turmoil, thus raising the probability of reasonable doubt.

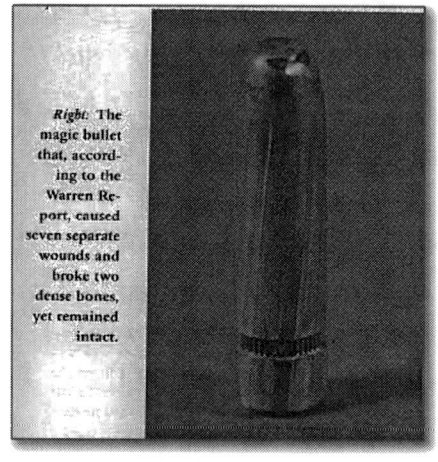

Right: The magic bullet that, according to the Warren Report, caused seven separate wounds and broke two dense bones, yet remained intact.

Dr. Wecht, who became among the first highly qualified 'forensic' pathologists to examine the autopsy materials in the National Archives, revealed in the 1974 edition of Legal Medicine Annual:

"The locations of wounds on the President's body were not precisely reported," states Dr. Wecht, specifically noting the President's wound to the upper back had inexplicably moved up to the lower neck area."

A further examination of the X-rays by Dr. Wecht showed that a customary procedure of wound dissection was not done on JFK's back. This is routinely performed to trace the path and trajectory of a bullet inside a body.

This one omitted procedure, on its own, brought confusion to the autopsy findings rather than clarification of exactly what happened.

Not even Dr. Humes could have known at the time that his earth-shattering about-face, which would never be contested in a court of law, enabled the Warren Commission to concoct the so-called 'Single Bullet Theory' (see Chapter 4).

Why? Because Dr. Humes was always under the impression that the nearly pristine bullet found at Parkland Hospital (see CE399 above), missing only 2.4 grains of metal at the nose, was the bullet he believed had penetrated only a few inches in the President's back and fell back out of the point of entry, to be found by a hospital employee.

Imagine the surprise when Dr. Humes learned that without any proof whatsoever, the Warren Commission abruptly decided that this bullet was actually found on a stretcher associated with Governor Connally and **NOT** President Kennedy.

How suddenly convenient!

The Commission could now say that the non-fatal first shot that struck President Kennedy, in fact, exited the Commander-in-Chief at the throat and went on to strike Texas Governor John Connally,

Texas Governor John Connally, sitting in front of JFK, believes he was hit by a separate bullet.

who was seated slightly to the left and in front of the President.

CREATION OF A 'MAGIC' BULLET

This bullet, according to the Warren Report, caused all the Governor's non-fatal wounds. These included three entry wounds, two exit wounds and two major broken bones.

This 'magic bullet' would allow the Warren Commission to take it a step further by declaring that *all* the non-fatal wounds sustained by the two men were caused by this one single bullet.

This became 100% necessary, because as the Zapruder film illustrates, the Governor is hit and reacts so soon after the President is hit and reacts, he is either hit by the same shot that first struck the president or the Governor is hit by a second shot fired almost simultaneous to the first shot.

We know the side of history that the Warren Commission chose. The Single Bullet Theory is what enabled the Commission to conclude that Lee Harvey Oswald fired all the shots from above and behind the limousine and that no conspiracy existed.

Without the single bullet theory being correct, there **must** be at least two gunmen and a conspiracy to kill the President!

Now that you know how flimsily history was shaped, it is most tragic that the head of the Warren Commission, Chief Justice of the United States Earl Warren, did not demand that all aspects of evidentiary law be upheld.

For instance, any forensic post-mortem, involving death by gunshot(s), is mandated to ascertain the nature of all wounds, including:

- Point of entry.
- Origin of the shot(s).
- Precise damage inflicted by the projectile(s).
- Point of exit, if any.
- Final destination of the projectile.
- Sequence of shots and wounds in the case of multiple firings.

Chief Justice Earl Warren headed government inquiry into JFK assassination.

Not only does the President's post-mortem not pass this test, it fails miserably on almost all points!

But with Oswald conveniently out of the way and the burden of establishing guilt beyond a reasonable doubt no longer required, the Warren Commission was free to suppress a most inconvenient truth.

And the Warren Commission was free to ignore evidence, change evidence or misrepresent evidence as it needed to present its case of a lone assassin of President Kennedy and a lone assassin of the assassin.

After all, they were encouraged by these two advantages:

1. Neither Lee Harvey Oswald, nor his family, were allowed legal representation during the Warren Commission hearings, just as Oswald was denied legal council while in custody by Dallas police, despite his pleas to see a lawyer.

Oswald's mother hired Mark Lane to represent Oswald at the hearings, but he was never allowed access to witnesses or evidence during the process.

Even in a Grand Jury procedure, a defendant has more rights than what the deceased Oswald was given.

This means that while the Commission heard plenty of circumstantial evidence against Oswald during the hearings, none of the witnesses or evidence was ever questioned or cross examined in defense of Oswald.

2. The Commission was free to reach its findings, knowing that a carefully edited report would be made available to the public, while thousands of documents and physical evidence would be classified as 'Top Secret' and stored in the National Archives for 75 years by Presidential decree!

While there are still hundreds of withheld classified documents not scheduled for release until 2038, The Warren Commission's case has slowly come crashing down over time, much in part thanks to the emergence of the Freedom of Information Act in 1967.

But something else even more remarkable happened.

The entire Zapruder film, not just the edited version released to support the single assassin theory, came to light 12 years later.

This 26-second film, taken by Dallas clothing manufacturer Abraham Zapruder, is the most famous amateur film ever taken.

In this Zapruder frame, JFK is hit in the back. The 'single bullet theory' says Gov. Connally is also hit, but could he still be holding a 10-gallon Stetson hat with his shattered right wrist?

Oddly, it presented the Warren Commission with both its greatest problem, as well as a solution to protect the national interests of the country.

Before getting to that remarkable film in chapter 6, there's one conclusion we can make based on the evidence thus far:

It is an injustice of epic proportions that qualified civilian forensic pathologists were not called upon to conduct the autopsy of the murdered President of the United States.

Nothing less than history may be different today

Through The 'Oswald' Window

Chapter 6

The Zapruder Film:

The Shocking 26-Second Home Movie that Won't Let History Be a Lie!

Warning: This chapter contains graphic images and descriptions of a violent nature that may be disturbing to see. Not recommended reading for persons under age 19.

President John F. Kennedy –
May 29, 1917 - November 22, 1963

It continues to shock us all these decades later.

Despite the increasing desensitizing of our society, thanks to violent war footage, watching desperate people leap 75 floors to certain death on 9/11, seeing ISIS captors decapitate heads on the Internet or ultra-violent video games, there's something about viewing President Kennedy's gruesome head shot that continues to haunt us.

Perhaps it's the shock value of its originality. Occurring at the dawn of television and four days of heart-wrenching national coverage that followed, the disbelief factor has waned over the years, especially after seeing Martin Luther King and Robert Kennedy suffer similar fates in a tumultuous 1968.

Assassination attempts on Presidents Gerald Ford and Ronald Reagan stunned us, but did they really shock us?

Did President Reagan's assassination attempt not shock us as much as JFK because he survived?

Maybe we were comforted that they survived and we didn't have to relive the tragedy of November 22, 1963.

Perhaps it was the sudden horrific end to 'Camelot' that keeps it so fresh in our minds. How can we not miss the youthful promise of a GQ President and his Princess bride?

Unlike Presidents who fulfill their terms in office, with JFK, we are unfairly left to wonder about what could have been.

Because of his premature passing, historians like to refer to him as *"a brilliant maybe."*

Would there have been a Vietnam? A Watergate? How would every Presidential election since have been different? After all, no less than three successive U.S. Presidential elections (1964, 1968, 1972) were affected by bullets as much as ballots.

Indeed, how would the world be different today if Dallas did not happen?

Or perhaps it was because true justice was denied when Lee Harvey Oswald was silenced by Jack Ruby and we were left with so many unanswered questions.

Less than 48 hours later, we were shocked a second time when we turned on our TV sets and saw the first ever murder committed on live television.

Live TV coverage not only made us viewers of history unfolding before our very eyes, we became eye witnesses to murder in real time when Ruby fired his gun and Oswald screamed out in pain.

THE FILM THAT WON'T LET US FORGET

Younger people are surprised to learn that the famous Zapruder film wasn't our first imbedded recollection of that awful day.

Actually, it had nothing to do with our early acceptance of a lone nut loser assassinating the leader of the free world.

Somehow, we were comforted to know that there was nothing more sinister at play.

The Zapruder film was not the official record of that event until the public was first allowed to see it in March of 1975 when Geraldo Rivera aired it on ABC's Good Night America.

Like millions of Americans, I saw it then for the first time. At frame 313, when the President's head explodes in a pink hazy

mist, there was a collective gasp at our television screens to match the gasps of horror from the live studio audience on set.

In 1979, Penn Jones Jr. provided me with a copy of his narrated Zapruder film.

When I played it to audiences at JFK assassination seminars for the next 20 years, that familiar haunting gasp would fill the room. The rare Penn Jones version of the Zapruder film is viewable at

Dallas clothing manufacturer
Abraham Zapruder.

www.youtube.com/watch?v=UBKliGNC49c.

From 1963 to 1975, the Zapruder film was suppressed to the public except for some black and white still frames published by Life Magazine in 1964 after buying the film for $150,000, followed by some color still frames published over the next few years.

And if you happened to be in the New Orleans courtroom in 1969 at the Clay Shaw trial for conspiracy to murder JFK, District Attorney Jim Garrison gave the Zapruder film its first ever public viewing.

Zapruder's Bell & Howell Zoomatic 8 mm Director Series Model 414 PD camera.

After the trial, some jurors said the Zapruder film established that there was a conspiracy, but that Garrison failed to prove Shaw had any role in that conspiracy.

RESEARCHERS DO WHAT MEDIA WON'T

In 1964, CBS News aired a documentary that supported the essential findings of the Warren Report, namely that Lee Oswald acted alone in shooting the President and Jack Ruby acted alone in shooting Oswald.

CBS did not present the Zapruder film to the public on that telecast because on the night of the assassination, it lost a bidding war to Life Magazine to acquire the rights to the film.

Nonetheless, with President Johnson locking away thousands of documents as 'Classified' or 'Top Secret' for 75 years, the public was limited to reading the Warren Report or following media stories, which rarely went beyond reporting the findings of the Commission.

When independent researchers like Mark Lane, Harold Weisberg, Josiah Thompson, Penn Jones Jr., Mary Ferrell and Edward Jay Epstein began to raise questions about the Warren Report findings, the main media would not give them the time of day…that is…until the Zapruder film finally came to the public's attention in 1975.

Even then, until the Internet truly became a world-wide web of information in the 1990's, very few people got to see the 486 frames of Zapruder's home movie.

Today, people accuse the Internet of misleading the public about the JFK assassination. They may be right, but that process began long before the birth of the computer age.

On the very night of the President's assassination, Dallas CBS bureau chief Dan Rather got a tip about the film's existence, located the owner and acted on behalf of CBS to purchase the film.

Life Magazine was also in the bidding and won, but Dan Rather became the first person to see the original Zapruder film and report on it.

Denied the right to show any part of the Zapruder film to the American public, Dan Rather went on CBS News with Walter Cronkite two days later and gave a chilling account of what he saw:

Go to YouTube.com and enter this address –

www.youtube.com/watch?v=LuHdK-4M1Wc

– courtesy of JFK Assassination Forum YouTube Channel

At 2:15 into the above CBS footage, Dan Rather states the greatest misrepresentation of all about the JFK assassination.

He reports, from copious notes taken at the film's private screening, that the President's head moves violently ***forward*** immediately after being struck in the skull.

This denotes a gunshot from the rear, which, of course, coincides with Oswald's alleged position in the sixth-floor window of the Book Depository Building.

Nobody of intelligence is suggesting that Rather's important account of the President's assassination was part of a cover-up to frame Oswald, but this is effectively what happened for 12 years until people began seeing what Rather inexplicably failed to see on the Zapruder film.

Undoubtedly, Dan Rather's memorable description of the shooting was a major contributor to the American people's acceptance for the first dozen years that Oswald was the lone assassin.

It is no coincidence that in the first decade following the assassination, the only people who had uncertainty about Oswald acting alone were conspiracy theorists like yours truly.

We were branded as nutty as Oswald.

SEEING IS DISBELIEVING!

But unlike most Americans, we conspiracy-minded types read all 26 volumes of the Warren Report, not just the summary edition made available in retail stores. The more we read, the more skeptical we became.

And we talked to witnesses and key people associated with that day, only to find that things were not always as the Warren Report stated.

I developed a written dialogue with Dr. Malcolm Perry, the first physician to tend to JFK at Parkland Hospital and who would alter history with a single incision to the President's throat (see Chapter 4).

Apart from our exchanged letters, Dr. Perry went stealth after developing a distrust of the Warren Commission, investigators and reporters.

Today, approximately 75% of the American public believes there was more than one gunman and hence a conspiracy to kill the 35th President of the United States. The Zapruder film's release had a lot to do with that.

Respectfully to Mr. Rather, we do not have the pressure or time constraint he was under when we view the Zapruder film today.

Yet, we are at a loss to explain how he could **not** see the President's head thrust violently *backward* and to the left as a result of the impact of the fatal head shot.

This, of course, would suggest a shot coming from the right-front of the limousine in the area of the grassy knoll.

One thing we have learned about the Zapruder film is that visual evidence does not necessarily constitute irrefutable fact.

Many people view the film and see conspiracy and many people view the film and see confirmation of a lone sniper.

The rarely seen Penn Jones narrated version of the Zapruder film is presented on the author's YouTube Channel, including slow-motion enhancements of the shooting sequence.

Simply follow the instructions under the image below. Viewer discretion is advised:

Go to www.youtube.com and type in this address –

www.youtube.com/watch?v=UBKliGNC49c

A FRAME-BY-FRAME LOOK

The above film footage presents a compelling case for conspiracy, but you may see it differently. Let's dissect the areas of controversy and take a still- frame look at what the Zapruder film reveals:

Frame #194

To give time its proper perspective, Zapruder's Bell & Howell camera captured 18 frames of film per second.

Zapruder Frame #194

Starting from frame 194, one second later takes us to frame 212 with both men still appearing unhurt.

In less than one more second, chaos erupts in Dealey Plaza.

Frame 194 shows President Kennedy looking at the crowd to his right on Elm Street and waiving to them. He is about to disappear momentarily behind a highway traffic sign.

At this point, neither the President or Governor Connally have been hit by a bullet, but the tragic sequence of shots will commence just over a second later.

The controversy begins here because that highway sign blocks Zapruder's view for a critical second.

Both men disappear behind the sign seemingly unhurt, but when the car emerges from behind the sign, the President is seen clearly reacting to a non-fatal shot that hits him in the upper back.

The crowd is beginning to thin out. It is sad to realize that in a matter of seconds, the President's limousine would pass

through Dealey Plaza and take an on-ramp to Stemmons
Freeway where the car would speed up to get to a luncheon
speech. Instead, the car sped past the lunch venue and went on
to Parkland Hospital.

Frame #223

In Zapruder frame 223, we see Governor Connally emerging
from behind the highway sign showing no apparent signs of
being hit by a bullet that first struck the President, who is still
blocked by the sign.

Zapruder Frame #223

Yet, the Warren Commission insists that Governor Connally is
hit by frame 223.

The bullet that struck Connally entered his back on the right side, broke off his fifth right rib, exited his chest just below the right nipple, hit his right wrist and shattered the distal radius bone before exiting the wrist and lodging itself in Connally's left thigh.

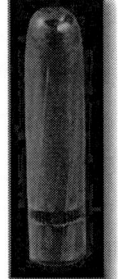

To say that one bullet caused all the non-lethal wounds in both men, the Commission concocted the 'Single Bullet Theory' (see Chapter 4). This enabled the Commission to conclude that Lee Harvey Oswald fired all the shots that day from above and behind the limousine.

Magic Bullet?

Does the Governor appear to be already hit in frame 223 by a bullet that caused him to sustain five wounds and two major broken bones?

And if the bullet that did all that damage to Connally first ripped through the President's chest as the Commission needs us to believe, could the bullet pictured above be the missile that did all that? The Commission says "*Yes!*"

Frame #225

Zapruder frame #225

Zapruder frame 225 is problematic for the Warren Commission because this image does not

153

illustrate what the official report says happened.

If Governor Connally is not hit by frame 225, there had to be a second gunman because when Connally is shown to be reacting to his wounds in frame 236 (see next page), his actions occur before the 'Oswald rifle' could be fired a second time.

Accordingly, the Commission was compelled to offer a 'Single Bullet Theory' or admit that Kennedy and Connally were hit by two different shots fired at almost the same time.

As you can see in frame 225, Connally appears to be non-flustered and showing no signs of pain or duress while the President emerges from behind the sign, just having been shot.

JFK is seen raising his hands to his neck. He has just been shot in the upper back, creating the effect of him being winded by a sudden punch between the shoulder blades.

His instinctive reaction is his breathing difficulties while Jackie looks at her husband, just beginning to be aware that something is terribly wrong.

Frame 230

Zapruder frame 230 illustrates the nightmare scenario faced by the Warren Commission.

President Kennedy is seen clearly reacting to his wound to the upper back

Zapruder Frame #230

by bringing both hands to his throat, yet Governor Connally appears uninjured.

The Governor told the Commission and the House Select Committee on Assassinations that he had not been hit by a bullet by frame 230. This photo supports his testimony that he had time to return to a forward position in his seat *"before I felt anything."*

If you have ever picked up a 10-gallon Stetson hat, you know it has some weight to it. The Governor is shown to be still holding on to the white cowboy hat with his right hand despite that wrist having a hole blown clean through it by frame 230.

The Commission stated that Mr. Connally was simply confused by the trauma of the moment and doesn't realize that he has been hit by frame 230.

Frame 236

Zapruder frame 236 is when we first see both men reacting to their survivable wounds. If no other shots had occurred that day, both men would have lived and history would be different.

Zapruder Frame #236

In frame 236, Governor Connally is finally seen reacting to his violent wounds. His right shoulder buckles downward, his mouth flies open in a loud gasp, his hair starts to become dishevelled and he has let go of his Stetson hat.

Just as The First Lady is beginning to sense her husband is in stress, Nellie Connally, who also testified that the first shot did not strike the Governor, is reacting to her husband's outburst.

The problem for the Warren Commission is the timing involved. We know that the earliest possible time President Kennedy could have received the bullet to his back is Zapruder frame 203, just as he disappears behind the highway sign.

Although the Commission also needs Connally to be hit when JFK is first hit, he does not appear to be struck by a bullet until frame 236. That's 33 frames after the first possible shot, or 1.83 seconds after the President is possibly hit.

Since we know it would not take 1.83 seconds for a high velocity bullet to travel the 4-foot distance between the two men...and it couldn't have possibly paused in mid air between the two victims for 1.83 seconds, this timing issue becomes a grave concern to the Commission.

Their answer is that Governor Connally had a delayed reaction to his wounds, although they could not prove it.

While there will always be experts who say this is possible, several forensic experts, such as Dr. Cyril Wecht (see Chapter 4) have stated that a delayed reaction by the Governor is highly improbable due to the violence of his injuries, including two shattered bones.

We also know that Connally was hit by a tumbling bullet, which is to say that his impact was blunter than a bullet entering nose first.

Frame 256

Without question, by Zapruder frame 256, both men are reacting to their wounds. In another three seconds, the fatal head shot will strike the President.

Zapruder Frame #256

In frame 256, the President is slumping forward with his hands at his neck. He doesn't make a sound, but Mrs. Kennedy is looking at him, beginning to realize that something is awry.

Mrs. Connally testified that "*I looked at the President and I saw no blood or anything...he just had a sort of quizzical look on his face.*" Then she goes on to say, "*Then there was a **second** shot that hit John* (her husband) *and he just fell into my lap like a wounded animal.*"

Although this happened so fast, it is interesting to note that Mrs. Connally makes a point of saying that she saw no blood. This observation becomes relevant when discussing the 'Magic Bullet' in Chapter 4.

Mr. Connally recoils to the right by the force of the impact, telling the Commission that he is fully aware that the limousine is under attack.

Frame 300

By Zapruder frame 300, chaos has engulfed the President's limousine. Mrs. Kennedy is fully aware that something is wrong with her husband. She leans to him, trying desperately to find out what is troubling him.

Zapruder Frame #300

Governor Connally's mouth is wide open. He begins to fall back toward his wife Nellie and she is also aware that something awful is happening.

Unfortunately for history, two key individuals who do not yet realize that the Presidential limousine is under fire are the two Secret Service agents in the front seat, driver William Greer and passenger Roy Kellerman.

By frame 300, approximately 5.4 seconds have passed since the first possible shot. This is a short time, but supposedly an eternity if you are a trained Secret Service agent.

One of the many bizarre conspiracy theories suggest that Greer turned around to look at JFK and shot him with a revolver. While the Zapruder film does show agent Greer briefly looking in the

President's direction in later frames, there is no gun or muzzle flash as wildly reported.

However, this does not exonerate the Secret Service completely. Reprimands were issued when it was learned that many Secret Service agents were up late drinking and partying the night before in violation of agency rules.

To what extent this involves agents Greer or Kellerman has not been made clear, but we must wonder if they should have recognized the first gunshot as they are trained to do.

Had they done so, is it possible they could have executed a safe getaway before the fatal head shot?

Frame 312

As we look at Zapruder frame 312, it is still hard to imagine that President Kennedy has just $1/18^{th}$ of a second left to live.

He wasn't declared dead for another 30 minutes, but the effects of the head shot are clear. Nobody could have survived that shot.

Zapruder Frame #312

The next ½ of a second is of paramount importance to history, but frame 312 is our last chance to see the President still alive.

Jackie Kennedy is now fully aware and trying to render aid to her fallen husband. Mrs. Connally is receiving her wounded husband in her arms. He would survive his injuries.

If we could stop history at this very moment, JFK would have gotten out of hospital within a few weeks to resume his presidency. If only…

Driver William Greer is shown looking back at JFK, but agonizingly too late for history's sake.

Just 1/18th of a second later, it happened…

Frame 313

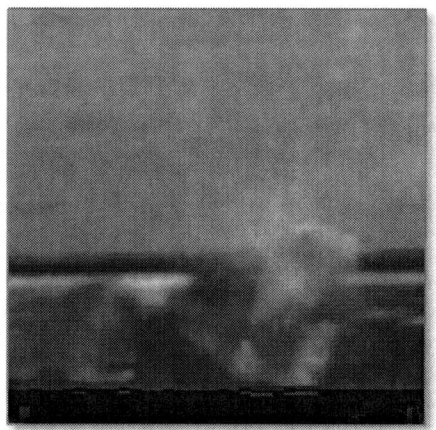

Zapruder Frame #313

The fatal head shot caused death, but it did not bring closure to a nation in mourning.

This moment in time, Zapruder frame 313, is forever seared into our memory. It will continue to shock people for generations to come, no matter how far removed they are from having lived it like my generation.

As Mrs. Kennedy tries to help her husband, the gruesome head shot rings out. The President's head explodes in a pinkish hue of blood and brain matter.

If only we could say that frame 313 is the end of one of America's most tragic events, allowing us to blame Oswald exclusively.

But we cannot end it there. Frame 314 and just a couple of seconds longer will not let history rest in peace.

Because of what we see next, history should be corrected. It must be set right for all of us to finally be at peace with what happened to a President and a nation.

If the Zapruder film ended at frame 313, history might forever tell a lie. Without more frames to look at, Oswald would undeniably be known as the solitary man who killed a President.

Since a proper forensic examination of the remainder of the President's brain was never conducted, we cannot state for certain that this graphic head trauma was caused by a shot from behind and above the President.

And until we can definitively ascertain the direction of the shot(s) that struck President Kennedy in the head, the case cannot be closed.

Thanks to Zapruder frames that follow #313, history may not be what we have been told it is. So, what do these frames tell us?

Frame 323

Thank goodness, the camera never blinks.

It is no coincidence that Zapruder film owner Life Magazine declined to publish frames in sequential order after #313.

Zapruder Frame #323

Add the Dan Rather misinterpretation of the head shot (see page 147), as well as the 1964 CBS News documentary that seconded the Warren Report.

It becomes clear that the mainstream media, from the outset, had no interest in challenging the single assassin conclusion.

The why is even more perplexing since it soon became evident that the best way to disbelieve the Warren Report is to read it. That was obvious to me as a 13-year-old.

Frame 323 (above) occurs just over ½ second after the fatal head shot. This frame reveals the single most compelling evidence that the death shot came from the front and right of the limousine.

If true, there were at least two snipers in Dealey Plaza that day. In frame 323, the President's head is clearly slammed violently back and to the left upon impact.

This is a physical impossibility if the shot struck President Kennedy in the rear of the skull as concluded by the Commission.

As Newton's Second Law of Motion contends, *"When a force acts on an object, the object accelerates in the direction of the force."*

In this instance, the force is the bullet and the object is the President's head. True to Newton's law, after the bullet strikes JFK's skull, the head moves severely in the direction of the incoming bullet.

This places the origin of the lethal shot somewhere behind the picket fence atop the grassy knoll, to the front and right of the limousine.

In addition to the more than 40 witnesses who place a shot from that location, the Zapruder film affirms it.

But if you are still unconvinced, there was another film taken that day on Elm Street on the opposite side of the street where Abraham Zapruder stationed himself.

Here is how to access the film taken by Orville Nix on YouTube:

Go to YouTube.com and enter this address –

www.youtube.com/watch?v=GU4mAVCprAU

- courtesy of JFK Assassination Truth YouTube Channel

As you can see in the Nix footage, President Kennedy's head moves considerably backward because of the shot. It is fast and completely reactionary to what physically happened to him.

If you go back to my seminar copy of the Zapruder film earlier in this chapter, you can also see the violent rearward head snap.

How the Warren Commission, Dan Rather or anyone else can see otherwise defies common sense and fact.

Frame 344

By Zapruder frame 344, which is 1.7 seconds after the head shot, President Kennedy is seen slamming into the back of his car seat.

Again, this is compatible with a shot from the right front of the car.

If the shot came from behind, we could expect

Zapruder Frame #344

to see the President's body thrown forward into the floor that divides his seat from the jump seat where Governor Connally was seated.

Tragically, Secret Service agent Clint Hill, seen mounting the back of the Presidential limousine, arrives too late to shield JFK from gunfire.

However, the next photo shows that he may have saved Mrs. Kennedy from being thrown onto Elm Street from an accelerating vehicle.

Mrs. Kennedy's actions to follow in the next couple of seconds added to the shock and horror of that day.

Frame 370

Thankfully, Jackie Kennedy has no recollection of what she was about to do or say in the moments following her husband being shot.

After the awful head shot, Nellie Connally says she heard Mrs. Kennedy scream out in anguish as follows: "*Jack! Jack! They've killed my husband! I have his brains in my hands!*"

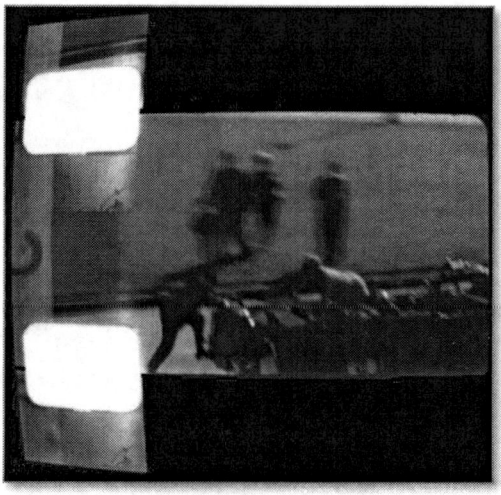

Zapruder Frame #370

Given the trauma of the moment, we cannot be sure that Mrs. Connally is quoting Jackie correctly, but we have the Zapruder film to verify the First Lady's gut-wrenching actions.

In Zapruder frame 370, Mrs. Kennedy can be seen jumping up on the trunk of the Lincoln limousine.

In a completely subconscious reaction to the horror of what just happened, Jackie Kennedy crawled onto the trunk of the car to retrieve a piece of her husband's head.

Fortunately, Clint Hill was able to reach the limousine, jumped up on the rear running board, grabbed Mrs. Kennedy and pushed her back into her seat.

Tortured Secret Service hero Clint Hill.

He then jumped on top of the President and First Lady and shielded them until they reached Parkland Hospital.

Clint Hill testified to the Commission that he saw Mrs. Kennedy reaching for a piece of skull on the trunk of the car. When at Parkland Hospital, a nurse had to pry the matter from Jackie's hand. She was clearly in a state of shock.

Apart from the drama Mrs. Kennedy's reaction adds to the horror of the assassination, it is further confirmation of a shot from the right front of the car.

The fact that she climbed on the trunk of the car establishes that the piece of skull flew backward after the impact, giving further evidence as to the origin of the shot.

Finally, it needs to be noted that neither Mr. or Mrs. Connally reported being showered by anything more than a slight mist after the head shot. Any bone or brain matter of substance or weight travelled slightly left and to the rear of the automobile.

In Chapter 7, a Dallas police officer gives a very compelling account of the head shot and where the shot came from.

Frame 397

This frame affirms the danger that Mrs. Kennedy unwittingly put herself in after the awful head shot.

She is seen completely out of her seat in the car, kneeling on the trunk and reaching for a piece of her husband's head.

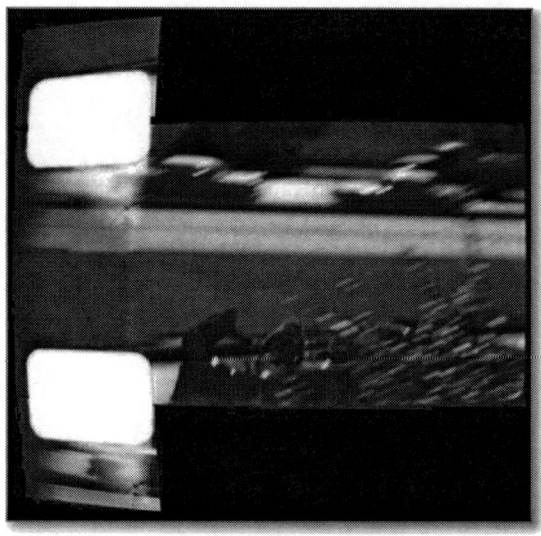

Zapruder Frame #397

Clint Hill takes her arm, all while the limousine is beginning to speed away, pushes her back into the seat and falls on top of Jackie and Jack Kennedy in the rear seat.

While not visible in this frame, the Texas First Lady is tending to her husband in her arms in the jump seats directly in front of the sprawled President in the back seat.

Neither recall JFK uttering a sound.

At the hospital, Hill put his suit jacket over the shattered head of his Commander out of respect and went back to his duty of protecting The First Lady.

On Air Force One about 30 minutes after Lyndon Johnson was sworn in as America's 36th President, Clint Hill joined Mrs. Kennedy as she stood vigil by his casket.

Her major concern was what might become of Mr. Hill now that she would no longer be in the White House. Clint Hill stayed on the Presidential detail and served five Presidents with distinction.

HISTORY MERELY DELAYED?

We have to wonder if we would be having the 'Lone Assassin' versus 'Conspiracy' debate all these years later if the Zapruder film became public viewing soon after the assassination.

It has swayed lots of people to the 'conspiracy' side, but the debate endures.

From the JFK assassination to the 9/11 terror attacks in New York and who knows what next, it appears that monumental events will always be subject to speculation and debate.

In fact, that 'what next' may have already happened.

At the time of this writing, a sense of incredulousness and anger grips America at the possible attempt by Russian Federation President Vladimir Putin to affect the 2016 election in favor of Republican Donald Trump over Democratic candidate Hillary Clinton.

Even more mind-boggling is that we can rarely agree on the specifics of an alleged conspiracy!

Such is the nature of cover-ups…and we may owe this phenomenon to the tragic events in Dallas on November 22, 1963.

Through The 'Oswald' Window

Chapter 7

The Top 8 Indicators That the Fatal Shot Did Come From the Grassy Knoll

---

Before you smirk, roll your eyes and utter to yourself, "*Oh no, not another one of those crazy grassy knoll conspiracy nut jobs*," consider this:

No less than science, medical evidence, instinctive reactions, some 40 eyewitnesses and ear witnesses, two visual records, and even old-fashioned logic supports the fatal shot as being fired from the grassy knoll.

The totality of the evidence can no longer be ignored as viable. And to present the likeliness of a second sniper positioned behind a picket fence atop a grassy incline, we don't have to invent another 'Magic Bullet' to support such a claim.

The infamous Grassy Knoll. Notice the trees lining the fence, especially the tree immediately above the Stemmons Freeway sign. It provides necessary shade and cover on both sides of the fence.

The result of a shot from this location is tragically clear and gut-wrenching. Had this second assassin not existed, or somehow missed his target, history might very well record that President John F. Kennedy survived that day and went on to...we can only imagine.

In placing a gunman at the infamous grassy knoll in Dealey Plaza, three witnesses give credibility to the more than 40 other people who thought a shot came from that location, as well as dozens of bystanders who ran

After the shots and JFK is rushed to a hospital, several people storm the grassy knoll, where they believe a shot came from.

up the hill after the President's limousine raced off because they thought something happened in that area (see photo above).

Just as there is no visual evidence of Lee Harvey Oswald firing from the southeast corner window on the sixth-floor of the Texas

172

School Book Depository Building, there is no visual evidence of a shooter on the grassy knoll that is irrefutable.

There are images of what could be a gunman in classic military firing position, but this alleged image is camouflaged by foliage from a tree. It is like looking at clouds in the sky and finding what appears to be a face.

FLASH OF LIGHT

There are three interesting eyewitness accounts that match the location of a potential marksman described above.

Lee Bowers Jr. worked in a railroad control tower, which places him on the same side of the picket fence that an assassin would have positioned himself for a shot at the President.

He testified that he saw two men standing under a tree at the picket fence. When the shots rang out, Bowers told the Warren Commission that he couldn't see the two men clearly, but saw a flash of light come from where the men were positioned.

Due to the pandemonium that erupted following the shots, Bowers lost track of the men. When he looked at where they had been standing, they were gone.

Interestingly, the position Bowers identified corresponds to a mature tree not far from the Stemmons Freeway sign, giving the two men shelter on either side of the fence.

The long hanging tree branches and leaves could easily mask a shooter from onlookers on Elm Street or on Bowers' side of the fence. The shading cast by the tree on that brilliantly sunny day would also act as visual protection for a gunman at that location.

Anti-Grassy Knoll advocates have argued that it would not have been easy to hide along the fence with a rifle exposed.

Witness Ed Hoffman stands at the picket fence where he says he saw a puff of smoke during the shooting.

If it was possible, Bowers may have described the perfect location, especially given the reports by two witnesses who attempted to view the motorcade in the shade behind the picket fence.

They were ushered away from the 'restricted' area by men in dark suits purporting to be Secret Service agents.

The Secret Service has denied having any men on foot patrol in Dealey Plaza and we can't question Bowers about who else he may have seen in the area.

Soon after the assassination, Bowers would die in a solitary auto accident, becoming one of the earliest 'mysterious deaths' linked to the JFK assassination outlined in Chapter 10.

A second witness, Ed Hoffman in the picture above left, is a deaf mute who was distracted from watching the motorcade by a puff of smoke emanating from a tree behind the picket fence atop the grassy knoll.

He described the plume of smoke as much more than what a cigarette or cigar would make. He also told authorities that as he raced over to the fence, he saw two men running from the scene and saw one of them throw what appeared to be a rifle into a car. He could not read the licence plate.

Were these two men the same men that Bowers reported seeing standing under the tree? Or were they the two men posing as Secret Service agents? Possibly, but Hoffman's story about the two men seemed to change with follow-up interviews.

He never waivered on seeing the smoke arise from the area. The FBI discarded the rest of his testimony because of his inconsistency, but Hoffman would continue to insist he saw the two men and a rifle, claiming that his disability prevented investigators from fully understanding what he was trying to convey.

So, the first of eight indicators that the lethal shot came from the grassy knoll is:

1. EYEWITNESSES

While nobody else reported seeing a potential assassin, nearly 40 additional witnesses swore that a shot came from the grassy knoll.

Gayle and Bill Newman shield their kids after watching JFK's limousine speed off to the hospital.

One of the more frightening accounts of the President's murder comes from Gayle and Bill Newman, along with their two young children.

The Newman family were waving to the President and First Lady from their position on the grass merely a few feet from the curb.

This location places the Newman family closer to JFK than any other witness who was not in the car. It also uniquely makes them both eyewitnesses and ear witnesses to the event.

Their testimony, if accurate, places them directly in the line of fire if a shot came from the fence behind them.

This is what they thought happened: When Billy Newman felt a bullet whizzing by his ear on its way to the President, his gut reaction was to tell his wife to grab their youngest son and hit the ground to get out of the line of fire.

The picture on the previous page shows the stunned Newman parents just having instinctively fallen to the ground, acting as a shield for their children.

Newman told reporters and FBI investigators that he thought the fatal shot came from behind him, which is the grassy knoll sectioned off by the picket fence.

He also states that he clearly saw the shot that missed him go on to strike the President in the '*side*' of the head and describes the horrific result.

Amazingly, you won't find Billy Newman's account of the assassination in the Warren Report because they declined to interview him.

Could it be because they didn't like what Newman had to say in his sworn statement before the Dallas County Sheriff's Office hours after the traumatizing event?

Here is Newman's sworn statement:

Before me, the undersigned authority, on this the 22nd day of November A.D. 1963 personally appeared William Eugene Newman, Address: 718 W. Clarandon, Dallas, Texas, Age 22, Phone No. WH 8-6082.

Deposes and says:

Today at about 12:45 pm I was standing in a group of people on Elm Street near the west end of the concrete standard when the President's car turned left off Houston Street onto Elm Street. We were standing at the edge of the curb looking at the car as it was coming toward us and all of a sudden there was a noise, apparently gunshot [sic]. The President jumped up in his seat, and it looked like what I thought was a firecracker had went off and I thought he had realized it. It was just like an explosion and he was standing up. By this time he was directly in front of us and I was looking directly at him when he was hit in the side of the head. Then he fell back and Governor Connally was holding his middle section. Then we fell down on the grass as it seemed we were in direct path of fire. It looked like Mrs. Kennedy jumped on top of the President. He kinda [sic] fell back and it looked like she was holding him. Then the car sped away and everybody in that area had run upon [sic] top of that little mound. I thought the shot had come from the garden directly behind me, that it was on an elevation from where I was as I was right on the curb. I do not recall looking toward the Texas School Book Depository. I looked back in the vacinity [sic] of the garden.

/s/ William E. Newman, Jr.

Subscribed and sworn to before me on this the 22nd day of Nov A. D. 1963

/s/ C. G. Gentry
Notary Public, Dallas County, Texas

We can only surmise that the Warren Commission was not

interested in the Newman account of the shooting because it did not support the notion of all shots coming from the 'Oswald' window above and behind the limousine.

Sam Holland stood on this bridge as JFK car approached, heard FOUR shots and saw a puff of smoke to his left on the grassy knoll.

SILENT WITNESSES OR WITNESSES SILENCED?

Whereas Dallas police, county sheriffs and FBI should have talked to as many as 40 witnesses about a possible grassy knoll connection, the apparent disinterest in these witnesses to history is appalling.

Sam Holland was one of few witnesses who got to appear before the Warren Commission.

Holland was standing on the Triple Overpass bridge as the President's car slowly approached him on Elm Street.

178

Like Ed Hoffman, Holland says that as the shots rang out, he saw a puff of smoke arise from the trees and the fence on the grassy knoll to his left.

Once the limousine sped under the Overpass and onto Stemmons Freeway, Holland says he raced over to the area of the smoke, but didn't see anything.

As he told the Commission:

Holland - *A puff of smoke came out about 6 or 8 feet above the ground right out from under those trees. And at just about this location from where I was standing you could see that puff of smoke, like someone had thrown a firecracker or something out, and that is just about the way it sounded. There were definitely four reports.*

Mr. Stern - *You have no doubt about that (hearing four shots)?*

Holland - *I have no doubt about it. I have no doubt about seeing that puff of smoke come out from under those trees either.*

Just like other witnesses who suggested a shot may have come from a location other than the Book Depository Building, or that possibly more than three shots were fired, Holland's testimony was simply dismissed by the Commission as inaccurate.

Given the enormity of the event, you would think that every effort would be made to track down all witnesses in Dealey Plaza to discover what they may have seen or heard as the President was killed before their eyes.

Not only was there no urgency to speak to all witnesses, a great many of the witnesses were never questioned by investigative authorities. Instead, independent investigators and reporters became the first to talk to many witnesses.

What at least 30 of these witnesses had to say to the press in the months following the assassination began to cast a shadow of suspicion about the Commission's lone gunman conclusion.

Several witnesses who were interviewed by police authorities and spoke of hearing a shot from the grassy knoll, seeing a puff of smoke or flash of light or smelling gunpowder in that area moments after the shots, were never called before the Commission or interviewed a second time.

This blatant disregard of material witnesses, as you will see in Chapter 9, did not just pertain to what people saw or heard that day.

It is shocking to learn what the FBI and Warren Commission did with all kinds of evidence that was at odds with the finding that Lee Harvey Oswald fired all three shots as the lone assassin of JFK.

2. EAR WITNESSES

What people saw that unforgettable day in Dealey Plaza is important, but so is what people heard.

The problem is that both eyewitness and ear witness evidence is unreliable. Even when we are looking at the same thing, we can see it differently.

And especially in times of trauma, two people can be standing a foot apart and hear a totally different scenario play out.

As it relates to the JFK assassination, two aspects of ear witness testimony become germane to the discussion of shots and trajectories:

- **Location** – Where did you hear the shots come from?
- **Number** – How many shots did you hear?

As stated above, nearly 40 people heard one shot come from the grassy knoll.

This includes more than a dozen police officers who are better trained in audio observation than the average person. This, at least, gives these reports some credibility.

What happened to Dallas motorcycle cop Bobby Hargis as the shots rang out is horrific. His account of what took place not only makes him a crucial eyewitness, his instinctive reactions are supported by science. His story is told later in this chapter.

WHAT HISTORY SOUNDS LIKE

As for the number of shots fired that day at the Presidential limousine, the fact that anywhere from two to eight shots were reported by assorted ear witnesses establishes that audio testimony is not an exact science.

The Warren Report concluded that a total of three shots were fired in 5.6 seconds, all coming from the so-called 'Oswald' window in the Book Depository Building above and behind the President's vehicle.

However, even ear witnesses who confirmed a total of three shots revealed a major problem for the Commission.

When asked to verbalize the shots they heard, several ear witnesses described the sequence of shots as follows (each dash equals one second of elapsed time):

BANG - - - - BANG/BANG

Note how close to each other the last two bangs are. Tests reported below reveal the second and third shots to be less than ½ second apart. So, what's the problem?

Two shots less than ½ second apart could not have come from the same weapon Oswald is alleged to have used. His Mannlicher-Carcano rifle was not an automatic firearm and could not discharge two shots in less than 2.3 seconds as confirmed by FBI ballistic testing.

Clearly, the second and third shots had to have come from two different assassins firing almost simultaneously to each other. How did the Commission handle the troublesome timing of the shots?

It simply discredited ALL ear witness testimony, except to point out that several people heard the three shots attributed to Oswald.

Fortunately, audio forensics have surfaced to refute the Commission's conclusion that only three shots were fired. Of course, the Commission had to limit the shots to a maximum of three or admit that a second gunman was involved.

In 1978, the House Select Committee on Assassinations (HSCA) heard acoustical evidence by Dr. James Barger and Dr. Mark Weiss from a police dictabelt recording of the limousine turning on to Elm Street.

The recording captured the sounds in Dealey Plaza, including police motorcycles and crowd noise. One of the procession's motorcycle cops unwittingly recorded the shots being fired and it was transmitted back to headquarters.

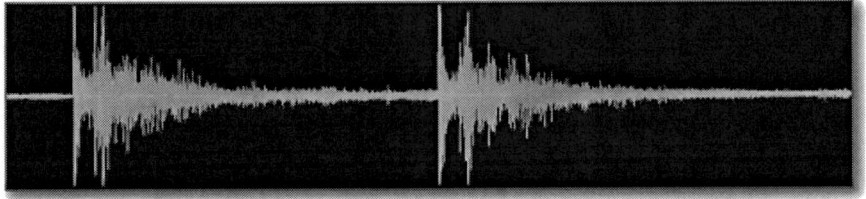

Acoustical science records distinctive sounds like the gunshots fired in Dealey Plaza.

The tape's potential relevance went unknown for more than a decade but was fortunately kept in a police evidence room.

Of particular interest on this tape are four distinct sharp sounds, which were identified as gunshots. But the biggest problem is the recording shows that only .44 seconds separate the third and fourth shots.

This acoustical evidence, measured to be accurate to within 95% of certainty, shatters the 'Single Bullet Theory' because the so-called 'Oswald' rifle could not be fired twice in that short timeframe.

Hence, we have two shooters and a conspiracy.

Equally important, the acoustical evidence places the third shot as having come from the grassy knoll, specifically behind the picket fence and approximately eight feet from the west corner of the knoll.

This happens to correspond to where Sam Holland and Ed Hoffman saw a sizeable puff of smoke, not to mention where

www.ThroughTheOswaldWindow.com

Author Dave O'Brien at the so-called 'Oswald' window.

Lee Bowers saw two unknown men lurking as the shots were fired.

Anti-conspiracy theorists have attacked the credibility of the acoustical evidence, but subsequent acoustical testing has substantiated the HSCA report by Barger and Weiss.

Although several ear witnesses reported hearing four shots, acoustical science was not available at the time to support or refute these claims.

This enabled the Commission to disregard any indication that there were more than three shots fired that day from one location, above and behind the President's convertible Lincoln.

Ironically, our third key indicator that a shot came from the grassy knoll is:

3. THE 'OSWALD' WINDOW

As described in Chapter 1, when I had the rare opportunity to take the position of the actual assassin and look out the window at the southeast corner of the sixth-floor of the Book Depository Building, I could sense that this position was not ideally suited for a 'lone gunman.'

Admittedly, this observation cannot be verified as fact since it is unlikely that anybody will ever again stand at that window (page 184) unless a new investigation is launched.

The best I can do with my seldom seen view of history is attempt to put myself in the mindset of a sniper at that location. There are two ways to go about it:

A) **One Assassin** – If I am the only assassin, is this location ideal to carry out a successful assassination of the President? Are there any disadvantages to this being the only sniper's nest?

B) **More Than One Assassin** – If I know I have one or more fellow assassins at ground level in Dealey Plaza, how does this effect the timing of my shots from that window?

Beyond what I could describe in Chapter 1 about my surreal moment at that window and the sensations that surged through me, I had to separate nerves from the reality of the moment, just like the actual assassin on November 22, 1963.

We know that at least two shots came from the so-called 'Oswald' window, although the Commission insists all three shots originated there.

As I stood at that window, looking down at the kill site, if I was about to shoot the President of the United States completely on my own, the last thing I want to do is permit JFK's car to turn left onto Elm Street before I begin the shooting for these reasons:

- My target is now moving away from me at 11 miles per hour, which enhances the degree of difficulty, greatly reduces my shooting time and puts the target in a better position to escape alive.

- The ideal kill shot is while the limousine is approaching me on Houston Street. The vehicle must slow significantly to make the 90-degree turn onto Elm Street and there are no obstructions as the target approaches me in the window. I can begin the shooting at will.

By letting the President begin to move away from me, the Oak tree shown at left becomes a major obstacle, which is described more succinctly in Chapter 9.

From a lone gunman's viewpoint, as the photo I took clearly demonstrates,

Photo by the Author

allowing JFK to disappear from my sightline for just these few critical seconds greatly diminishes the time I have to get off a minimum of three shots.

More importantly, this unavailable time puts the target several yards farther from me and closer to Stemmons Freeway. Once under the triple overpass that Sam Holland stood on, the car is near the highway, virtually out of my range and sightline completely.

Since I must wait until the President emerges from behind that tree to fire my first shot, this gives the target less exposure time to danger…or does it?

ENTERING A CROSSFIRE

There's only one scenario that gives me, as an assassin, comfort in passing on a Houston Street shot and allowing President Kennedy to turn onto Elm Street. And that is...

***Knowing that the target is not
potentially escaping danger
but actually approaching even more danger.***

How would I know that?

By knowing that a fellow assassin is positioned at ground level in Dealey Plaza, waiting for JFK to arrive in his sightline through his rifle telescope.

If it's not all on me to successfully assassinate the President from that window, I am under a lot less pressure because a time constraint is no longer a major issue.

A second assassin on the grassy knoll not only makes a shot unnecessary from the Book Depository window while the car is on Houston Street, it demands that I not take that much easier shot.

Otherwise, I have not allowed the President to enter the trap of crossfire in Dealey Plaza.

Had all the shots come from that controversial window, what physical reaction do you think the President would have had upon receiving a bullet to the back of his skull?

If you are imagining a sudden thrust forward, you would be correct. But that did not happen, which presents us with a 4th major indicator of a shot from the right-front of the car:

Mrs. Kennedy tries to help her husband 1/18th of a second before the deadly head shot.

4. JFK'S VIOLENT BACKWARD HEAD MOVEMENT

As both the Abraham Zapruder film and the Orville Nix film graphically illustrate in Chapter 6, President Kennedy's head moves violently back and to the left because of the fatal head shot.

This is science at its most basic. If you slap the back of your head with your hand, what direction does your head move?

Naturally, your head moves in the same direction as the impact caused by your hand. If you want your head to move backward, you must strike your forehead with your hand.

Despite this simple self-demonstration, the Warren Commission asks us to believe that when the President receives his head shot with a force much greater than what we can do with our own hand, his head defies science and moves rapidly forward.

With the exception of CBS newsman Dan Rather, upon viewing the Zapruder and Nix films, Kennedy's head snaps viscously back and slightly to the left immediately upon impact of a bullet.

The eyewitness testimony of Bill Newman and others support the physical reaction of the President as it relates to that shot coming from the grassy knoll, to the right and front of JFK at the time of Zapruder frame 313 (see Chapter 6).

It has been argued that the President was thrown back against the backrest of his seat because the driver of the vehicle, Secret Service agent Bill Greer, jumped on the gas peddle when he realized the automobile was under attack.

While Mrs. Kennedy is in the same position as she was in frame 312 on previous page, notice how JFK has been slammed back against the car seat after catastrophic head shot.

There are two things wrong with this explanation:

A) **Coincidental Timing –** We cannot escape the film evidence that shows President Kennedy's severe rearward head movement occurring immediately after Zapruder frame 313, the recorded moment of impact.

In the two Zapruder frames shown in this section, we see the President 1/18th of a second before the head shot (frame 312), followed by frame 321 (above), less than ½ second later.

JFK is propelled violently back into his seat.

B) **Delayed Reaction** – Both the Zapruder and Nix films show that the President's limousine slows at the moment of the head trauma and doesn't speed up for another few seconds.

Had agent Greer accelerated the car just before the head shot, the bullet may have missed the President's head. Additionally, Secret Service agent Clint Hill may not have made it to the back bumper of the car, possibly causing Mrs. Kennedy to be thrown out onto the road.

This Segway's us to the next key indicator of the mortal shot coming from the grassy knoll:

5. MRS. KENNEDY'S INSTINCTIVE REACTION

One of the most heart-wrenching moments of the assassination is what happens in the seconds that immediately follow a shot striking President Kennedy in the side of the head.

Tragically, it is one of those moments in history that cannot be sugar-coated, much like young John Jr. saluting his fallen father as his coffin passes by during the funeral procession.

In a moment that time cannot diminish, JFK Jr. salutes his slain father as his casket passes by on the way to Arlington National Cemetery.

Mrs. Kennedy subconsciously leaping out onto the trunk of the car to retrieve a piece of her husband's skull is also one of those timeless images that makes the JFK assassination as horrific today as when it happened.

The moment is well documented in Chapter 6, but in this section, her reaction clearly speaks to the origin of the shot that killed her husband.

The fact that she saw a piece of her husband's skull fly 'back' onto the trunk of the car, causing her to instinctively go after it, scientifically supports the notion that the shot responsible for this damage came from the right-front of the car.

It stands to reason that a shot from behind would have sent skull and brain matter forward into the limousine. According to Mr. and Mrs. Connally, seated directly in front of the Kennedy's, this did not happen.

While this is persuasive proof of the origin of the kill shot having come from the grassy knoll, our #6 indicator leaves little doubt.

6. OFFICER BOBBY HARGIS

Bobby Hargis was a Dallas motorcycle cop assigned to the presidential motorcade. He had a unique position at the time of the shooting, riding just behind the left-rear bumper of the President's car.

This puts Hargis over the left shoulder of Jackie Kennedy as the motorcade moves along Elm Street at 11 miles per hour.

Motorcycle cop Bobby Hargis over Jackie's left shoulder.

On April 8, 1964, officer Hargis was questioned by Warren Commission council Samuel Stern. Let's have Hargis tell his story in his own words:

Mr. Stern - *Did something happen to you, personally in connection with the shot you have just described?*

Mr. Hargis - *You mean about the blood hitting me?*

Mr. Stern - *Yes.*

Mr. Hargis – *Yes. When President Kennedy straightened back up in the car the bullet hit him in the head, the one that killed him and it seemed like his head exploded, and I was splattered with blood and brain, and kind of a bloody water. It wasn't really blood. And at that time the Presidential car slowed down. I heard somebody say, "Get going!"*

Mr. Stern - *Someone inside…*

Mr. Hargis - *I don't know whether it was the Secret Service car, and I remembered seeing Officer Chaney.*

Chaney put his motor in' first gear and accelerated up to the front to tell them to get everything out of

Officer Hargis is pictured off his motorcycle. Hargis is looking toward the grassy knoll where he thinks a shot came from. Note a second unidentified cop running in the same direction.

the way, that he was coming through, and that is when the Presidential limousine shot off, and I stopped and got off my motorcycle and ran to the right-hand side of the street, behind the light pole.

Mr. Stern - *Just a minute. Do you recall your impression at the time regarding the source of the shots?*

Mr. Hargis - *Well, at the time it sounded like the shots were right next to me. There wasn't any way in the world I could tell where they were coming from, but at the time there was something in my head that said that they probably could have been coming from the railroad overpass, because I thought since I had got splattered, with blood...I was just a little back and left of...just a little bit back and left of Mrs. Kennedy, but I didn't know for sure.*

Mr. Stern - *You were clear that the sounds were sounds of shots?*

Mr. Hargis - *Yes sir. I knew they were shots.*

The testimony of officer Hargis is consistent with Mrs. Kennedy's reactive leap out of her car seat to grab a piece of skull sitting on the car trunk.

As Hargis says, matter and a bloody liquid flew back at him after the head shot, indicating to him that the relative shot came from the front and right of his position.

At this point, Hargis had a split-second decision to make. Does he accompany the President's car to Parkland Hospital? Or does he remain at the crime scene?

As we discover, he stays behind because something makes him think a shot came from the grassy knoll area to his immediate right. His police instincts take over and he wants to investigate.

In the picture on the previous page, Hargis is seen just having dismantled his motorcycle and looking toward the grassy knoll. Other pictures show Hargis running up the hill toward the picket fence.

He claims that he saw a lot of people running around atop the hill, but nothing suspicious.

Again, we have an instinctive reaction, much like Jackie Kennedy, to a shot originating from the right-front of the limousine at the time of Zapruder frame 313.

The direction of the brain and skull matter hitting him made the origin of the shot obvious. Otherwise, he would have headed off in another direction to investigate or even raced off to the hospital if he had no inclination as to where the shooter of the fateful shot was stationed.

Like all 'unfriendly' witnesses in Dealey Plaza, the testimony given by officer Bobby Hargis was categorically dismissed by the Warren Commission.

It simply didn't fit the narrative that Lee Harvey Oswald fired all 'three' shots from the Book Depository window.

7. TELLING GRASS LANDING

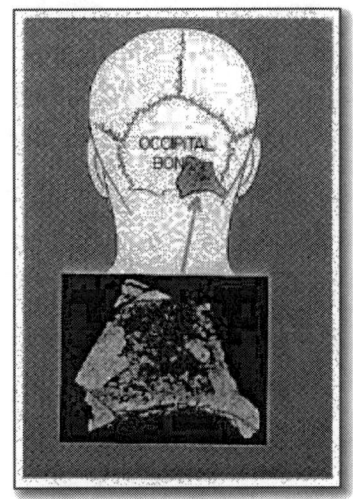

Another rearward proof of trajectory following the head shot is provided by a sizeable piece of President Kennedy's skull found in the grass in Dealey Plaza

A 2.5-inch piece of skull was discovered by local resident Bill Harper minutes after the shots. He turned his gory finding over to authorities, which proved to be unhelpful to the Warren Commission.

A found piece of JFK's skull in Dealey Plaza indicates a gunshot from the right-front of the car.

Medical experts determined that the bone came from the occipital region of JFK's head, as shown above.

More relevant, we know the exact spot on Elm Street where the kill shot struck Mr. Kennedy, frame 313 of the Zapruder film.

It has been calculated that the skull fragment Harper found flew back and slightly to the left a little more than 30 feet upon the bullet's impact.

This is irrefutable evidence of a high velocity projectile to the side of his head with such violent force, the skull piece was sent backward more than 10 yards!

The direction of the discharged piece of skull is consistent with the brain and blood matter that spattered police motorcyclist Bobby Hargis. It also affirms the reaction of Mrs. Kennedy after the head shot, as sadly described above.

These three instances establish, beyond doubt, that the shot that killed President Kennedy came from the grassy knoll to the right-front of the slowly-moving limousine.

Lastly, we come to the 8th indicator that the death shot came from a second location:

8. PARKLAND MEDICAL EXPERTS

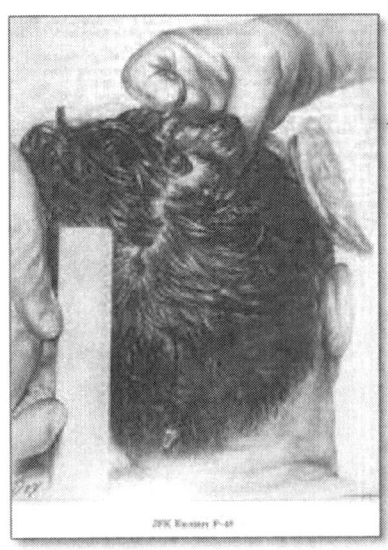

Artist Ida Fox drawing of JFK's head wound, showing circular entry wound just below top of the ruler, as well as flap of skull caused by bullet exit.

The Warren Commission, in an effort to offer medical evidence of a rear shot to the President's head, employed schematic artist Ida Fox to illustrate that wound, as well as other wounds on JFK.

This was done to tone down the graphic nature of the wounds sustained by the President rather than publish actual autopsy photographs and X-rays.

It turns out that there were more sinister reasons to show mostly artistic renditions of the wounds.

As the Ida Fox drawing at left illustrates, President Kennedy seemingly took a bullet to the crown area of the skull, which exited just above the right ear.

You can see the alleged result of the explosive exit wound. There is a hole above the right ear, as well as a sizeable flap of skin near the point of exit.

There is only one thing wrong with this artist conception of the head wound – Factually, it is a complete fabrication!

MEDICAL MISREPRESENTATION

In reality, there is no small entry wound at the back of the skull.

And instead of a gaping exit hole appearing on the right side of the head as presented in the Fox drawing, there is a fist-sized blow-out at the right rear of the President's skull in the occipital region.

The diagram at right is an accurate depiction of President Kennedy's massive head wound to the right rear hemisphere.

This is in complete contrast to the Ida Fox depiction of the fatal head wound.

How do we know which wound representation is correct?

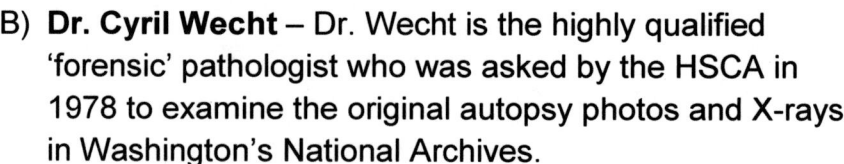

Second version of JFK head wound based on actual photos and expert medical witnesses.

A) **Expert Eyewitnesses** – The testimony of several medical professionals at Parkland Hospital. These people either rendered aid to President Kennedy or at least viewed his body upon arrival.

B) **Dr. Cyril Wecht** – Dr. Wecht is the highly qualified 'forensic' pathologist who was asked by the HSCA in 1978 to examine the original autopsy photos and X-rays in Washington's National Archives.

First, let's examine the overwhelming consensus by the Parkland doctors, who are as follows:

Dr. Charles Crenshaw points to location of JFK's head wound.

- Dr. Charles Crenshaw (left)
- Dr. Richard Dulaney
- Dr. Kenneth Salyer
- Dr. Paul Peters
- Dr. Charles Carrico
- Dr. Ronald Jones
- Dr. Robert McClelland (below)

When these medical experts were interviewed by Robert J. Groden for his book 'The Killing of a President,' all of them pointed to the right rear of their own skull to illustrate the location of the major wound they saw on the President.

These descriptions are all akin to the sketch on page 198 and bear no resemblance to the drawing by Ida Fox.

In addition to the experienced doctors documented here, several other emergency room and trauma room attendants saw the President's body on the operating table.

Dr. Robert McClelland indicates large open wound on the President's head.

These people, like nurse Audrey Bell, unanimously confirm the description of the head wound on the President by the doctors at Parkland.

Nurse Bell described the wound to Groden as "*A massive wound at the back of his head.*"

WECHT CONFIRMATION

Of all these professional witnesses ignored or discounted by the Warren Commission, Dr. Cyril Wecht finds the observation of Dr. Robert McClelland to be unimpeachable.

In an interview with Dr. Wecht on January 8, 2017, he points to Dr. McClelland's credentials as a chief surgeon at Parkland who has treated countless gunshot wounds during his career.

Dr. Cyril Wecht tells author artist drawings of JFK head wound were complete misrepresentations to support 'Single Bullet Theory.'

"*The autopsy report is salacious,*" Dr. Wecht flatly states.

As for the Ida Fox diagram of the President's head wound, Dr. Wecht reports that the original autopsy color photos and X-rays he examined prove the Fox representation to be completely false.

O'Brien – "*Dr. Wecht, how do we explain the Ida Fox drawing of the President's head wound?*"

Dr. Wecht – "*The Ida Fox drawing is absolutely made up. There is no question about it. It's not just one opinion. You've got a dozen or more doctors. They all describe what they saw.*

"*We had a program in Pittsburgh, live television for an hour with chief surgeon Dr. McClelland. He was right on point with what I am saying.*

"*There is no question there was damage to the back of the brain, including the cerebellum and the large area of scalp that was damaged in the rear.*

"*What they depicted later on* (Ida Fox and other Warren Report images) *is totally made up.*"

Was Ida Fox a witting part of a conspiracy and cover-up? It is highly unlikely.

It is more likely that Fox was given doctored photos and she simply drew what she saw. Unfortunately, her drawings became part of the public record that sought to falsify history.

Aggregately, the evidence in this chapter leads to one conclusion:

President John F. Kennedy died as a result of a gunshot to his right temple that came from the grassy knoll in Dealey Plaza.

And the presence of a second assassin changes history as follows:

The assassination of President Kennedy
was the result of a conspiracy.

And this correction of history opens the door to an even more disturbing revelation:

Following the assassination of President Kennedy,
a cover-up by the U.S. Government was
enacted to suppress the truth until at least 2038.

Chapter 8

The Three Arrested Tramps, the Disappearing Cop and Other Oddities of the JFK Assassination

---

So far in this book, the JFK assassination has provided no shortage of deceit and mystery, but as the old saying goes:

"You Ain't Seen Nothing Yet!"

These 'Three Tramps' were arrested after JFK was shot, but no police records exist.

In addition to the President of the United States being murdered that terrible day in Dallas, a number of unexplained oddities took place in Dealey Plaza that keep us talking as if happened more currently.

They add to the intrigue of the event and keep us spellbound to one of history's greatest mysteries.

If there are innocent and sensible explanations, most have alluded the passage of time.

Until they are solved, we must continue to ask what association they may have to the death of President Kennedy and the altered course of history that has brought controversial Donald Trump into the White House.

One occurrence that day should be reviewable by Dallas police records, but no accounts exist of the arrest of:

The Three Tramps

In the immediate aftermath of the shots in Dealey Plaza, police arrested several 'suspicious' people in the area, believed to be 11 or more. These were primarily 'persons of interest' that they wanted to question.

The most intriguing arrest that day, other than the alleged assassin Lee Harvey Oswald, was the detention of three straggly dressed men who were oddly clean shaven and well groomed. They became known as 'The Three Tramps' (see photo on previous page).

Despite being taken into police custody, which would ordinarily result in them being officially booked and sequestered for interrogation, there is no police record of them being detained or questioned.

In of itself, that is strange. But when you consider that Dallas police kept no notes or recordings of their hours of interrogation of Oswald before he was gunned down in their protection, a pattern of shoddy police practices emerges.

Is Watergate felon E. Howard Hunt (right) also the Dealey Plaza 'tramp' in the hat?

We know these three men were stopped by police, placed into cop cars and were taken to a police precinct, had mug shots and fingerprints taken, but after that, they become ghosts.

Is that because they were innocent 'railyard bums' from behind the grassy knoll who saw nothing and couldn't contribute to the investigation?

This is possible. However, JFK researchers claim they have since matched the faces to some notorious characters, starting with E.

This letter, allegedly written by Oswald, seeks direction, but for what purpose? Was this letter written to E. Howard Hunt or JFK hater Texas oil billionaire H.L. Hunt?

Howard Hunt.

FROM DALLAS TO WATERGATE?

If that name is familiar, it's because Hunt was a former clandestine CIA operative linked to the Bay of Pigs invasion against Cuba in 1961.

A little more than a decade later, Hunt was convicted and served jail time for his involvement in the Watergate break-in at Democratic party headquarters.

Hunt always publicly denied being in Dallas that fateful Friday right up to his death on January 23, 2007. Afterward, his children wrote his biography, quoting a deathbed confession that he was in Dallas that day.

Photo analysis seems to confirm that Hunt may be the 'tramp' in the hat holding a paper lunch bag, although the House Select Committee on Assassinations could not verify it.

It is possible that Hunt may have known Oswald through an associate named David Ferrie, who was in the New Orleans chapter of the Civil Air Patrol with Oswald.

The Hunt-Oswald link surfaces with a vague letter that Oswald allegedly penned to a "Mr. Hunt" on November 8, 1963 (see previous page).

The timing of the letter, as well as a request of clarification of his position, presents another unresolved question mark.

This intriguing letter was sent to JFK researcher Penn Jones Jr. as an anonymous tip, so its origin remains a mystery.

The House Select Committee on Assassinations tried to authenticate the letter in 1978, but could not conclusively say it was or was not Oswald's handwriting.

If it was addressed to E. Howard Hunt, could it have anything to do with Oswald's role in the JFK assassination just 14 days later?

Hunt associate David Ferrie also worked for Louisiana mob boss Carlo Marcello during his deportation trial. Marcello was eventually deported to Guatemala without due process by Bobby Kennedy's Justice Department.

It is believed that Ferrie, who was a commercial pilot, secretly flew Marcello back into the U.S. several months later.

Ferrie, as outlined in Chapter 12, trained anti-Castro Cubans for the Bay of Pigs invasion, where he likely also got involved in gun-running operations to arm the rebels with Jack Ruby, who we now know was an associate of both Marcello and Florida top mobster Santo Trafficante.

The Florida mafia kingpin was a funder of CIA sanctioned plots to assassinate Cuban dictator Fidel Castro, hoping to reinstate deposed leader Batista back in power and regain control of his casino operations in Havana.

In addition to his official CIA activities, E. Howard Hunt also got personally involved in political causes on a hire-for-pay basis, from the mafia attempts against Castro to the secret cash payouts to the Watergate burglars.

His wife Dorothy may have paid the ultimate price for his shady

Is the lead 'tramp' behind the cop the notorious Frank Sturgis of Watergate infamy?

transgressions. As reported in Chapter 10, Dorothy Hunt is believed to have been carrying $200,000 in hush money when her plane crashed in 1972, killing all aboard. The cash was never recovered at the crash site.

If E. Howard Hunt was in Dealey Plaza the day Kennedy was shot, as he confessed in a recorded deathbed statement to his son, it raises the possibility of a disturbing mafia-CIA rebel alliance at work that day.

DASTARDLY BEDFELLOWS

This is particularly true if a second 'tramp' is Frank Sturgis, the infamous Hunt CIA associate tied to both anti-Castro activities and Watergate as one of the burglars caught.

Sturgis referred to himself as a *"CIA whore"* and told the 1975 Church Committee hearings into CIA activities that he was a CIA assassin for *"domestic projects."*

The CIA was strictly mandated to foreign affairs, but Sturgis said that when the CIA got into bed with the mafia over the anti-

Castro Cuba project, CIA agents also started working as private contractors for the mafia.

Sturgis boasted about working in Havana with Hunt for mafia chieftains Santo Trafficante and Meyer Lansky, both of whom hated Kennedy for his last-minute pull-back of military air cover for the Bay of Pigs invasion.

Frank Sturgis became joined at the hip with Hunt. The two had the same clandestine links for decades, only Sturgis has told friends and researchers that he was in Dallas the day *"Kennedy was hit."*

He told Gaeton Fonzi, author of 'The Last Investigation,' that he was one of the assassins in Dealey Plaza.

Frank Sturgis says he was in Dallas, but is he the lead 'tramp' shown above left?

Known for his colorful rantings, the CIA hitman simply can't be trusted about his claim as a sniper.

However, if Hunt was one of the tramps in the photograph, even if Sturgis is not the lead tramp shown above, there's a good likeliness that he was with Hunt in Dallas.

When we connect the political dots between Kennedy, Cuba, the mafia and organized crime, it can be safely said that Hunt and Sturgis were not in Texas on that day to see a Dallas Cowboys football game.

WHO'S YOUR HOLLYWOOD DADDY?

Is convicted murderer Charles Harrelson the middle 'tramp' at JFK kill site?

Rumors persist that the middle tramp in the above photo is not nearly as famous as his son, actor Woody Harrelson.

Charles Harrelson is the convicted hitman of Sam Degelia in Hearme, Texas in 1968, receiving $2000 to do the killing.

While on parole for that killing, Harrelson murdered District Judge John Wood in 1979 and served the rest of his life in prison, dying of an apparent heart attack in 2007.

But before his murderous ways, Harrelson was known to associate with criminal elements linked to organized crime and the intelligence community.

He was a buddy of Russell Mathews, who was friendly with none other than Jack Ruby, all fellow Texans at the time. And Ruby's ultimate boss was Carlos Marcello, who despised the Kennedy brothers (see Chapter 12).

How Harrelson got involved in the JFK assassination is not known, nor is the nature of his connection to Hunt or Sturgis unless this is the trio appearing in Dealey Plaza as 'The Three Tramps.'

Several years later, city records were released purporting to identify the three tramps as other people completely. While possibly true, there were several arrests in Dealey Plaza after the shooting with very poor record-keeping by police.

Who the actual 'Three Tramps' are at the JFK kill site remains a mystery. If they are Hunt, Sturgis and Harrelson, along with Oswald allegedly positioned in the Book Depository Building as a sniper, it is hard to imagine their deep-rooted connection to be a coincidence that happened to rendezvous in Dallas for a date with history.

The Disappearing Motorcycle Cop

At the very beginning of the famous Zapruder film, something very strange takes place.

A police motorcyclist, riding at the right front of the Presidential cavalcade, does not accompany the procession onto Elm Street.

Instead, this motorcycle cop continues along Houston Street

and disappears from the Zapruder footage. This can be seen in Zapruder frame #203 at left, as well as my seminar copy of the film in Chapter 6.

This police officer has never been identified or located, leaving us with no answers for

Notice the police motorcyclist at the point of the arrow. This cop initiated the motorcade's turn onto Houston Street, then left the scene rather than stay in place with the other two cops for the fateful turn onto Elm Street.

his sudden departure from the scene moments before the shots rang out.

Conspiracy theorists point to this cop as having a singular sinister role in the JFK assassination.

Given his position as the lead motorcycle cop on the right side of the motorcade at the critical time it reached the intersection of Main Street and Houston Street, this officer initiated the history-making right-hand turn onto Houston Street.

Like a row of dominos, once the lead motorcyclist turned onto Houston Street, the rest of the motorcade followed, just as they had all along the parade route.

Once on Houston Street, the Presidential entourage had no choice but to turn left onto Elm Street to still be able to get onto Stemmons Freeway and get to the Trade Mart for Kennedy's luncheon speech.

Tragically, the turn onto Elm Street brought the President much closer to the Texas School Book Depository Building and the grassy knoll.

The debate all these years later is the confusion about the actual parade route. Did this officer innocently lead the President into his death trap or was it by horrific design?

There are two conflicting parade routes published in the major Dallas newspapers that contribute to this controversy. They are of too poor quality to be legible here.

The first map appeared in the Dallas Morning News the day before President Kennedy's visit to Dallas. It shows no turn onto Houston Street or subsequent turn onto Elm Street.

A HARD KILL MADE EASIER

Instead, this map shows the motorcade continuing along Main Street and onto Stemmons Freeway. Had this route been taken, it would have been significantly more difficult for the sniper in the sixth-floor window of the Book Depository to carry out the assassination, especially on his own.

Conveniently, when the motorcade followed the mystery cop onto Houston Street, as shown on the parade route published by the Dallas Times-Herald, the President's limousine is now compelled to turn left onto Elm Street, making JFK an easier target, especially for a sniper positioned on the grassy knoll.

Of course, the Warren Commission found no significance to the confusion of the parade route despite what was about to happen.

But what about the spectators that showed up that day? Why were several dozen standing along Elm Street awaiting the President to pass by, including Abraham Zapruder, the amateur filmmaker?

Some of these people report that they saw the Times-Herald map, came to Dealey Plaza and positioned themselves accordingly.

Others say they saw no map, but heard on TV or radio that the President would go through Dealey Plaza.

These people came to Dealey Plaza, looked around and simply took a spot they felt would give them a good look at the President and Mrs. Kennedy.

And there were people who evidently saw the Morning News map. There is footage of people standing on the Main Street side of Dealey Plaza waiting for the President.

When they see the motorcade turn right onto Houston Street rather than continue along Main Street in front of where they are waiting, you can see these people turn around and run toward the Elm Street side of Dealey Plaza. Many get there in time to witness the President being murdered.

Was the disappearing cop doing his duty and performing his task correctly when he led the motorcade onto Houston Street?

Or did he initiate the turn onto Houston Street knowing that the Presidential procession would follow his lead and the motorcade would have to turn onto Elm Street to exit Dealey Plaza?

Even more importantly, did he know the consequences that would come from his decision to steer the parade cars directly into to the crossfire that awaited President Kennedy?

The Strange All Points Bulletin

Just 15 minutes after President Kennedy was shot and rushed to Parkland Hospital, an all points bulletin went out over the police radio system in search of a suspect that turned out to be Lee Harvey Oswald.

The wording from the police dispatcher is as follows:

"Attention all squads, the suspect in the shooting at Elm and Houston is supposed to be an unknown white male, approximately 30, 165 pounds, slender build, armed with what is thought to be a 30-30 rifle, - repeat, unknown white male, approximately 30, 165 pounds, slender build. No further description at this time or information, 12:45 p.m."

The Warren Commission credited this radio dispatch for the capture of Oswald, not as the President's assassin, but the killer of Dallas policeman J.D. Tippit almost exactly 30 minutes after the transmission.

Otherwise, this is a vague description of an assassin that could match literally thousands of people.

So, how did this description go out on police airways just 15 minutes after the shooting? How was any information known about the assailant of the President so soon after the event?

Timing becomes an issue for any of three possible explanations by the Warren Commission or Dallas police. For instance:

1. **Oswald Rifle Found** – At first, it was thought that a radio description went out for a suspect after the Oswald rifle was found on the sixth-floor in the Book Depository Building, where Oswald worked.

   This is foolish twofold. If they could identify who owned the rifle, the name of the owner could be dispatched, as well as a much more detailed description.

   Secondly, the radio dispatch for a suspect went out at 12:45 p.m., but Oswald's rifle was not found in the building until 1:22 p.m., more than 45 minutes later.

2. **Tippit, Not Kennedy** – Another version to explain this early police transmission for a suspect is that it applied to the Tippit murder, not JFK.

How was Oswald targeted as the assassin as soon as 15 minutes after the shooting?

   This is equally nonsensical because the transmission clearly states the transmission is about the shooting at Houston and Elm Streets.

   Also, officer Tippit was murdered at 1:16 p.m. A police transmission pertaining to the slain cop did not go out until a suspect was seen going into the Texas Theater at 1:45 p.m.

3. **Eyewitness Identification –**

Howard Brennan was the Warren Commission's star witness. He claims he saw Oswald shoot from the sixth-floor window.

Warren Commission star witness Howard Brennan.

Unfortunately, Brennan never spoke to anyone about his sighting until after 1 p.m., still leaving us with no cause for the all-points bulletin.

Also, Brennan's credibility as an eyewitness is debatable. It took him two looks at Oswald in police lineups before he selected Oswald as the person "*Who most resembles the man I saw in the window.*"

His identification of Oswald becomes dubious after this exchange took place with Warren Commission council David Belin:

Belin – "*In the meantime* (before the police lineup), *had you seen any pictures of Lee Harvey Oswald on TV or in the newspapers?*"

Brennan – "*Yes sir, on television.*"

Obviously, it would have been much better had Brennan identified Oswald as the shooter ***before*** seeing Oswald's face splashed all over the media.

Brennan also told Belin that he saw the sniper moving about in the window and fire from a standing position.

But, as you can see me at the so-called 'Oswald' window on this book's back cover, it is quite impossible to shoot from that window from a standing position, even at Oswald's moderate height of 5'9".

Can you imagine how his testimony would have stood up under cross examination at an Oswald trial?

4. Employee Roll Call –

Dallas detective James Leavelle helped arrest Oswald, was the first to speak to him in captivity, escorted Oswald when he was shot and was the last person to see Oswald alive.

Yet another explanation for Oswald emerging as the early suspect in the President's assassination is a roll call of Book Depository employees after the tragedy occurred.

It was alleged that Oswald was the only person who did not show up for the roll call, pointing him out as a prime suspect to police.

Detective James Leavelle (above left), who was handcuffed to Oswald when he was shot by Ruby, confirmed this to British journalist Christopher Bucktin in the Mirror newspaper.

"*It was only after a head count at the Book Depository, where Oswald had a job, that police knew who they were looking for in the JFK killing,*" Leavelle says.

First, a firm time cannot be established for a roll call of employees to fit the narrow 15-minute window before the police description went out.

Secondly, of the 73 documented Book Depository employees, 17 of them state they did not immediately report back to work. Some even say they were denied entry because the Book Depository was in police lock-down.

Carolyn Arnold is one such witness who claims she saw Oswald on the first floor of the building mere minutes before the shooting, then went outside to see the President.

She didn't return in time for a roll call, but because Arnold was a female, it seems she was automatically dismissed as a suspect.

To this day, a believable cause for a suspect wanted in the shooting of JFK just 15 minutes after the event, which led to the arrest of Lee Harvey Oswald, is not adequately explained.

The Umbrella Man

The 'Umbrella Man' makes the list of JFK assassination oddities not because it remains an unsolved mystery. It isn't.

Thanks to the 1978 House Select Committee Hearings on Assassinations, we know that the Umbrella Man appearing in the Zapruder film is Louie Steven Witt, a Texas warehouse manager.

Make no mistake, the Umbrella Man would have always been part of JFK assassination lore.

He is the only man who showed up in Dealey Plaza that beautifully sunny day and unfurled a black umbrella at a most suspicious time.

Despite his emergence in 1978, there remain some curious questions about his actions that day.

Most importantly, the identity of the Umbrella Man and

explanations for his odd behavior as the President passed by should have been known before Oswald was shot two days later.

The 'Umbrella Man,' now known to be Louie Steven Witt, sits on a curb beside a man he says he doesn't know after folding up his umbrella. His use of an umbrella during the shooting remains suspicious.

He made no effort to run away after the shooting. He merely went back to work. He didn't try to leave the state or the country.

Louie Steven Witt simply went home and did everything possible to maintain a low profile. He did this very effectively for 15 years!

220

It is incredulous that Witt was not one of the most wanted 'persons of interest' following the assassination.

As the limousine emerges from behind the traffic sign, you can see 1/2 of an open umbrella to the right of the sign. For years, this person was only known as 'The Umbrella Man.'

The moment you view the Zapruder film, you see his umbrella pop up just as the President's limousine begins to emerge from behind the highway sign (see right).

This most unusual act is accompanied by the haunting cracks of rifle fire that shattered history. Is this nothing more than a tragic coincidence?

Yet, no effort was made to ascertain the identity of this fellow in the Zapruder film despite the existence of still photos of him standing, and then sitting after the shots, beside a dark-skinned man on the curb.

Witt was never contacted by the Dallas police. He was never contacted by the FBI and he was never summoned before the Warren Commission. How is this possible?

Because of the apparent disinterest in who the Umbrella Man was and why he did what he did that day, in this one instance, the flames of conspiracy were allowed to rage unnecessarily.

Because his bizarre appearance and actions went unexplained for so many years, conspiracy theorists tried to fill in the blanks.

For instance, here are two examples:

221

A) **Signal to Assassins** – Many people believe that the Umbrella Man had the important role of signaling to the assassins that the President was in position for the shots to begin.

He happens to unfurl his umbrella slightly in advance of the first shot, striking the President in the upper back.

When JFK emerges from behind the highway sign directly in front of the Umbrella Man, you can see him reacting to that shot. More importantly, he is now exposed to a sniper stationed behind the picket fence on the grassy knoll.

B) **Umbrella Was a Weapon** – Although we never see the umbrella lowered and pointed at President Kennedy, this fairy tale persists because such a weapon existed in 1963.

An umbrella was devised that could shoot poison darts, no doubt for the James Bonds' of the world, but while this scenario is silly, it is what happens when suppositions are allowed to fester.

It turns out that Louie Steven Witt went to Dealey Plaza with his umbrella to heckle the President, who he admits he was not fond of.

Although his explanation is vague, he told the HSCA hearings that the umbrella represented something to do with Joe Kennedy and Hitler going back to the days when JFK's father was the U.S. ambassador to the United Kingdom.

He thought that the umbrella would catch the attention of the President and would irritate him.

Witt claims that he did not know the dark-skinned man to his right and never spoke a word to him.

Further, Witt makes for a terrible assassination witness. He could not recollect much of anything that he observed that day.

Was Louie Steven Witt anything more than he claims to be? It is highly unlikely.

Yet, his possible role in the assassination of President Kennedy will never escape suspicion because police authorities at the time and the Warren Commission didn't do their jobs.

Conspiracy theories didn't emerge simply because of the magnitude of the event. They emerged because of the sloppy investigative work of the crime.

So, allow me to fan the conspiracy flames even more:

Did the Dallas Police, the FBI and the Warren Commission ignore the obvious presence of 'The Umbrella Man' because an investigation might link him to the assassination, thus proving that Oswald did not act alone?

Since no one of authority even talked to Witt prior to his 1978 appearance before the HSCA hearings, we can't categorically dismiss this possibility.

After all, it fits a disturbing pattern by investigative agencies and the Commission. As you will see in Chapter 9, there was a concerted effort to ignore, dismiss and even suppress evidence that might suggest more than one lone crazy nut gunman.

Oswald's Denial to His Death

One of the frustrations associated with the killing of President Kennedy is a lack of a substantiated motive by Oswald that explains him acting out on his own.

The Commission simply asked us to accept their finding that Oswald was pro-Communist and was a misfit in society.

He was a loner by nature, so it makes sense that this anti-American hatched a plan to assassinate the leader of the free world.

Lee Harvey Oswald proclaimed his innocence right to the end.

And yet the Commission did establish Oswald had one particular passion after his failed romance with communism that brought him back home to America – the tropical island of Cuba.

Once back on U.S. soil in New Orleans, Oswald set up the 'Fair Play for Cuba Committee' and handed out supportive literature on street corners.

His position angered anti-Castro Cubans in the area, with whom he clashed on the streets. He even debated their spokesman on radio.

The Commission found that in the months leading up to the JFK assassination, Oswald walked into the Cuban embassy in Mexico City and tried to obtain a visa to go to the island nation.

To accentuate Oswald's apparent distaste for U.S. aggression against Cuba, such as the botched Bay of Pigs invasion, the Commission further found that JFK's lone assassin also tried to murder outspoken military general Edwin Walker, who advocated that Castro be taken out by force (see Chapter 2).

Along with this hot button topic, the Commission continued to assert that he was pro-Communist, which put him at odds with U.S. foreign policy. He brought home a Russian bride, whose father was well placed back home in the military.

While in police custody, Oswald admitted to the press that he had Marxist leanings, but made no other declarations other than to insist "*I'm just a patsy!*"

"*VIVA FIDEL!*"

If Oswald carried out the assassination of President Kennedy because of his political beliefs, or any other personal reason, he had plenty of opportunities to declare himself a hero to the cause, both privately and publicly in the last 48 hours of his life.

Withstanding hours of police interrogation, Oswald refused to confess to shooting the President or Dallas patrolman J.D. Tippit despite his rifle and revolver having been found and linked to both crimes.

He never issued a verbal or written manifesto about his anti-American views or even suggested a personal dislike of President Kennedy.

As investigators continued to tighten the noose around his neck by presenting him with incriminating circumstantial evidence that pointed to his guilt, Oswald remained unflappable and defiant.

There would be no confession to either murder.

One veteran Dallas police detective found Oswald's demeanor to be most unusual. James Leavelle was part of the arrest team when Oswald was captured at the Texas Theater.

The first words out of Oswald's mouth as he was being led away was "*I didn't shoot anybody!*"

As Leavelle told The Mirror reporter Christopher Bucktin, he was also the first officer to get a few alone minutes with Oswald at the police station. Again, Oswald said nothing of substance.

"I tried to build a report (with Oswald) but he didn't seem to have a care in the world," states Leavelle. "He was very calm and collected. Not the actions of someone who just killed the most powerful man on the planet."

Publicly, the accused presidential assassin had several chances to take the bully pulpit and shout out his actions on behalf of a cause.

With a slain Oswald still handcuffed to detective James Leavelle, the officer would climb into the ambulance with the accused assassin. There would be no deathbed confession.

But there was no *"Viva Fidel!"* or *"Long live Communism!"* declarations from Oswald.

If he thought that he could be embraced as a Cuban or Russian patriot and hero, he decided to pass on the opportunity.

He likely didn't know that he was about to die, but with police charging him with two murders and it seeming apparent that he was the only suspect being pursued, why was his only outburst about being a patsy?

Instead, he seemed preoccupied with his self-preservation. He protested not being able to speak with a lawyer and asked the media to put out the word about his need for legal representation.

If Oswald's actions in Dealey Plaza were the result of some pent-up hatred for President Kennedy or a cause that he was emotionally connected to, he never let it show even when his fate as an accused double murderer must have appeared gloomy even to him.

Oswald's behavior and defiance despite the dire circumstances he found himself in is one of the oddities of the JFK assassination that will never be explained. Still, he had one last chance…

DEATHBED CONFESSION?

When Oswald may have felt his life slipping away, he had one last opportunity to confess his crimes and declare a reason.

Detective James Leavelle once again found himself near the

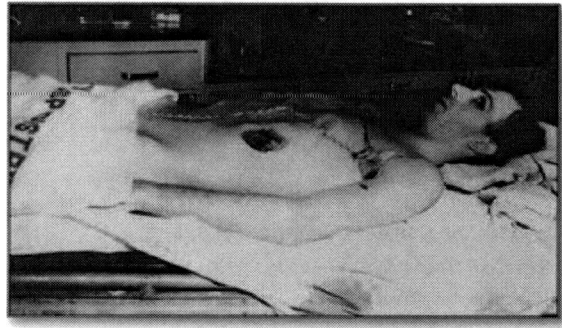

presumed assassin when he jumped into the ambulance with Oswald as it pulled out of the police station and raced to the same hospital that treated President Kennedy.

Lee Harvey Oswald would be silent forever.

Just moments earlier, Leavelle was handcuffed to Oswald when Jack Ruby plunged out of a crowd and shot Oswald in the abdomen. With handcuffs still connected to the two men, the stunned detective followed a silent Oswald into the ambulance.

As he drew his final breaths, Oswald had a chance to confess to being the assassin of a U.S. President, to stake his place in history.

He had one final opportunity to declare himself a lone gunman or possibly even name any confederates he may have had.

We will never know if Oswald was consciously aware of his situation or his pending fate. He may not have been able to express himself because of his condition.

But Oswald did open his eyes and remained alive for another 90 minutes.

In the British Mirror interview, Leavelle recalls his last moments with Oswald.

> *"People ask 'did he admit it?'*
> *or 'did he confess?'...*
> *But he never uttered a word."*

Perhaps Oswald believed to his last breath that he would get his ultimate platform to tell all at a trial in the months ahead.

Jack Ruby denied him that. History's custodians, the Warren Commission, did what a trial wouldn't have done – suppress the truth to the American public.

Oddities such as these serve a conspiracy theory well, but they can't tell us for certain if and why Lee Harvey Oswald assassinated President John F. Kennedy or if he acted on his own.

Through The 'Oswald' Window

Chapter 9

From Camelot to Cover-Up:

Ballistics Tests, Medical Findings And Photo Evidence Either Ignored or Altered to Suppress the Truth for 75 Years

Cover-Up:

'An attempt to prevent people discovering the truth about a serious mistake or crime'

Chief Justice Earl Warren hands the Commission's report to President Lyndon Johnson. The cover-up is official!

Consider the handling of the following evidence by the Warren Commission and you decide if there was a cover-up in the aftermath of the JFK assassination.

So far, this book has detailed blatant deceit pertaining to the President's autopsy, from the use of unqualified pathology surgeons to glaring errors and omissions that failed to account for all the wounds on his body.

We have learned that several witnesses were ignored by investigators and the Warren Commission, especially those who brought reasonable doubt to the single assassin conclusion.

You will discover in Chapter 12 that researchers and the House Select Committee on Assassinations have established disturbing links between Lee Harvey Oswald, Jack Ruby, organized crime and rebel elements within the Central Intelligence Agency.

Immediately after the fatal head shot, President Kennedy is knocked back and to the left, suggesting a shot from the right-front that the Warren Commission decided to ignore.

To our aghast, we have found that the observations of several doctors and nurses at Parkland Hospital were ignored by the Warren Commission as if the mortally wounded President had never been there.

And you will see that a bullet wound to the back can mysteriously move up, a side head wound can remarkably move back and a bullet can cause seven wounds, break two bones and still look nearly brand new.

BUT WAIT, THERE'S MORE!

All the above, as well as what is to follow, will reveal one frightening point of commonality that will become obvious to you.

Let's start by revisiting the bizarre handling of the Zapruder film that caused the Warren Commission major headaches:

Zapruder Film Fiasco

As we found out in the Chapter 6 analysis of the Zapruder film, the Commission hid behind the façade of public decency when it decided not to publish color stills of the graphic film.

Although the Commission had the means to work from the original Zapruder film to ensure clarity and crispness, the frames they presented in the Report appear darker than necessary.

Clearly, they did not want people to see much in the way of details.

After finally getting to view the entire silent color Zapruder film, we can see things that the black and white stills simply don't show us, such as the clear delay in reaction by JFK and Governor Connally.

By obscuring this one image alone, the Commission felt safe enough to declare, in fact, that both men were hit by the same first shot fired that day.

And that declaration gave birth to the famous 'Single Bullet Theory' (see Chapter 4) that enabled the Commission's most important conclusion – Lee Oswald acted alone.

While the Commission could only produce still frames in its report, apart from the extra cost of printing color images, we must ask if there was another agenda at play.

What is most remarkable is that even the sequential Zapruder black and white still frames show the President's head moving violently backward after the lethal head shot, as does the compelling Orville Nix film.

Upon viewing the darker black and white version of frame 313 and subsequent frames, why didn't the Warren Commission, as we do, ask what suddenly appeared to be obvious? – Was there a second gunman in Dealey Plaza that day?

The Commission did answer that question, of course, with an emphatic "*NO,*" but in doing so, the Zapruder film demonstrates the most obvious example of the panel's willingness to ignore evidence of a second shooter.

We also know the Warren Commission had access to the original Zapruder film or at least a quality first generation copy. We must assume that they viewed the film as often as they wished more than a decade before the public got to see it.

I invite you to go back to Chapter 6 and view the Zapruder film as I presented it at seminars in Canada.

After viewing it, what do you see the President's head do in response to the violent head shot?

All these years later, we are at a loss to explain why the Commission members didn't see what you see.

In addition to disregarding what our eyes tell us, the Zapruder film also underwent some 'purposeful' or 'accidental' altering along the way.

Three distinct mistakes were made with the 158 individual frames printed in Volume 18 of the Warren Report:

1. A splice was visible in frames 207 and 212, opening the door for allegations of film editing to hide something.

2. Frames 208, 209, 210 and 211 went missing, again inviting allegations of us not meant to see something, particularly when several successive frames are suddenly gone.

3. Frames 314 and 315 were reversed. This is potentially significant since the Commission asserts that the President's head did move forward after the head shot (frame 313), denoting a shot by Oswald from the Book Depository Building.

   Had this occurred just about anywhere else in the Zapruder film, the public would have been none-the-wiser, but the reversal of frames a nano-second after the critical head shot is too coincidental to believe as an accident.

   Amazingly, the Commission chose to believe the slight frontal movement caused by the frame switch rather than the savage rearward motion of the President clearly seen in the Zapruder motion picture.

Withheld Autopsy Photos and X-Rays

In addition to that iconic film, photos and X-rays of the deceased President's body proved to be problematic for the Warren Commission, so they went to extraordinary lengths to misrepresent or outright suppress these materials to maintain that all shots were fired by Oswald from above and behind President Kennedy.

There is no better example than how the Commission dealt with Mr. Kennedy's autopsy photos and X-rays.

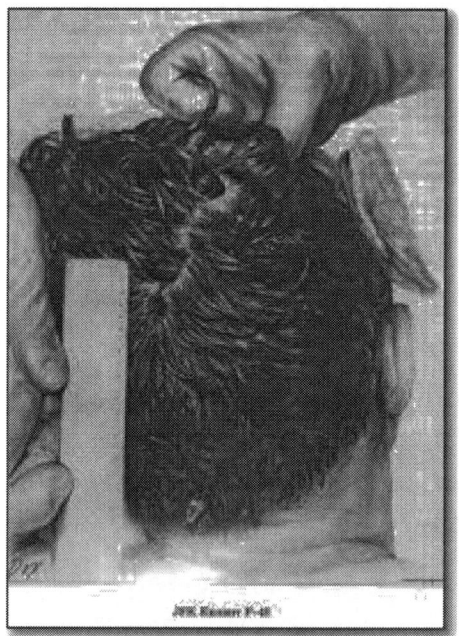

Ida Fox drawing shows a small rear entry hole and a large exit hole above the right ear.

As discussed in Chapter 5, the Commission sought to desensitize the gruesome head wound photos by expunging the actual color pictures and replacing them with black and white artist renditions.

There was only one problem with this; The artistic drawings published in the Warren Report completely distort the accuracy of the wounds sustained by President Kennedy.

As remarkably doubtful as this should be, we can now show you the two contrasting images.

At left is a black and white drawing by Ida Fox, showing a small bullet entry wound in the crown area of JFK's head, as well as the large exit wound above his right ear.

Clearly, the Commission used this artistic representation to suggest President Kennedy received the death shot from above and behind him.

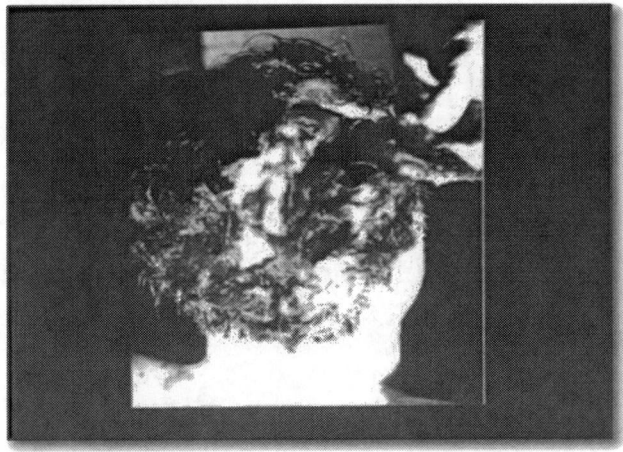

This photo of JFK's head wound was concealed by the Warren Commission, with a falsified artistic drawing as a replacement that does not resemble the actual wound.

However, a Freedom of Information Act lawsuit forced the release of some of the original medical photographs. We are stunned to see that they are nothing like the black and white version adopted by the Commission.

Above right, we see a massive, outward blast at the right rear of the President's skull, not a neat, circular entrance wound as portrayed in the Fox sketch.

And on the next page, we see a second color photo of the President's deadly head wound from another angle that again in no way resembles the Ida Fox drawing.

We might be inclined to applaud the Commission's decision to

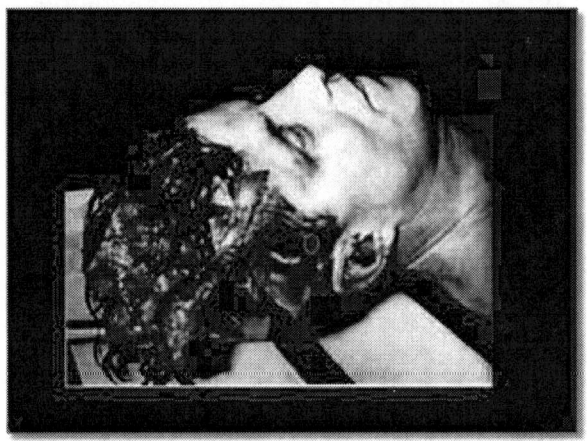

not publish the actual photos had they at least replaced them with accurate black and white representations.

But it becomes clear that the true motive of using artwork instead of photographs was to mask the truth.

Otherwise, the Commission would have to concede that a shot struck JFK in the side of his head and blasted out the right rear occipital portion of his skull, thus admitting to a second sniper and a conspiracy.

THE MOVING BACK WOUND

Another quandary the Commission had to deal with was the non-fatal wounds JFK suffered that day.

At issue were two wounds, an entry wound that struck President Kennedy in the upper back and a supposed wound at his throat just below the Adam's apple.

The Commission needs this throat wound to be the point of exit for the bullet that went on to hit Governor Connally and cause all his non-fatal injuries.

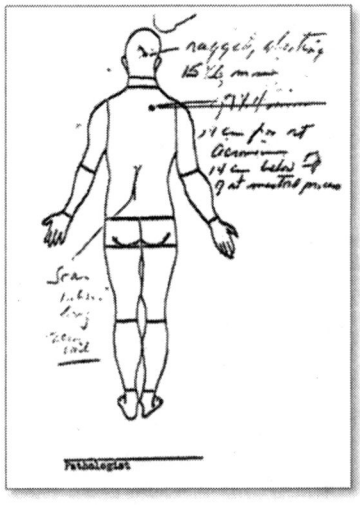

Once again, although much less gruesome than the severe head wound, the Commission relied on artist drawings of the back wound rather than actual photos.

The only drawing they should have used was the standard autopsy sketch at left, made by Dr. Thornton Boswell to show the back wound to be located 5 ¾ inches below the collar line and two inches to the right of the spinal column.

Unfortunately, no photos exist of the front neck wound on JFK because Dr. Malcolm Perry obliterated the wound at Parkland Hospital by making a tracheal incision at the point of that wound to insert a breathing tube.

However, despite the original autopsy report that said the entry wound in JFK's back didn't even transit his body, the Commission needed that bullet to exit at Kennedy's throat so it could claim that both men were hit by the same projectile (see Single Bullet Theory in Chapter 4).

How did the Commission pull this off? By once again using artistic diagrams to misrepresent the wound on JFK's upper back.

It did publish the Dr. Boswell autopsy chart above, but for reasons that continue to defy logic, the Commission decided that the diagram on the next page best describes the trajectory of the bullet that hit both men in the limousine.

Have you noticed that in the artist's version at left, Commission

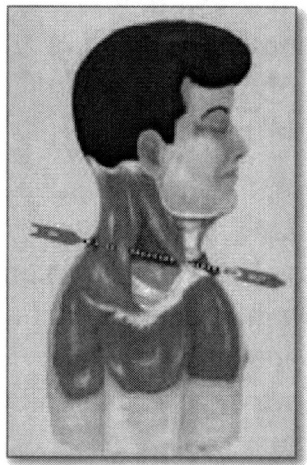

exhibit 385, JFK's back wound has mysteriously moved up nearly five whole inches to the base of the neck?

Why?

This was done to better fit the 'Single Bullet Theory.' The Commission couldn't have a bullet striking JFK at a downward angle of 45 to 60 degrees (fired by Oswald), deflecting up in his chest despite not hitting any bones or hard material in order to exit at the throat at an upward angle, then somehow deflect downward in mid-air to find the Governor's back.

Schematic drawing showing a different point of entry than the Dr. Boswell chart above.

Instead, the 'Single Bullet Theory' would work much better if it was demonstrated that the bullet hit JFK in the base of the neck, at a point slightly higher than the bullet's exit at the throat.

And to pull both the head wound and neck wounds together to affirm shots from above and behind the target, the Commission also presented the second artist

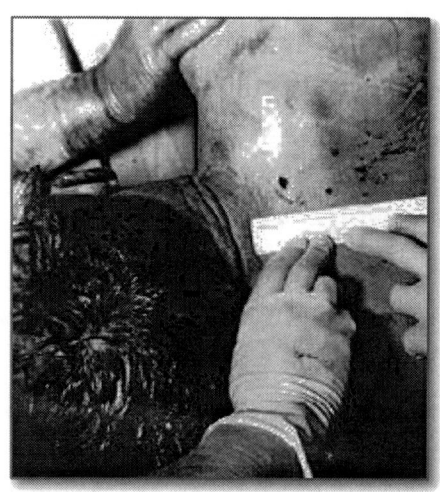

Artist drawing of a higher back wound and a head wound that has disappeared.

240

drawing on page 240 to show a higher point of entry in the upper back AND a head wound to match the Ida Fox drawing earlier in this chapter.

NO X-RATED X-RAYS

The Commission also decided that X-rays, most of which are still locked away in the National Archives in Washington, were too difficult to interpret for the laymen public.

Not surprising, it decided that artistic renditions of X-rays would be better, also giving the artist license to add arrows and such to point out the trajectory and wound damage it wanted to convey.

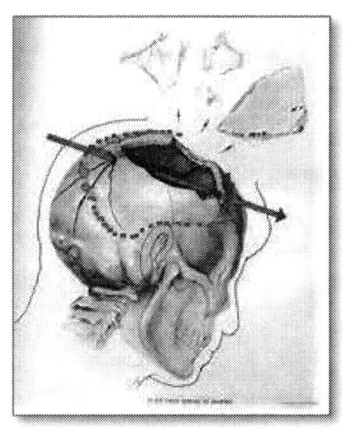

Once again, artist depiction does not match photos.

The artist illustration at left shows a bullet entering the rear of the skull and blasting away a portion of the head up top, which is again in complete contrast to the color photographs of the President's major wound at the back of the skull.

Dr. Cyril Wecht, one of America's leading forensic pathologists who has seen the actual photos and X-rays under lock and key, shared his observations with me on January 8, 2017:

Dr. Wecht – "*There's no doubt there was damage to the brain and the occipital area (right rear) with damage to the cerebellum.*

"This was described by all the doctors at Parkland and they even demonstrated with their hands pointing to the area of damage.

"Keep in mind that some of the doctors were not only experienced trauma surgeons, one was chairman of neuro surgery.

"These guys couldn't be part of any kind of plot. They describe what they saw.

"So, who do you believe? These guys at Parkland who describe what they saw or the bullshit that emanates later on after who knows what's been done with the body?

"And you've got these two guys, Humes and Boswell, who have never done a single gunshot wound autopsy.

"The autopsy report is just salacious. What more can I say?" – Dr. Wecht

---

There is one more disturbing thing that can be said about the handling of medical evidence in this case.

A lot of vital material has gone missing, which does not appear to be in the National Archives in Washington. These include:

- **The President's Brain** - This is tragic. Normally, the brain would be placed in a formalin solution for several days until it hardens, allowing it to be cut into thin slices so that bullet trajectories and damage can be documented.

Without this vital piece of evidence, the Commission was free to speculate on the nature of the head wound and limit its cause to one shot from the rear.

- **Slides of Preserved Brain Tissue** – Without the brain to study, the missing slides become a significant loss. For instance, they can show fragment patterns that suggest bullet trajectory.

- **Photos and X-Rays of the Body** – While some have been released via lawsuits, many photos and X-rays do not appear to be in the National Archives. Unless found, they may not be released to the public in 2038 with other classified documents.

- **Tissue Slides at Bullet Wound Locations** – Tissue slides could reveal metallic residue for ballistics examination or help ascertain if a wound is a point of entry or exit. This is vital to determining the origin of shots.

With all this information missing or non-existent, it is possible that Lee Harvey Oswald's defense team may have been able to establish reasonable doubt at a public trial.

FBI Ballistic Analytics Data

If there is any FBI analysis of bullet(s) or fragments found to match them to the wounds on either man or the Oswald rifle, they appear to be missing or were never done.

A 6.5 mm full metal jacket bullet like these was found at Parkland Hospital and linked to Oswald's rifle, but what about several fragments recovered that day?

The one exception is CE399, the nearly pristine bullet found at the hospital.

Tests verified it had been fired from the Oswald rifle, but other tests should have been applied to connect the so-called 'Magic Bullet' to the wounds inflicted upon Kennedy or Connally.

This way, by matching fragments to the found Parkland bullet, the Commission could say conclusively that this bullet caused all or some of the wounds on the two victims.

Because such tests were either not done or suppressed, the Commission cannot definitively say that CE399 was fired from the Oswald rifle specifically on November 22, 1963.

This oversight invites conspiracy theorists to act as defense attorneys for Oswald posthumously, raising questions of incompetence or even cover-up as a trial would have done.

For instance, it could be argued in a court of law that CE399 was fired from the Oswald rifle prior to the Dallas event into a container of gelatin, retrieved and planted as evidence against the accused assassin.

How then did this bullet become found and associated with the JFK assassination? As noted in Chapter 3, Jack Ruby was seen at Parkland Hospital within 15 minutes of the President's arrival.

Such speculation is akin to giving the Warren Commission a dose of its own medicine. In the final analysis, truth seems to pay the ultimate price.

So, why this oversight? They simply couldn't risk getting back results they didn't want.

As you will see, the Commission learned this lesson the hard way. And the moral of that lesson was to limit any information pertaining to the 'Magic Bullet' they allege caused all the survivable wounds on JFK and Connally.

Once they were told that CE399, the bullet found on a stretcher at Parkland Hospital, was fired from Oswald's rifle, the Commission believed this was enough to establish that they had their lone assassin dead to rights.

To be more accurate, the Commission's lone assassin suspect was dead, leaving him no rights as an accused person in a murder case.

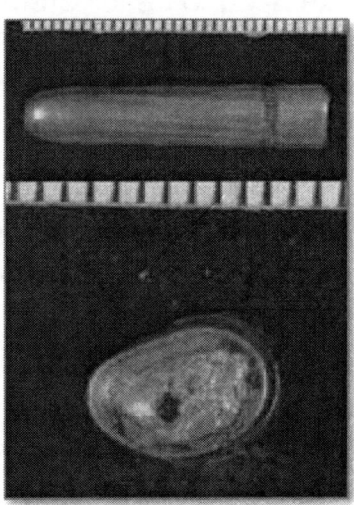

The 'Magic' Bullet, CE399, shows natural squeezing at base but remained 98.5% intact.

To that end, it is astonishing to learn that either no such tests were ordered or test results were suppressed by the FBI and never shared with the Commission.

At the time, both spectroscopic and neutron activation analysis could have been applied to fragments, showing them as having come from CE399.

Some researchers believe these tests were done, but the results were buried by the FBI at the direction of Director J. Edgar Hoover, no fan of the Kennedy boys.

For the Commission's 'Single Bullet Theory,' such tests could be a double-edged sword as follows:

A) **No Link to CE399** - The last thing they needed was to show that fragments recovered from either Kennedy or Connally could not have come from the recovered 'Magic' bullet at Parkland Hospital.

B) **A Weighty Dilemma** - Further, they could not have all the fragments recovered add up to more than the 2.4 grains of metal missing from the found bullet (CE399).

The need to tread carefully with CE399 was raised by experienced Dr. Robert Shaw, one of the surgeons who tended to Governor Connally's multiple wounds, in a dialogue with Commission council Arlen Specter:

Mr. Specter – *"What is your opinion as to whether bullet 399 could have inflicted all the wounds on the Governor then, without respect at this point to the wound of the President's neck?"*

Dr. Shaw – *"I feel that there would be some difficulty in explaining all of the wounds as being inflicted by bullet Exhibit 399 without causing more in the way of loss of substance to the bullet or deformation of the bullet."*

The best way to avoid either of those scenarios was to simply not do certain standard FBI ballistic tests or make sure any unfavorable results never come to light.

APPEAL TO THE CONNALLYS

Dr. Cyril Wecht is a leading forensic pathologist who is outspoken against the 'Single Bullet Theory.'

One final effort to resolve the 'Magic Bullet' issue was undertaken by Dr. Cyril Wecht and some of his fellow forensic pathologists.

Dr. Wecht, who is both a forensic pathologist and a lawyer, is a former President of the American Academy of Forensic Science and the American College of Legal Medicine.

In the conversation we had, Dr. Wecht explains his efforts this way:

"A group of us got a hold of (Attorney General) Janet Reno when Governor Connally was critically ill.

"She passed along a request to Mrs. Connally to ask her permission for some of the fragments in her husband to be removed so they could be tested and matched up (to CE399) and regrettably, she refused.

"From the first press conference Governor Connally ever gave from the hospital, and Mrs. Connally too, they insisted for their entire lifetimes that he was struck by a different shot.

"Unfortunately, the fragments were taken to the grave.

"I remember talking with Parkland's chief operating nurse Audrey Bell back then about several fragments given to her from the operation on Connally, which she passed on to the FBI.

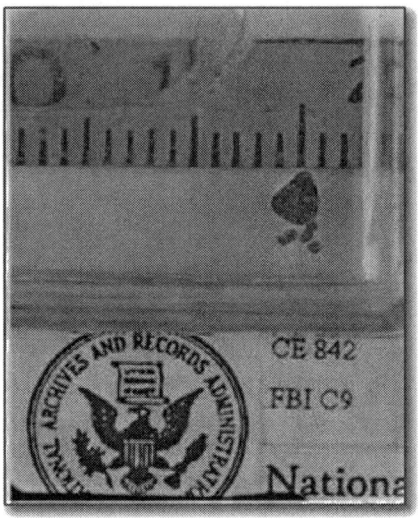

As Dr. Cyril Wecht notes to this author, these fragments (CE842) were taken from Governor Connally's wrist and given to nurse Audrey Bell, who turned them over to the FBI.

"So, we have these fragments given to the FBI and fragments seen in Connally's chest and wrist X-rays that he took to the grave with him.

"And yet, according to the Warren Commission Report, all of these grains together only weighed 1.5% of the original weight of the bullet at its store-bought condition of 161 grains.

"As it was found under a stretcher at Parkland Hospital by a maintenance man, the bullet weighed 158.6 grains.

"2.4 grains are exactly 1.5%. There's no way in the world that a bullet having moved in that fashion, breaking two large bones, destroying four inches of Connally's fifth right rib, producing a commuted fracture of the distal radius bone, a very dense bone, especially in a 6'4" guy like Connally.

"And the bullet is completely intact? The only deformity is at the base from the impact of the firing mechanism. The entire copper jacket is intact with no deformity at all.

"There you have the Magic Bullet, leaving the fragments of itself, quantitating to only 1.5% of the original weight, with no deformity other than that caused by the firing mechanism at the base."

As Dr. Wecht points out, given his vast experience with gunshot wounds and ballistic testing, it is absurd to expect the firing mechanism to cause deformity and damage at the base while the entire bullet jacket causes seven wounds and two major broken bones and emerges with only a sliver of metal missing at the nose.

As you are about to learn, some ballistic tests backfired on the Commission, so when it came to the essential 'Single Bullet Theory,' it was decided that little or no talk about test results would equal no controversy.

They were wrong.

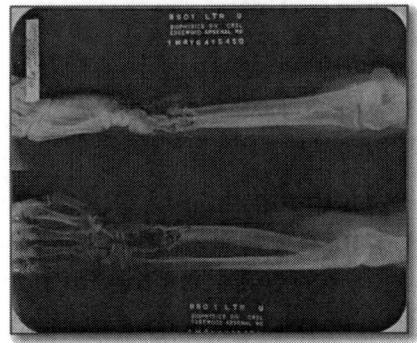

Ballistics test (CE854) on wrists of cadavers show very similar results to damage sustained by Gov. Connally.

Trying to Produce a 'Magic Bullet' Clone

The Warren Commission did try to produce a 'Magic Bullet' clone in hopes of establishing that the damage attributed to CE399 was possible.

The tests didn't go so well.

Using Oswald's rifle and identical 6.5 mm copper jacketed bullets, test shots were fired into the wrist of two cadavers (previous page), showing identical damage to the distal radius bone as sustained by Governor Connally.

Yet, pictured here is Commission Exhibit 856, the bullet recovered from the test firing.

As you can see, this missile is hardly the 'Magic Bullet' the

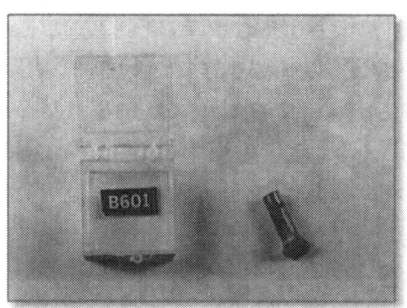

Commission says caused a similar compound fracture in Governor Connally, PLUS broke off four inches of a rib and inflicted five additional wounds in 'two' men!

CE856 shows the test bullet fired into the wrist of a cadaver. This one wound alone caused more damage to the bullet than the bullet (CE399) the Commission says smashed Connally's wrist and produced six other wounds.

How did the Warren Report deal with this ballistic finding? It simply chose to ignore it, figuring that nobody would notice the contradiction until all files were released in 2038.

The House Select Committee on Assassinations (HSCA) also tried such a test, but as HSCA/JFK Exhibit 294 reiterates (next page), the bullet on the far right was fired into the wrist of a cadaver and came out misshapen and much more damaged than the Commission's 'Magic Bullet.'

Dr. Cyril Wecht likes to refer to this exhibit when speaking in public about test results not supporting the Warren Report findings.

In our dialogue of 01/08/17, Dr. Wecht explains HSCA/JFK Exhibit 294 at right:

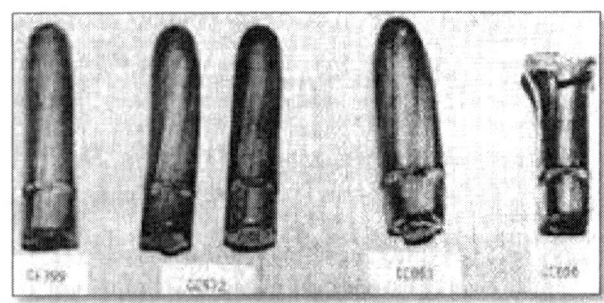

Only when bullets were fired into cotton wadding (second & third bullets from left, striking no hard substance, did the bullets look anything like (CE399) the 'Magic Bullet' at far left.

"*They shot two goat carcasses to simulate Connally's rib fracture and two human cadavers to simulate Connally's radial fracture and other bullets into cotton wadding, striking nothing, to see what the bullets would look like.*

"*The government slides, not mine, show the bullet with the least damage from each group.*

"*The bullet from the goat carcass (second from right) is much broader. You almost think it is a different caliber.*

"*And the bullet through a radius (bullet far right) shows the typical, classical deformity. The bullet peels back when it strikes bone.*"

Despite their own testing, the Commission decided that CE399, in this historic instance, did not peel back or deform as shown in the test bullets.

Entry Versus Exit Wound Ballistics Blunder

One final ballistic test pokes major holes (pun intended) in the Warren Commission's defense of its necessary 'Single Bullet Theory.'

At issue is the characteristics of entry wounds compared to exit wounds using Oswald's Mannlicher-Carcano 6.5 rifle and identical bullets as CE399, the famous 'Magic Bullet.'

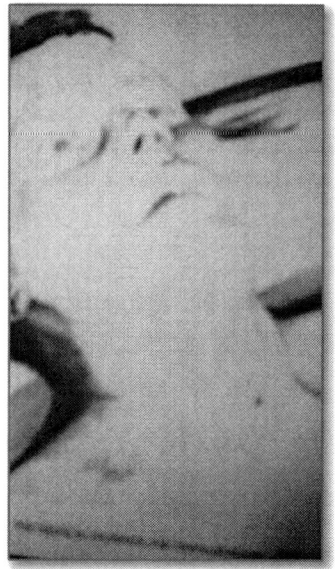

This drawing, published by Robert J. Groden (The Killing of a President) shows a small hole in JFK's throat. It has characteristics of an entry wound, but the Commission says it is an exit wound.

Typically, an entrance wound that doesn't strike a hard substance like bone at point of impact creates a clean puncture wound.

At point of exit, the hole tends to be bigger and more jagged because it is blasting out of the body.

The Commission was hoping to establish that a bullet fired from the Oswald rifle could produce a clean exit wound the same size or even smaller than an entry wound.

This became important to the 'Single Bullet Theory' because we know the President received a bullet entry wound in the upper back that was clean, neat, circular and small, about the diameter of the bullet itself.

252

But as noted in Chapter 5, Dr. Malcolm Perry, the only doctor to see a hole in the President's throat before he destroyed it with a tracheotomy incision, described the hole as small and circular, about the diameter of a pencil, as shown in the diagram at left.

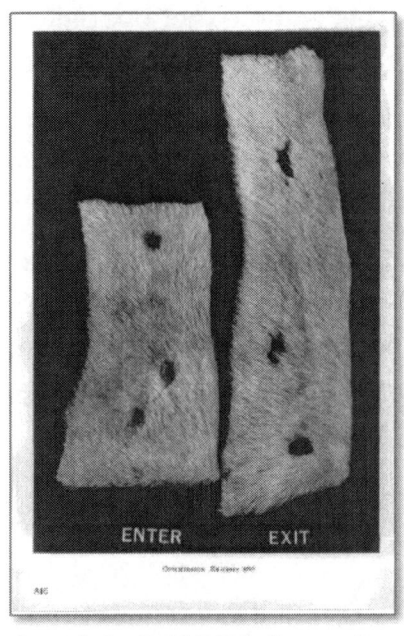

Without the President's throat wound being an exit wound, bullet CE399 couldn't possibly have struck JFK in the upper back, exited his throat and traveled on to cause all the wounds on Governor Connally.

The very foundation of the 'Single Bullet Theory' rests on this trajectory and requires the throat wound to be one of exit.

Commission Exhibit 850 disproves its own claim that the so-called 'Magic Bullet' exited JFK's throat and struck Gov. Connally.

The Commission set out to show that the JFK throat wound, as recalled by Dr. Perry, was typical of 6.5 mm bullets fired from the Oswald rifle.

But in the image at right, Commission Exhibit 850 shows quite the reverse characteristics.

Using goat skin to simulate human skin, Oswald's rifle and the same type of ammunition, we can see that in every instance, bullet exit holes (right) were almost '*double*' the size of bullet entry holes (left).

This is the exact opposite test result needed by the Commission to uphold its 'Single Bullet' hypothesis.

Yet again, despite its own ballistics results, this is the one instance the Commission insists the exit wound was smaller than the entry wound.

Even when the Commission encountered evidence of its own doing that pointed to a second gunman in Dealey Plaza, it inconceivably chose to ignore such evidence to staunchly declare Oswald as the lone assassin of JFK and attempted murderer of Mr. Connally.

Photo Fraud to Hide the Truth

One of the most alarming examples of outright evidence tampering was a black and white photo taken by James 'Ike' Altgens, a Dallas-based photo journalist and reporter for the Associated Press (AP).

The dramatic moment of the first shot was captured by AP photographer James Altgens.

Altgens was positioned in front of the President's limousine and captured the moment the first shot was fired, as well as JFK's reaction to that shot striking him in the upper back.

At left is a close-up of the Altgens photo that focuses on JFK in the limousine. Seated directly in front of the President is Governor Connally, who is turned to his right in response to hearing a shot from behind him.

The President's face is partially blocked by the mirror on the car's windshield. His mouth is closed. His left arm is up at his throat and bent at 90 degrees.

You can see his clenched fist at his mouth. The white cuff of his shirt is visible as well as the dark suit covering his arm.

On the President's forearm, you can see the white glove of Mrs. Kennedy's left hand. She has just realized that her husband is in some kind of distress and is attempting to come to his aid.

The President is clearly reacting to the first shot that, in of itself, would not have killed him.

Based on this view into the Presidential Lincoln, the only controversy is whether Governor Connally has also sustained his five wounds and two bone fractures at this moment.

The Warren Commission says "Yes," but this debate is more fully discussed in Chapter 4. Another monstrous controversy occurs when we look at the full scope of this famous photograph.

MISSING THE BIG PICTURE

At right is CE900, published in Volume 18 of the Warren Report. This shows the Altgens photo made available to the public as well as the Warren Commission's effort to re-enact the moment of the assassination that Altgens captured (lower image).

An entire re-enactment of JFK's assassination was done by the Commission and FBI based on numerous photographs and the Zapruder film, but the Altgens photograph gives us the ultimate evidence of deception and cover-up.

At right is the same Altgens photo on its own. You can see two Secret Service agents looking behind them in reaction to hearing the gunshot as Altgens clicked his camera.

256

This version of the Altgens photo was presented in the Warren Report...but there was more to this photo that the Commission could not show if it didn't want to admit to more than one assassin.

Secret Service agent Clint Hill (sunglasses) is shown still standing on the running board of the vehicle behind the President's car, looking into the Presidential convertible.

Agent Hill was assigned to The First Lady's protection.

Within another couple of seconds that proved to be too late, agent Hill will leave his position, run to the limousine, jump up onto the trunk and push Mrs. Kennedy back into the seat with her mortally wounded husband.

This unforgettable moment, at right, was also caught on film for history by Altgens.

As discussed in Chapter 7, Jackie Kennedy's instinctive reaction to the tragic head shot, prompting her to climb out onto the trunk of the Lincoln despite the obvious danger, contributes to the debate of a second sniper

positioned to the right-front on the grassy knoll.

But the 'full' Altgens photo, not the cropped version printed by the Warren Report on page 93 of volume 18, provides a history-shattering revelation on its own!

TRUTH DENYING TRIFECTA!

Below is the full, unedited Altgens photo, which reveals three egregious attempts to alter the truth about what happened that awful day in Dallas.

This full Altgens photo was suppressed by the Warren Commission for three distinct reasons, described below.

If you take a minute to compare the entire Altgens photo with the cropped version released to the public in the Warren Report, three important differences appear that were purposely withheld for what was to be 75 years.

First, positioned at the left-rear bumper of the Presidential limousine is motorcycle cop Bobby Hargis. He is the inside cop riding alongside agent Hill. He has been edited out of the Commission's offering of this photo.

It is hard to believe that the omission of officer Hargis is incidental because of what happened to him as a direct result of the President's head shot just seconds after this moment was caught on camera.

His momentous account of what happened to him in Chapter 7 is one of the more compelling indications of the fatal shot originating from the grassy knoll.

This photographic omission of officer Hargis was the first step by the Commission to downplay his place in the true assassination story.

The troubling testimony of Bobby Hargis was buried in Volume 6 of the Warren Report and his actions in Dealey Plaza were never expounded upon in the key summary edition released to the public.

CAR POSITION PROBLEM

Up next, take note of the limousine's position on Elm Street.

The left front tire is touching the white lane marker that divides the road.

This will prove to be of vital importance to the sequence and origin of shots, a key factor that couldn't have been missed by the Warren Commission.

As revealed in Chapter 1, I became one of few journalists or researchers ever allowed access to the so-called 'Oswald' Window in February of 1979. One picture I took of the kill site from this historic window will become very prominent in this discussion.

After viewing the full Altgens photo, I made a second trip to Dealey Plaza in 1983. Using this uncropped photo as my guide, I could ascertain that the Presidential limousine's left-front tire is touching the *sixth* white lane marker from the intersection of Houston and Elm Streets.

OMINOUS SIGN

Another way of ascertaining the limousine's position on the road is what the Zapruder film '**doesn't**' show us.

Just before JFK disappears from view on the Zapruder film, he is shown smiling and waving to the crowd on his right.

Less than a second later, Zapruder frame 225 shows the President emerging from behind the Stemmons Freeway sign.

His smile is gone and his hands are coming to his neck in response to being hit by a bullet. This is the moment captured by the Altgen's photo.

Knowing that President Kennedy was hit behind the highway sign, during my second visit to Dealey Plaza in 1983, I positioned myself at the Stemmons Freeway sign, precisely where 'the umbrella man' stood that day.

From that position, looking out onto Elm Street, I could see the same white road marker that the Altgens photo shows being touched by the car's left-front tire. This affirms Kennedy's position on Elm Street when he receives his initial non-fatal wound.

This enables us, as the Commission must have done in their re-enactment, to position the JFK automobile exactly on Elm Street as you see it, knowing that the first shot has sounded, clearly wounding the President.

I took a position at that sixth white road marker in the middle of the road in 1983 and made an astonishing discovery when I looked up to the sixth-floor southeast corner window of the Book Depository Building.

This brings us to the third piece of crucial evidence conveniently removed by the cropped version of the Altgens picture that the Commission presented:

TREE TROUBLE

As you can see in the unedited Altgens photo shown earlier, there is a large oak tree that blocks out the first couple of floors of the Book Depository Building where Oswald worked. What you can see is the white main entrance of the building on Elm Street.

If you go back to the Commission's cropped Altgens photo, the oak tree is completely removed from the snap shot. Was the tree merely thought to be irrelevant?

Or was there a dire need by the Commission to apply the 'out of sight, out of mind' concept to this tree?

If you saw what I saw in Dealey Plaza, first from the 'Oswald' window in 1979 and then on Elm Street in 1983, the answer becomes obvious and bewildering for seekers of the 'Oswald alone' scenario as historical truth.

As mentioned above, thanks to the unreduced Altgens photo, I was able to position the left-front tire of JFK's Lincoln on the sixth white lane marker on Elm Street from the corner of Houston Street.

I then looked up to the Book Depository sixth-floor window and was stunned by what I discovered -

I could not see the alleged 'Oswald' window!

Do you know why?

Because that oak tree visible in the uncut Altgens photograph blocks the view of that window from the known position on the road where President Kennedy received his bullet wound to the upper back!

More important to history, this also means that a sniper perched in the sixth-floor southeast corner window could not have had an unobstructed shot at President Kennedy at that precise moment, at that spot on the road when we can clearly see JFK reacting to being hit.

THIRD ASSASSIN?

To further illustrate this point, at right is the photo I took from the 'Oswald' window that clearly shows the sightline obstruction this oak tree causes an assassin at this location.

Clearly, even the most skilled shooter would have to wait until the target limousine clears the foliage of the oak tree before taking a shot.

From the vantage point of the Book Depository window, it appears that when the car's driver-side front tire touches the sixth white road marker, JFK is not visible to the assassin.

Therefore, it becomes unlikely that the shot causing JFK to raise his hands to his neck came from the infamous sixth-floor 'Oswald' window.

It needs to be noted that there is no indication of any road work or construction on Elm Street until 2013. At that time, the notorious 'X' on the road to mark the fatal head shot was removed, only to be returned due to public protest.

During my visits in 1979 and 1983, Elm Street was as it appeared on that fateful November 22, 1963.

Another issue is the potential change to the oak tree due to the passage of time. Did what I saw in 1979 or 1983 accurately reflect the circumstances in 1963 within reason?

The answer is yes. Even in 1963, the large oak tree was mature and in full bloom. It had ceased growing, meaning that the mature branches would simply thin out or fill in during the modest changes of season in Dallas.

In other words, every November 22 for several years following the assassination, the oak tree is in full bloom with lots of foliage.

So then, where did the shot come from that struck President Kennedy in the upper back?

The oak tree is problematic for a sniper in the Book Depository window, but not for a potential sniper in the Dal-Tex Records Building.

The Dal-Tex Records Building sat adjacent to the Book Depository at the intersection of Houston and Elm Streets.

Some conspiracy theorists speculate that a shot came from a window partially concealed by a stairwell in the Dal-Tex Records Building.

The above photo by ConspiracyZonePodcastPeople.com shows a possible bullet trajectory from the Dal-Tex Records Building that suggests such a shot would not be impeded by the oak tree.

A close-up within the photo appears to show an unknown person at that possible sniper perch who, as far as we know, has never been identified or was ever interviewed as a witness by investigative authorities.

This indicates that no hidden files exist that may come to light in 2038 that might address a possible shooter in the Dal-Tex Records Building. We are unlikely to ever know for certain if the Book Depository assassin had one accomplice or two.

THE JACK RUBY IMPACT

All the above witness, medical, ballistics and photographic evidence was greatly impacted the moment Jack Ruby shot and killed Lee Harvey Oswald.

Had Oswald lived, a public trial would have demanded witnesses be cross examined. It would have put medical findings under greater scrutiny by experts.

Photographs could not have been altered without accountability and thorough ballistics tests would have been required.

All the above would have been submitted evidence as proof of Oswald's guilt or innocence.

But with him out of the way, and no Oswald representative allowed to question witnesses and test results submitted to the Warren Commission, there was no pressure or requirement to meet the standards of American jurisprudence.

Instead, history was sullied by a whitewash report, a cover-up controlled by Lyndon Johnson's Justice Department and J. Edgar Hoover's FBI.

And despite the efforts of hundreds of sleuth researchers over the years, most have only obfuscated the truth for the sake of any conspiracy theory they can think of.

If no conspiracy, foreign or domestic, was to be found, who gave this directive to the Warren Commission?

Blueprint for Cover-Up?

Soon after Lee Harvey Oswald was pronounced dead, one oddity may have given birth to the Warren Commission and the narrowly-focused investigation that would follow.

On the day that both Oswald and President Kennedy were buried, assistant Attorney General Nicholas deB. Katzenbach wrote an astonishing memorandum to Bill Moyers, special assistant to newly sworn-in President Lyndon Johnson.

Here is the unedited transcript of that memo to the new administration:

———————————————

November 25, 1963

Memorandum to Mr. Moyers

It is important that all of the facts surrounding President Kennedy's Assassination be made public in a way which will satisfy people in the United States and abroad that all the facts have been told and that a statement to this effect be made now.

> 1. The public must be satisfied that Oswald was the assassin; that he did not have confederates who

are still at large; and that the evidence was such that he would have been convicted at trial.

2. Speculation about Oswald's motivation ought to be cut off, and we should have some basis for rebutting thought that this was a Communist conspiracy or (as the Iron Curtain press is saying) a right–wing conspiracy to blame it on the Communists. Unfortunately, the facts on Oswald seem about too pat — too obvious (Marxist, Cuba, Russian wife, etc.). The Dallas police have put out statements on the Communist conspiracy theory, and it was they who were in charge when he was shot and thus silenced.

3. The matter has been handled thus far with neither dignity nor conviction. Facts have been mixed with rumour and speculation. We can scarcely let the world see us totally in the image of the Dallas police when our President is murdered.

    I think this objective may be satisfied by making public as soon as possible a complete and thorough FBI report on Oswald and the assassination. This may run into the difficulty of pointing to inconsistencies between this report and statements by Dallas police officials. But the reputation of the Bureau is such that it may do the whole job.

    The only other step would be the appointment of a Presidential Commission of unimpeachable personnel to review and examine the evidence and announce its conclusions. This has both advantages and disadvantages. It [sic] think it can await publication of the FBI report and public reaction to it here and abroad.

I think, however, that a statement that all the facts will be made public property in an orderly and responsible way should be made now. We need something to head off public speculation or Congressional hearings of the wrong sort.

Nicholas deB. Katzenbach
Deputy Attorney General

———————————————

Within a few days, a compromise was reached. A Presidential Commission was appointed by LBJ and the FBI became its chief investigative arm.

And since the FBI and the CIA had no cooperative working relationship at the time, the CIA was left to handle the delicate matter of Oswald's Soviet defection and Communist leanings, making sure that no Soviet involvement would be found.

This memorandum raises some fascinating considerations:

- **Mandate Pre-Ordained?** – In point #1above, just 48 hours after the assassination, Katzenbach does not recommend a way to go about establishing the facts and the truth about what happened in Dallas.

Instead, the second top law enforcement official in the land has already branded Oswald

Attorney General Robert Kennedy (right) with Ramsey Clark (left) and Nicholas deB. Katzenbach, both of whom would serve as Attorney General in the Johnson White House.

as the 'lone assassin' and emphasizes the need to satisfy the public about this fact.

- **Forget Other Possibilities** – Oswald's obvious ties to the Soviet Union, as well as his pro-Castro ideals, need to be discarded. Despite these possible foreign involvements in the assassination, any links to these entities need to be quickly squelched.

- **Information Control** – The urgency expressed by Katzenbach to cut off public speculation shows the need to control information. And the expressed concern about a congressional inquiry removes the control of information from the executive branch of government. Hence his recommendation of a blue-ribbon panel investigation.

- **Memo's Origin?** – Were the views expressed in the Katzenbach memo his own personal thoughts? Did the memo follow a private meeting with the new President?

  Even more intriguing, was this memo in any way influenced by Katzenbach's direct boss, Attorney General Robert Kennedy, the deceased President's brother?

Unfortunately, we are left with yet more unanswered questions to one of the greatest mysteries of the 20th century.

Chapter 10

The Mysterious Deaths of More than 100 People Linked to JFK Assassination

---

By the time Martin Luther King Jr. and Bobby Kennedy were assassinated in 1968, nearly 40 other lesser known people had also died, from apparent natural causes to mysterious circumstances and even unsolved murders.

They all had this one historic thing in common:

All of them can be linked to the assassination of President John F. Kennedy on November 22, 1963.

These people ranged in age and all aspects of life. Some were witnesses to that horrible event.

Some were instantly thrust into history as an emergency room attendant at Parkland Hospital, or perhaps a co-worker of either Lee Harvey Oswald or Jack Ruby.

Still others had a chance rendezvous with history and immortality like J.D. Tippit, the Dallas police officer who allegedly confronted an escaping Oswald 45 minutes after the assassination and paid for that brief encounter with his life.

It won't surprise you that more than five decades later, hundreds of people with some kind of link to the JFK assassination have died.

All the Warren Commission members are dead. All the doctors who tried

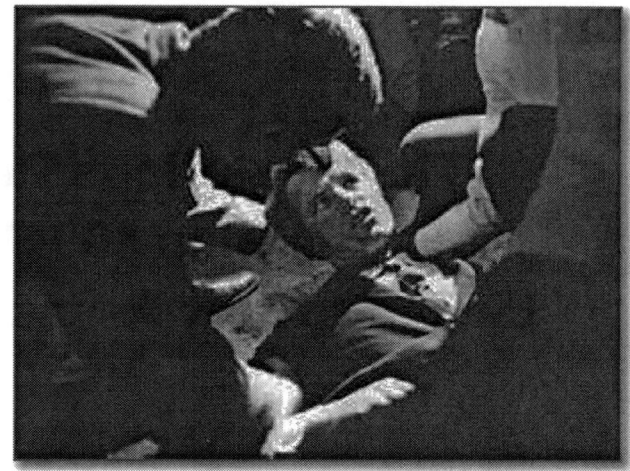

Bobby Kennedy died bearing the guilt of his brother's assassination.

to save his life are dead. Governor John Connally is dead.

The assassin's assassin is dead. And the majority of witnesses on that fateful day are dead, most of them naturally surrendering to time.

Time catches up to all of us, but for approximately 100 of these people, it wasn't time that took them. They can never be erased from their tiny spot in our history books.

Rather, it was unusual circumstances, unexplained suicides and even cold-blooded murder that claimed far too many of these lives.

ODDS DEFY BELIEF

Penn Jones Jr. - A pioneer researcher of the JFK assassination and chronicler of mysterious deaths.

Just three years after President Kennedy was killed, Midlothian, Texas journalist and researcher Penn Jones Jr. began documenting the unusual deaths of people somehow associated to that tragic day.

He noted that 18 people had died (not counting Lee Harvey Oswald or Jack Ruby) by the end of 1966, all of them linked by a small or significant part they played in the death of the country's 35th President.

Penn Jones was one of the earliest critics of the Warren Commission findings, starting a newsletter titled 'The Continuing Inquiry' that inspired this young journalist and brought us together for an 'official' JFK assassination tour in Dallas in 1979.

His work brought serious questions to light about the Warren Report findings and gave birth to other noted researchers and authors.

At first, the deaths reported by Jones were dismissed as natural or at best, a curious coincidence.

The London Sunday Times decided to look into this coincidence by employing an actuary to study the odds. It then published its bombshell findings, noting that:

The odds of 18 material witnesses dying under any variety of circumstances within three years of the JFK assassination is... 1 in 100,000 TRILLION!

To put that into perspective, the odds of you winning a $500 million New York Mega Millions lottery is:

1 in 258,890,850

Suddenly, the 18 JFK-related deaths within 36 months caught people's attention and prompted a very compelling question:

How do we explain this astounding actuarial finding?

Keep in mind that just three years removed from that shocking event, the vast majority of Americans believed the key findings of the Warren Report, namely that:

A) Lee Harvey Oswald acted alone in shooting President Kennedy.

B) Jack Ruby acted alone in shooting Lee Harvey Oswald.

So, beyond a bizarre coincidence, what else might explain why these 18 people, and counting, would die so soon after the President?

If the above conclusions by the Warren Commission are correct, then nothing but coincidence can explain these deaths, despite the massive odds against it happening.

However, if President Kennedy died because of a conspiracy and a cover-up ensued (see Chapter 12), perhaps these deaths are more than mere happenstance.

Beyond the first three years that followed the assassination, many other mysterious deaths occurred, including some famous and infamous names.

Here's a look at some of the peculiar deaths relating to the JFK murder, starting with the President's own brother.

Robert F. Kennedy

We all know how Bobby Kennedy was killed, but is there a why behind it that ties into the death of his older brother?

Robert F. Kennedy Jr., the late Attorney General's son, says "Yes."

Did Robert Kennedy seek the presidency to access JFK death files?

In 2013, RFK Jr. told Charlie Rose of CBS News and PBS that his father never believed that Oswald acted alone.

His father suspected that organized crime may have been involved because of the heat his Justice Department was putting on the mob.

It was a terrible burden to think that he may have caused his brother to be killed.

RFK Jr. stops there, but his comments raise the possibility of one very personal reason why his father decided to seek the presidency in 1968.

JFK's successor, Lyndon Johnson, appointed the Warren Commission and when it submitted its 26-volume report, Johnson declared thousands of documents as "Classified' or 'Top Secret' and imposed a 75-year ban on these materials, sealed away until 2038 by presidential signature.

The only way Bobby Kennedy could access those documents and get to the truth was to become President of the United States. That's part of what motivated him to seek the highest office in the land when he was gunned down in Los Angeles.

Was Sirhan a lone assassin? Or were there powerful forces at play, such as those described in chapter 12, that couldn't risk the truth coming to light?

One intriguing hint comes from Louisiana mob boss Carlos Marcello himself. He wanted the Attorney General killed, but understood that by killing President Kennedy instead, he was also getting his wish.

E.R. Buddy Walthers

Walthers was a Dallas Deputy Sheriff who was at Dealey Plaza when President Kennedy was shot.

The photo on the next page shows Deputy Sheriff Walthers (standing with dark hat) searching the grass on Elm Street, the opposite side of the grassy knoll, immediately following the shots in Dealey Plaza.

Walthers told some of his fellow officers that he found a badly

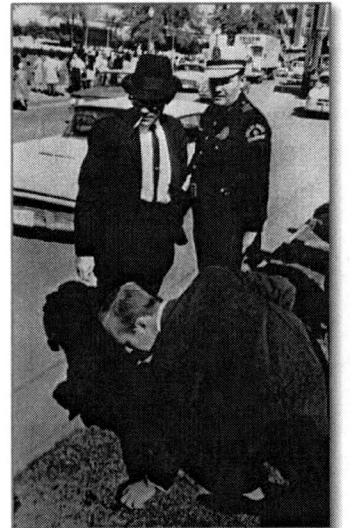

damaged .45-caliber bullet in the grass, but turned it over to a man identifying himself as a Secret Service agent (the man crouching in the photo?).

This was problematic for the Warren Commission because this bullet could not have been fired from the Oswald rifle found in the Book Depository Building.

Strangely, Walthers had a change of tune. When he appeared before the Warren Commission, he said he had no recollection of finding a bullet at the assassination site.

Dallas Deputy Sheriff Buddy Walthers (standing left) says he found a bullet in the grass that did not match Oswald's rifle.

Privately, Walthers continued to vary his story, depending on who he was telling it to, right up until January of 1969 when he was shot on duty and killed.

Lee Bowers Jr.

Working that day in a railroad control tower, Lee Bowers had a unique view of the goings on in Dealey Plaza. His elevated position allowed him to see the hidden side of the picket fence on the grassy knoll.

More than 40 witnesses reported hearing a shot come from behind the picket fence up on the knoll, putting a potential shooter on the side of the fence that Bowers could see.

Bowers testified before the Warren Commission that he saw two unfamiliar men along that fence line, standing under a tree.

It was bright and sunny at 12:30 p.m. when the shots rang out, but the shade and branches from that tree blocked the activity taking place.

Grassy Knoll witness Lee Bowers Jr., one of the first mysterious deaths associated with the JFK assassination.

One man was heavy-set and middle aged and the other man was in his 20's and wore a plaid shirt or jacket.

Bowers reported to the Commission that he heard three shots and saw a flash of light or puff of smoke come from the area of the two men.

This 'puff of smoke' sighting was seconded by witness Sam Holland, who was standing on the triple overpass bridge on Elm Street as the motorcade approached. The grassy knoll and picket fence were to his left.

When Holland took on-site police to where he saw the puff of smoke, it coincided with where Bowers saw the two men and a small cloud arise. There were footprints in the area.

Immediately after the shots, pandemonium ensued. Bowers was distracted by the commotion and when he looked back at the spot where he saw the smoke, the two men were gone.

On August 9, 1965, Lee Bowers lost control of his car in good driving conditions and hit a concrete bridge abutment.

Before he succumbed to his injuries, he told hospital workers that he felt woozy after he stopped and bought a coffee. Tests only confirmed that he was free of alcohol.

Hank Killam

Hank Killam is linked to Jack Ruby by his wife Wanda, who served drinks and cigarettes at Ruby's nightclub.

Killam is also linked to Lee Oswald by John Carter, who briefly roomed with Oswald in Dallas and worked with Killam as a house painter.

In the months that followed the JFK assassination, Killam felt unsafe in Dallas. He fled to Pensacola, Florida to be near family.

His brother Earl called him "The Man Who Knew Too Much" and said that his brother felt he was being followed and harassed.

Just before his strange death, Earl quotes his brother as saying, *"They're going to get me. I've run as far as I'm going to run."*

Earl Killam also told researchers that his brother Hank, in early November of 1963, overheard John Carter on the phone saying that JFK would be killed in Dallas.

Hank Killam chose a strange way to kill himself.

On March 17, 1964, the police report says Killam 'walked' through a plate glass window of a department store in Pensacola, severing his jugular vein and causing him to bleed out before an ambulance arrived.

The death was ruled a suicide. When coroner A.H. Northup reviewed the files after the case was closed, he described the wound as a single deep gash in the throat and called it "a very strange way to try to kill himself."

The was blood inside the store and signs of a struggle, but no witnesses were ever found.

Dorothy Hunt

Dorothy Hunt was the wife of E. Howard Hunt, the former CIA operative who was convicted of being part of the Watergate break-in. Many believe Hunt is one of the 'three tramps' taken into police custody in the minutes following the JFK assassination.

Mrs. Hunt died in a plane crash on December 4, 1972 when a United Airlines plane went down from Washington to Chicago.

This occurred as the Watergate affair was gaining steam. As aired by Toronto CFTR radio reporter Clint Nickerson on the program 'Thou Shalt Not Kill,' 10 other people linked to Watergate also perished in the crash, along with a suitcase of suspected payoff cash that was never recovered at the scene.

Did Dorothy Hunt die with Watergate payoff money?

CBS news reporter Michele Clark was accompanying Dorothy Hunt on the flight. It is believed that Mrs. Hunt had a CIA document on her that Ms. Clark was going to publish.

It apparently divulged that the CIA was directly linked to political assassinations abroad, specifically failed attempts against Fidel Castro and the successful murder of South Vietnam leader Ngo Dinh Diem just 20 days before President Kennedy went to Dallas.

The National Transportation Safety Board ruled pilot error although data recovered from the plane suggests he was silent and unresponsive for a good couple of minutes before the crash.

Hale Boggs Sr.

Another plane crash took the life of Hale Boggs Sr., the Louisiana congressman and House Majority Whip when JFK was killed.

Congressman and dissenting Warren Commission member Hale Boggs Sr. with President Johnson.

On October 16, 1972, Boggs' plane left Anchorage for Juneau, Alaska but never arrived. The plane, nor the bodies of Boggs or three others, were ever found.

Boggs became one of the seven Warren Commission members recruited by President Lyndon Johnson.

He refused to sign off on the 'single bullet theory' (see Chapter 4) and publicly voiced dissatisfaction with the Warren Commission proceedings, specifically the lack of cooperation from the FBI, which was the chief investigative arm of the Commission.

When the Warren Report was released, Boggs, as well as Senators Richard Russell and Sherman Cooper, disagreed with the Commission's findings that both Oswald and Ruby acted alone.

They sought to write a minority report to distance themselves from the Warren Commission findings, but were denied. Boggs would not stay silent about his dissention before his death.

Sam Giancana and Johnny Roselli

Both Sam Giancana and Johnny Roselli lived the gangster lifestyle in Chicago and both mobsters died by the means they used to kill others.

Giancana was top boss of the Chicago crime syndicate who famously shared a lover with JFK (see Judith Campbell Exner in Chapter 12).

He also struck a deal with Joe Kennedy to stuff the ballot box in Illinois and help his son win the presidency. It worked.

Chicago top mobster Sam Giancana.

Roselli was a 'capo' (Made Man) in the Giancana family who helped his organization gain control of illicit activities in Hollywood and Las Vegas. He became good friends with Frank Sinatra, who was close with JFK and Peter Lawford.

Giancana and Roselli were recruited by the CIA to help privately fund assassination attempts against Fidel Castro, who Roselli would later claim turned the tables on Kennedy.

Both Giancana and Roselli were called to testify about the Castro plots before the U.S. Select Committee on Intelligence in 1975.

Roselli was to appear a third time on April 23, 1976 pertaining to a possible conspiracy to kill President Kennedy. He never showed up or was ever again seen alive.

Giancana never lived to testify a first time. He was found dead June 19, 1975 in his basement kitchen with a gunshot wound to his head, as well as six circular shots around his mouth, a Mafioso warning to others to keep their mouth shut.

Mobster Johnny Roselli was recruited by CIA to help assassinate Fidel Castro.

As for Roselli, his decomposing body was found in a 50-lb metal drum off the shores of Miami on August 9, 1976.

Before his death, Roselli told noted investigative reporter Jack Anderson that Jack Ruby was ordered to take out Oswald.

Dorothy Kilgallen

One of the more famous deaths associated with the Kennedy assassination is that of Dorothy Kilgallen.

In the early 1960's, Kilgallen was a noted journalist for the Journal American and CBS news. But millions of Americans knew her best as a regular panelist on the popular TV game show 'What's My Line?'

As a reporter, Kilgallen wrote an article exposing a sexual relationship between President Kennedy and Marilyn Munroe.

Two days later, on August 5, 1962, the iconic Hollywood actress was found dead of a suspected overdose.

Investigative reporter and celebrity Dorothy Kilogallon dies suddenly on the eve of a major Jack Ruby scoop.

Several weeks before the Warren Report was released to the public, Kilgallen secured a copy of Jack Ruby's June 07, 1964 testimony before the Warren Commission.

She reprinted Ruby's testimony in the Journal American, which caused alarm bells to go off as it appeared he was hiding more than he was revealing.

Kilgallen was skeptical and was able to use her journalistic clout to get an exclusive private sit down with Jack Ruby in a Dallas courtroom.

Dorothy Kilgallen came out of that meeting and proclaimed,

"What Jack Ruby told me will shatter the world!"

She would not disclose details of that meeting pending a full story that would soon appear in publication.

It did not happen.

Just two weeks later, on November 8, 1965, Ms. Kilgallen was found dead in her Manhattan apartment. The death was ruled a suicide by alcohol and barbiturate poisoning.

Close friends claim that Dorothy Kilgallen was not a drinker and question the timing of killing herself when she appeared so excited about having the 'scoop of the century!'

Two other oddities add to the suspicious cause of death.

No notes from the Jack Ruby interview were ever found in her apartment or office. And a good friend, Mrs. Earl Smith, died two days after Ms. Kilgallen from blunt trauma to the throat. That murder remains unsolved.

Joseph A. Milteer

Joseph Milteer was President of the Georgia chapter of the White Knights of the Ku Klux Klan. He was also a right-wing activist for the National States Rights Party and the Constitution Party, both racist organizations with some powerful backers in the south

Radical Joseph Milteer predicted JFK's death with alarming details.

Two weeks before JFK's trip to Dallas, Milteer was recorded talking to Miami police undercover cop William Somersett, posing as a militant sympathiser.

In the recording, Milteer is heard saying the murder of the President was *"in the working,"* and that the best way to do it is *"from an office building with a high-powered rifle,"* even commenting that *"they will pick up somebody within hours afterwards to throw the public off."*

Somersett passed along these comments to the Secret Service and called them credible. Before a planned motorcade in Miami was publicly announced, it was called off.

After the events in Dallas, Somersett contacted Milteer, who seemed jubilant and remarked *"everything ran true to form. I guess you thought I was kidding when I said he would be killed from a window with a high-powered rifle."*

The Warren Commission became aware of Milteer's prediction quite late in its mandate and did not pursue it.

Joseph Milteer died in his home in 1974 when a portable Coleman heating stove exploded.

JIM GARRISON'S DEAD WITNESSES

In 1966, New Orleans District Attorney Jim Garrison began an investigation into the JFK assassination after learning that Lee Oswald had spent time in the area, was related to local mob bookmaker Dutz Murret, and was associated with known criminal David Ferrie.

Garrison brought conspiracy to murder charges against Clay Shaw, a New Orleans businessman and associate of David Ferrie, whom Garrison had linked to Louisiana organized crime boss Carlos Marcello.

Shaw was found not guilty and the Garrison investigation was widely discredited for its lack of evidence.

Garrison publicly defended his case against Shaw and claimed that more people may have faced charges if the government hadn't been able to squelch so many of his subpoenas for documents and witnesses.

During his investigation, key witnesses to be called by Garrison died, keeping the possibility alive in the eyes of conspiracy theorists that District Attorney Garrison may have been on to something.

Here are a few of those witnesses who may have taken secrets with them to their graves:

Eladio Cerefino del Valle

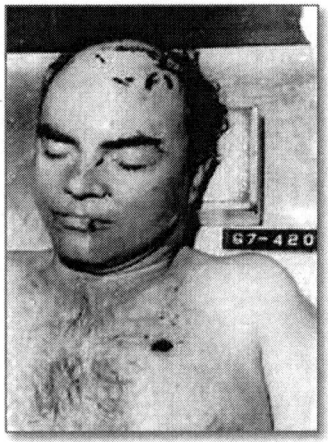

When Cuban defector Manuel Garcia Gonzales was seen in a photo with Lee Harvey Oswald, del Valle identified him as an Oswald co-conspirator in the assassination of JFK.

According to Garrison, del Valle was going to swear in court during the Shaw trial that Oswald also knew Ferrie.

Jim Garrison witness Eladio del Valle suffers violent death before Clay Shaw trial.

A photo (see Chapter 12) shows the two men together at a Civil Air Patrol camp in 1955.

Garrison claims that Ferrie had a homosexual relationship with Shaw and that Ferrie was the private pilot who flew Marcello back into the U.S. after Bobby Kennedy had him deported to Guatemala.

Eladio del Valle was key to Garrison linking Oswald to both the CIA through Ferrie and top Mafioso Carlos Marcello via both Ferrie and Oswald's uncle Dutz Murret.

Before he was called to testify, del Valle was found mutilated in the trunk of his red Cadillac. He was severely beaten, shot once above the heart and stabbed in the head.

Pilot David Ferrie could link Oswald, Ruby and mobster Carlos Marcello, but died before testifying.

David Ferrie

Just one day before Eladio del Valle was murdered, key JFK assassination suspect David Ferrie died in his home, penning two suicide notes on the day the coroner ruled death was caused by intracerebral hemorrhage.

Ferrie was an odd-ball character, wearing fake eyebrows and a flaming red wig, who worked as a private investigator for one of Carlos Marcello's lawyers.

A 1955 photo proves Ferrie and Oswald knew each other when the two were members of the New Orleans chapter of the Civil Air Patrol.

David Ferrie was a former disgraced Eastern Airlines pilot who Garrison believes privately flew Marcello back into the U.S. in defiance of Bobby Kennedy's less than legal deportation order.

Garrison also asserted that Ferrie was assigned to get Oswald out of Dallas after the assassination, only to return home when Oswald was apprehended while attempting to rendezvous with Ferrie.

In 1978, the House Select Committee on Assassinations learned that a cellmate of Louisiana mob boss Carlos Marcello taped him in the exercise yard.

Marcello admits to meeting Oswald through David Ferrie and got Ferrie to bring Oswald into the assassination plans.

In the Oliver Stone movie JFK, David Ferrie, played by Joe Pesci, is shown in a panic over having to testify at the Clay Shaw trial, claiming it would be the death of him.

Ferrie's death was a key blow to the Garrison trial not just because of his connection to Shaw, but the flamboyant District Attorney was also hoping to go after Carlos Marcello for conspiracy to murder the President of the United States.

Maurice Gatlin

Maurice Gatlin and associate David Ferrie (above) died while under investigation by New Orleans D.A. Jim Garrison.

Maurice Gatlin was also a pilot under contract with Guy Banister, who Garrison was building a case against because of his connections to David Ferrie, Lee Oswald, Carlos Marcello and the CIA.

Banister is an ex-FBI agent and New Orleans cop who started his own private investigative firm.

Banister's office was in the same building identified on literature as the home office for Oswald's 'Fair Play for Cuba Committee.'

Gatlin got involved with Banister as a gun-runner and money delivery man and could tie crates of guns, grenades and ammunitions to Banister's office.

The New Orleans States-Item newspaper reported that Banister was a key supplier of munitions for the 1961 Bay of Pigs Invasion.

If plane drops of munitions were required, Garrison believed that Ferrie and Gatlin were the pilots involved.

Several people reported seeing Banister's office always filled with crates of munitions, as well as repeated sightings of Ferrie and Oswald at Banister's place of business.

Garrison believed that Gatlin could place Ferrie, Oswald and Banister together and tie them to CIA black-ops pertaining to the Bay of Pigs and Fidel Castro assassination attempts.

Garrison also believed that Gatlin could connect these three individuals to mafia chieftain Carlos Marcello via his deportation lawyer G. Wray Gill.

When Marcello had to sneak back into the U.S., his lawyer had two veteran private pilots at his disposal – David Ferrie and Maurice Gatlin.

Gatlin had come to Garrison's attention in the early stages of his investigation, but died before being interviewed by the D.A.'s office. Gatlin apparently suffered a heart attack, which caused him to fall six floors from a hotel balcony.

Of course, the most famous JFK-related death is when Jack Ruby shot Lee Harvey Oswald on November 24, 1963.

It became the first murder ever caught on live television, making millions of Americans actual witnesses to history.

The Warren Commission concluded that Ruby acted alone in taking out revenge against the President's assassin. This is subject to much debate, which is discussed in Chapter 3.

Note: This chapter is dedicated to Penn Jones Jr., friend, JFK assassination mentor, and relentless seeker of the truth.

Hopefully, one day, we can finish the job he so relentlessly researched.

Through The 'Oswald' Window

Chapter 11

12:30 p.m. CST:

What Happened in Those Six Seconds That Changed American History Forever?

The horrifying Zapruder film, with the key moments dissected frame-by-frame in Chapter 6, acts as a timeclock.

It tells us that from the crack of the first shot until chaos ensues in a matter of seconds, history would never be the same.

Here we are several decades later and those 6 seconds continue to haunt us, not just because of what happened in that brief span of time, but because of what might have happened if we could erase those six seconds from history.

WHAT IF?

Six seconds is an eye blink in terms of history, yet that precious fleeting period of time has impacted the unfolding of our historical record to date.

Abraham Zapruder filmed the last not survivable moments of President Kennedy's life.

For instance:

Would President Kennedy have been re-elected in 1964? If so, how might history be different?

Ponder this:

• Would Richard Nixon still have won the presidency in 1968 or would the 'Camelot' effect have kept the Democrats in power?

• Without a Nixon victory in '68, we can safely surmise that there wouldn't have been a Watergate scandal in 1972. Might an impeachment and a shamed resignation been avoided if not for those six seconds in Dallas?

• Can we say for certain that Martin Luther King or Robert Kennedy would have been assassinated in 1968?

- And history still debates whether JFK would have continued the conflict in Vietnam as both Lyndon Johnson and Richard Nixon did for nearly a decade.

When President Kennedy died on November 22, 1963, a total of 186 U.S. military deaths had occurred in Vietnam during his presidency.

By the end of the Johnson and Nixon years, a total of 58,220 U.S. servicemen and servicewomen gave their lives in Vietnam!

Had he decided to withdraw rather than escalate, as many of his inner circle believes, that alone makes the JFK assassination historically impactful.

Historians can raise far more 'what ifs' than mentioned here. We can only speculate about how those six seconds might have affected the years to follow.

The Abraham Zapruder home movie and other evidence allows us to examine what happened that tragic day in Dallas.

But only to a point.

Because of the following, we may never know all the facts pertaining to the assassination of President Kennedy:

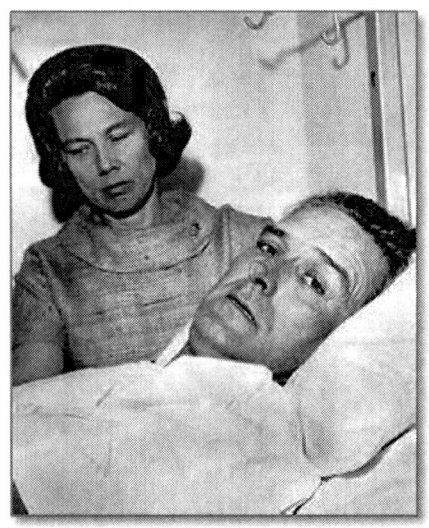

John and Nellie Connally both disputed the 'single bullet theory' their entire lives.

• **Stemmons Freeway Sign** – For a little over a second, a large green highway sign blocked Zapruder's view of the President and Governor Connally.

During that brief time, the first shot rang out, denying us the exact moment JFK was hit, as well as possibly a lost second or two of Connally's response to that shot.

He says he was not yet hit while behind the highway sign, but would a clear view say otherwise?

- **Poor Investigation** – Of the nearly 600 witnesses in Dealey Plaza at 12:30 CST, less than 25% were ever questioned by police, the FBI or the Warren Commission.

Might just one of these ignored witnesses shed new light on history? Because of an early belief by authorities that Lee Harvey Oswald acted alone based on circumstantial evidence, eyewitness and ear witness accounts became less relevant.

Even worse, witnesses who did not support the lone gunman scenario, such as Nellie Connally and Governor Connally himself, were simply labelled as mistaken by the Commission.

- **Faulty Autopsy** – An autopsy's mandate is to ascertain exact cause of death. It is alarming to discover the errors and omissions of the President's autopsy performed by unqualified pathologists. This includes not accounting for all the wounds on the body!

Because of an incomplete post-mortem as detailed in Chapter 5, we cannot definitively say how many shots struck President Kennedy or where they came from.

- **No Oswald Trial** – Had Lee Oswald lived to stand trial, we would not have nearly as many unanswered questions and a more thorough investigation into the murder would have been necessary to establish guilt beyond a reasonable doubt.

- **Zapruder Film** – The famous film itself raises some key questions rather than give us visual answers to everything, such as why did a motorcycle cop cause the turn toward the Book Depository Building and then disappear off the Zapruder screen? (see Chapter 8)

Even a frame-by-frame analysis of the Zapruder film creates enduring controversy, leaving two official government investigations to arrive at somewhat different conclusions.

Which version of history do you believe? Did Oswald act alone? Have a look here once again at the Zapruder film footage I showed at seminars:

Go to www.youtube.com and type in this address –

www.youtube.com/watch?v=UBKliGNC49c

WARREN COMMISSION'S FINDINGS

Before we look at those traumatizing 6 seconds of gunfire and try to piece together the final moments of President Kennedy's life, let's start with the Warren Commission's five essential conclusions:

1. **Location** – The shots that killed President Kennedy and wounded Governor Connally were fired by Lee Harvey Oswald from the southeast corner window on the sixth floor of the Texas School Book Depository Building, which was above and behind the Presidential limousine.

2. **Shots/Results** – Lee Harvey Oswald fired three shots, finding his target twice.

3. **Cop Killer** – Lee Harvey Oswald, while attempting to flee from the JFK assassination scene, shot and killed Dallas patrolman J.D. Tippit.

4. **Assassin Assassinated** – Two days after the President's assassination, accused assassin Lee Oswald was murdered by Dallas Nightclub owner Jack Ruby.

Three spent cartridge cases found at the 'Oswald' window equals three shots fired at JFK?

5. **Lone Assassins** – No conspiracy, foreign or domestic, existed in either the assassination of President Kennedy or his slayer, Lee Harvey Oswald.

The following describes the sequence of shots from the Oswald sniper's nest according to the Warren Report:

Shot #1

The bullet struck President Kennedy at the back of his neck, exited his throat just below the Adam's apple, went on to strike Governor John Connally in the upper back, broke off four inches of his fifth right rib, exited his chest on the right side just below the nipple, went on to strike his right wrist, causing a compound fracture of the distal radius bone, exited his wrist and went on to

imbed itself into the Governor's left inner thigh.

According to the Warren Commission, this bullet worked its way out of the point of entry in the thigh due to the commotion at Parkland Hospital.

It fell onto the Governor's stretcher and later fell to the floor,

CE399, also known as the 'Magic' Bullet, was found at Parkland Hospital and allegedly caused all the non-fatal wounds on two men.

where a hospital staffer found it and turned it over to the FBI.

This missile trajectory became known as the 'Single Bullet Theory,' which requires this bullet (above) to cause seven wounds on two men, including two major broken bones, while losing only 2.4 grains of metal at it's nose.

Shot #2

The second shot missed the Presidential limousine and all its occupants completely.

The Commission was unable to determine if the second shot was a clean miss of the target or may have struck a branch or leaves of the oak tree in its pathway.

The Warren Report postulates that the second shot, or a fragment of that bullet, hit further down the street near the triple overpass, striking a curb and causing a piece of cement to fly up and hit bystander James Tague on his right cheek.

Shot #3

The third shot, per the Warren Commission, struck President Kennedy in the back of his head, blasting out the right side of his skull above the ear and killed him (see schematic drawing at right).

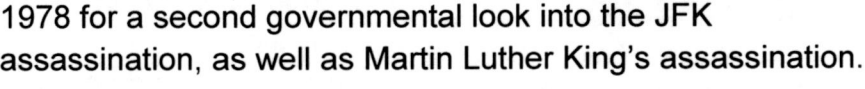

THE HSCA FINDINGS

The House Select Committee on Assassinations (HSCA) convened in 1978 for a second governmental look into the JFK assassination, as well as Martin Luther King's assassination.

During my one month of covering the hearings in Washington, it became clear that the public historic record would change.

Here are the essential findings of the HSCA:

1. **Conspiracy** - President John F. Kennedy was likely killed as a result of a conspiracy.

2. **Second Gunman** – In addition to three shots from above and behind the President, a shot came from behind a picket fence atop the grassy knoll in Dealey Plaza. There was a total of four shots directed at the President's limousine.

3. **Unknown Shooter** – The identity of the second gunman is unknown. Lee Harvey Oswald fired three shots from the sixth-floor window in the Book Depository Building, causing all the wounds inflicted on the two men.

4. **Nature of Conspiracy** – In addition to two assassins, certain elements of organized crime had the means and

motive to kill President Kennedy, but no evidence beyond a reasonable doubt could be found to bring those involved to justice.

How did Oswald leave the Marines, defect to Russia and renounce his U.S. citizenship, but return two years later as if he went on vacation?

5. **CIA Cover-Up** – The CIA lied to the Warren Commission about Lee Harvey Oswald's military intelligence career, as well as other information it had on the accused assassin, such as Oswald's brief defection to the Soviet Union.

6. **FBI Cover-Up** – The FBI withheld information about Lee Harvey Oswald from the Warren Commission, such as its failure to flag and surveil Oswald leading up to the President's visit to Dallas.

In addition to these findings, the HSCA also decided that the first shot may have occurred earlier than when the limousine disappears behind the highway sign, thereby increasing the shooting time to just over eight seconds, but it was not able to prove the timing of the shots as a certainty.

SEQUENCE AND RESULTS OF FOUR SHOTS

The HSCA identified one more shot than the Warren Report, claiming that the four shots occurred as follows:

Shots #1 and #2

The HSCA agreed that one bullet caused all the non-fatal wounds sustained by President Kennedy and Governor Connally, but could not state for certain if this bullet was the first or second shot fired.

Therefore, either the first shot or the second shot missed the limousine completely and its occupants. Either the first or second bullet fired did the following:

That bullet struck President Kennedy at the back of his neck, exited his throat just below the Adam's apple, went on to strike Governor John Connally in the upper back, broke off four inches of his fifth right rib, exited his chest on the right side just below the nipple, went on to strike his right wrist, causing a compound fracture of the distal radius bone, exited his wrist and went on to imbed itself into the Governor's left inner thigh.

Shot #3

Based primarily on acoustical evidence, the HSCA believes the third shot came from the grassy knoll to the right-front of the President's car.

It further believes that the grassy knoll shot missed the intended target, but could give no

Could an assassin behind the picket fence on the grassy knoll have quickly escaped or hid via this storm drain?

information as to what this bullet may have hit in Dealey Plaza or where the bullet ended up.

Z-313

We can see how JFK died, but still debate the location and shooter of this shot.

Shot #4

Occurring less than ½ a second after the third shot, the HSCA believes that the fourth shot was fired by Oswald from the Book

Depository window.

The HSCA believes this shot struck President Kennedy in the rear of the skull, caused a massive exit wound on the right side of his head and killed him.

MODERN DAY PERSPECTIVE –
FOUR SHOTS, THREE ASSASSINS

As you can see, time has not helped to correct the facts or even lessen the confusion pertaining to this historic event.

The first government investigation claims a lone gunman to be responsible. The second official government inquiry suggests two gunmen but cannot name the second sniper or other conspirators involved.

Over time, the Warren Commission has proved itself to be mostly incompetent, but it was also hampered by intelligence organizations more interested in protecting their own failings pertaining to the accused assassin, Lee Harvey Oswald.

Fifteen years later, the HSCA re-wrote history when it pointed to a second shooter and a conspiracy, but mostly due to the passage of time, it could not answer the two essential questions it created:

1. In addition to Oswald, who was the second assassin?

2. Along with a second gunman, who were the conspirators involved?

Further, the HSCA Report, much like the Warren Report, not only failed to resolve key unanswered questions, even more questions and perplexities emerge from these studies.

There are still way too many unanswered questions about who targeted JFK.

Because of the mountainous doubt about the Warren Report raised in this book, as well as the HSCA Report to a lesser extent, what follows is the most likely assassination scenario based on the latest information at hand.

Did JFK Jr's beliefs about his father and uncle's assassinations keep him out of politics?

Let's start with the essential conclusions:

1. **Shots Fired** – There were four shots fired at President Kennedy.

2. **Number of Shooters** – There were three gunmen in Dealey Plaza.

3. **Location of Assassins** – One assassin took position at the southeast corner window on the sixth floor of the Texas School Book Depository Building.

A second assassin fired from the second floor of the Dal-Tex Records Building, immediately adjacent to the Book Depository Building. This location was also behind the President's car, but not as high up as the Book Depository shooter.

A third assassin was located behind a picket fence atop the grassy knoll, which was to the right-front of JFK at the time of the fatal head shot.

4. **Nature of Conspiracy** – President Kennedy was assassinated because of a conspiracy that involved three assassins, all of which are unknown.

JFK was assassinated by an alliance of 'rebel elements' of both the CIA and organized crime, brought together by a common cause that is detailed in Chapter 12.

SUPPLEMENTAL CONCLUSIONS

Lee Harvey Oswald

- **Not an Assassin** - Lee Harvey Oswald was involved in the JFK assassination, but was not one of the assassins. His role, as a Book Depository employee, was to set up a sniper's perch at the sixth-floor window for one of the three shooters.

- **The Set-Up** - Oswald did not know that his rifle would be left behind close to the Book Depository window to implicate him as the President's assassin.

Oswald did not know that rounds of ammunition would be previously fired from his rifle and three cartridge cases would be left at the window to tie his rifle to the assassination (see photo on page 301).

The large package that Oswald brought into the Book Depository Building on the morning of the assassination was a rifle, but not his Mannlicher-Carcano.

Instead, it was a rifle he thought would be used at the sixth-floor sniper perch he set up, a weapon that would not be traced to him.

- **The Patsy** - As he told police in custody, Oswald was in the second-floor lunchroom at the time of the assassination. Oswald was a "patsy" as he unwaveringly claimed in the last 48 hours of his life.

   Oswald became alarmed at the immediate police presence in the Depository Building within 90 seconds of the shooting. As a co-conspirator, he panicked, left the building, went home and picked up a revolver.

- **The Murderer** - Lee Oswald shot and killed Dallas Police officer J.D. Tippit, fearing he had been implicated in the President's assassination. He may even have suspected that he was being set up as the fall guy at the time of the Tippit confrontation.

Enter Jack Ruby

- **Bullet Plant** - Unbeknownst to Oswald, a previously fired bullet (CE399) that could be matched to his rifle, was planted as evidence at Parkland Hospital.

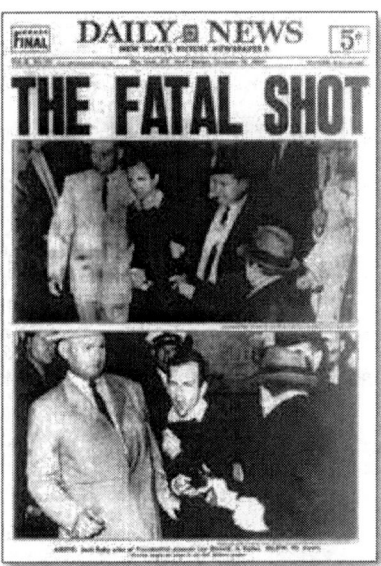

Bereaved vigilante or mob hit?

- **The Planter** - Oswald's similar gangster and CIA associates (see Chapter 12) makes it likely that mobster thug Jack Ruby went to Parkland Hospital after the shooting and planted CE399. This planted bullet was linked to the Oswald rifle found in the Book Depository Building.

- **The Stalker** - Because of Jack Ruby's relationship with Dallas police officials, he could make multiple appearances without suspicion at the police station where Oswald was being held.

- **The Silencer** – Because of Jack Ruby's mobster ties, as well as his association with Dallas police officers and officials, he was directed by organized crime bosses to silence Oswald before trial could be arranged.

- **The Association** – Both Jack Ruby and Lee Oswald can both be linked to Louisiana crime boss Carlos Marcello and/or Florida mafia chieftain Santo Trafficante, as well as Chicago top gangster Sam Giancana (see Chapter 12).

These three mafia kingpins were involved in the JFK assassination as outlined in Chapter 12.

- **CIA Rebels** - Certain rebel elements of the CIA, namely E. Howard Hunt and Frank Sturgis, were also associated with both Ruby and Oswald and were involved in the JFK assassination as outlined in Chapter 12.

SEQUENCE & RESULTS OF FOUR SHOTS FIRED FROM THREE LOCATIONS

Shot #1

This photo by the author from the 'Oswald' window suggests the first shot couldn't have come from this location because the Zapruder film shows JFK reacting before he emerges from behind the tree foliage.

Based on an oak tree blocking out the assassin's view from the sixth-floor window of the Book Depository Building at the time of the opening shot (left), we must consider that the first shot came from the second floor of the Dal-Tex Records Building, close to and adjacent to the Book Depository.

Given the apparent reaction by President Kennedy on film upon being struck by the non-lethal shot that hit him in the upper back, the limousine's position on Elm Street at the time of that shot is inconsistent with a shot from the so-called 'Oswald' window.

Shot #2

This shot came from the sixth-floor window of the Book Depository Building by an unknown assassin.

Upon being hit in the upper back by the first shot, President Kennedy slumped forward in his seat. Although President Kennedy was the only target, his movement resulted in Governor Connally being exposed and hit by the second shot fired.

This shot struck Connally in the upper back, broke off four inches of his fifth right rib, exited his chest on the right side just below the nipple, went on to strike his right wrist, causing a compound fracture of the distal radius bone, exited his wrist and went on to imbed itself into the Governor's left inner thigh.

Shot #3

This is the fatal shot that came from behind a picket fence on the grassy knoll, located to the right-front of the President's car.

As Mrs. Kennedy was trying to render aid to her stricken husband, this missile entered President Kennedy's head just above his right ear, causing a massive exit wound at the right-rear of his skull.

The impact of this head shot prompted similar physical reactions from three different people that indicate the death shot could only have come from the front:

1. **JFK's Head Movement** – The President's head moves violently backward and to the left as an immediate and direct result of the impact.

The stoic First Lady.

2. **Mrs. Kennedy** – To retrieve a piece of her husband's skull, Mrs. Kennedy instinctively climbs out onto the trunk of the limousine in pursuit of the flying debris that was propelled backward upon impact.

3. **Officer Hargis** – Riding at the left-rear bumper of the Presidential limousine, over Jackie's left shoulder, motorcycle copy Bobby Hargis is hit so strongly by the President's blood and brain matter, he instinctively identifies the shot as having come from the right of the car on the grassy knoll.

Shot #4

Occurring less than ½ second after the fatal head impact, the fourth and final shot came from the Book Depository Building sixth-floor window.

The violent rearward movement of JFK's head after the third shot causes this shot to miss its mark, as well as other occupants in the limousine.

It is likely that this shot struck pavement ahead of the limousine and caused a cement fragment to hit bystander James Tague on his right cheek.

Decades later, James Tague points to where a bullet or cement fragment struck him during the shots in Dealey Plaza.

Within a few seconds of the fourth shot, The Zapruder film shows Secret Service agent Clint Hill jump onto the trunk of the limousine, take hold of Mrs. Kennedy, push her into the back seat and spread himself on top of her and the wounded President while the car sped to Parkland Hospital.

Sadly, just 30 minutes later, the 35th President of the United States was pronounced dead.

WHY WE MAY NEVER KNOW THE TRUTH

As you can see, inconsistences are the only consistency of JFK's assassination all these years later.

Evidence, such as the President's brain, have gone missing, denying us answers to questions that have endured far too long.

Despite scientific and medical advances, such as DNA, as well as tests that might reveal truths about bullets, fragments and bullet

Unfortunately, the JFK assassination has become a cottage industry.

trajectories, we are at a loss to explain why such tests have yet to be applied.

History is worth our every effort to set it straight. It is why we cannot rest so long as the truth remains elusive.

It is completely unrealistic to one day expect President Kennedy's perfectly preserved body to be exhumed so that a proper forensic examination can correct the blundered autopsy performed the night of his death.

As of now, we must be content with occasional updates of the event in hopes that one day, history will finally be able to tell the truth.

To that end, the final chapter discusses the frightening alliance that appears most likely responsible for killing President Kennedy.

Hopefully, this book contributes to the discussion and helps to bring us a step closer to the true facts pertaining to the greatest crime of the 20th century.

HISTORY TRUMPED?

For conspiracy theorists, there is the hope of October 26, 2017 when thousands of sealed documents are scheduled for release via the JFK Assassination Records Act of 1992.

But with the uncertainty enveloping the Trump White House and the awful 'impeachment' word being bandied about, it is unclear if and how President Trump will release these historic papers.

This long-awaited event will be documented on the author's web site – ThroughTheOswaldWindow.com.

Perhaps our one remaining hope is the original 2038 scheduled release of thousands of still classified documents sealed in the National Archives in Washington.

Until then…and possibly beyond, we will continue to discuss the assassination of President John F. Kennedy for what we still don't know about it.

How sad for history.

Through The 'Oswald' Window

Chapter 12

Oswald, Ruby and the Robert Kennedy Revenge Alliance that Assassinated JFK

Who assassinated President John F. Kennedy on November 22, 1963?

All these decades later, the murder of the 20th century remains, for the most part, an unsolved mystery.

The Warren Commission Report of 1964 says that Lee Harvey Oswald, acting alone, fired all the shots that tragic day in Dallas.

It further concluded that Dallas nightclub owner Jack Ruby also acted individually when he shot and killed Oswald two days later, a murder recorded live on television for the first time ever.

The House Select Committee on Assassinations (HSCA) report of 1978 also says that Oswald was the lone assassin, but had conspiratorial help in planning the assassination.

But the HSCA report says that Ruby did not likely act strictly on his own when he gunned down Oswald in the basement of the Dallas police station.

So, while the official government versions of President Kennedy's assassination have changed over the years, we are left to piece the puzzle together very slowly as the Freedom of Information Act forces merely a trickle of classified documents from the National Archives in Washington.

If this is ever going to change, it could occur in October of 2017 when the JFK Records Act of 1992 will prompt the release of some 3,600 classified documents pertaining to the events surrounding November 22, 1963.

However, skeptics are quick to point out that the same Act permits federal agencies to further delay release of JFK documents if they perceive the documents would cause "identifiable harm" that is greater than the public's right to know.

The Archives also houses more than 40,000 JFK documents that are heavily redacted to the point of uselessness. The

Assassination Archives and Research Center is attempting to have the documents un-redacted and deemed subject to release through the same JFK Records Act.

COMRADE OSWALDOVICH?

If this is accomplished, one area of intrigue is Oswald's apparent trip to Mexico City just eight weeks before he allegedly shot JFK.

In 2017, A&E's History Channel ran a six-part docuseries titled JFK Declassified: Tracking Oswald, verifying that Oswald visited both the Cuban and Soviet embassies in late September.

Show host Bob Baer, a former CIA counterintelligence officer and contributor to CNN, along with retired LAPD Lieutenant Adam Bercovici, suggest that Oswald may have met with KGB operative Valery Kostikov, the Soviet Union's covert director of sabotage and assassinations. He was stationed in Mexico City at the time.

However, the meeting did not go well, according to KGB officer Oleg Nechiporenko, who claims to have been at the meeting.

He asserts that Oswald demanded a VISA to return to the Soviet Union and when told he would have to apply at the Russian Embassy in Washington, he became angry.

Oswald started crying and even pulled out a revolver (there were no metal detectors back then). *"He was a time bomb,"* Nechiporenko told Baer.

Baer's team was given limited advanced access to classified CIA and FBI files on Oswald scheduled to be released on October 26, 2017.

A September 28 meeting at the Soviet consulate in Mexico City suggested a possible affiliation between Oswald and the KGB, which Nechiporenko denied.

Given Oswald's emotional outburst, Bob Baer's instincts and training in the CIA put him in agreement. Oswald was not a KGB agent or informant.

Due to the print schedule of this book, as CIA and FBI classified files are released in 2017 pertaining to Oswald's life in Russia and his activities in the weeks before the assassination, they will be discussed on the author's website – www.ThroughTheOswaldWindow.com.

TWO CONSPIRACIES

But we are no longer guaranteed that the truth will ever come out because there were 'two' conspiracies at play the moment Oswald was killed. He died proclaiming his innocence, leading us to believe he would have pled "not guilty" in a court of law.

We are left to ponder these two conspiracies:

1. The conspiracy to assassinate the President of the United States.
2. The conspiracy to cover it up.

For decades, conspiracy theorists, me among them, have been mocked and ridiculed for daring to shed doubt on the official findings of the Warren Report.

But over time, the intermittent release of information has favored conspiracy over the lone nut theory.

So, what happened that fateful day?

And more importantly, what happened in the aftermath that caused the truth to be so sensitive to 'national security' that President Johnson felt it necessary to impose a 75-year ban on thousands of relevant documents, most notably FBI, CIA and Naval Intelligence files?

I believe the truth can be found somewhere between the findings of the Warren Report and the HSCA report, starting with this one essential finding based on my unique perspective from the so-called 'Oswald' window:

Lee Harvey Oswald was involved in the assassination of President Kennedy, but he did not fire any shots from the Book Depository sixth-floor window, or any other location for that matter.

So far, history has been divided into these two schools of thought:

A) Oswald acted completely alone.

B) Oswald fired three shots from the Book Depository window, but a shot also came from the grassy knoll, denoting a conspiracy.

My own study of the assassination, since I was 13 years old in 1965, compels me to offer up a five-part option 'C' as follows:

C) Two shots came from the Book Depository window, but were not fired by Lee Harvey Oswald.

A single shot came from the Dal-Tex Records Building, on the northeast corner of Houston and Elm Streets, directly across from the Book Depository Building. This shot was not fired by Oswald.

The fatal shot came from the behind a picket fence on the grassy knoll, to the right front of the President's limousine. This shot was not fired by Oswald.

A clandestine alliance of people conspired to assassinate JFK, all of them rogue elements of powerful organizations unified by events in early 1960's Cuba.

The late Fidel Castro was not directly involved in the plot to kill his American adversary.

However, if rebel CIA operatives and betrayed anti-Castro Cubans had suddenly targeted JFK after the Cuban Missile Crisis, Castro would have taken delight in knowing that the people that once tried to assassinate him were now gunning for the U.S. President.

Oswald was involved in the assassination, but not as a shooter.

I believe his role, as a Book Depository employee, was to ready the sixth-floor southeast corner window as a sniper's perch for one of the three designated assassins.

When he lived to be arrested and proclaimed himself to be a "Patsy," Jack Ruby was sent in by the conspirators to silence Oswald because a public trial could not be allowed.

And there is a bombshell associated with point 'C' above, which is:

Robert Kennedy unwittingly played a key role in the assassination of his own brother!

Did Robert Kennedy unwittingly bring about his brother's assassination?

It was something that would haunt him for the rest of his short life until he met the same fate as Jack.

Some Kennedy circle insiders have hinted that a big motivation for Bobby Kennedy seeking the presidency in 1968 was because that, only as President, could he see all the classified JFK assassination files stored away by presidential seal.

Let's start with this deadly alliance, especially the two most infamous characters known to be involved.

A MOST CLANDESTINE ALLIANCE

In Chapter 3, we learned how Jack Ruby used his Dallas police connections to become the perfect hitman for the Mafia.

History changed in 1978 when the House Select Committee on Assassinations (HSCA) ruled that the Warren Commission Report of 1964 was wrong.

In changing the historical record, HSCA chief council G. Robert Blakey stunned the world when he told ABC News "I see Jack Ruby's assassination of Lee Harvey Oswald as a mob hit."

Unfortunately, the HSCA report also left a lot of unanswered questions because it could not categorically name the people or organizations behind the assassination of the President.

And it could not name the second shooter it concluded fired at least one shot from the grassy knoll area.

Running out of time and money, the HSCA at least tried to identify the many components of the assassination plot, but could not piece them together.

Consequently, still decades later, the JFK assassination, in large part, remains a mystery.

However, if we delve into the Warren Report, the HSCA report and examine the thousands of documents since released to the public via the Freedom of Information Act, we can start connecting some very interesting dots, such as a most telling alliance.

THE OSWALD-MARCELLO-RUBY CONNECTION

Marcello thug Jack Ruby	*Marcello 'Patsy' Lee Harvey Oswald?*	*Mob boss Carlos Marcello.*

After the Texas Court of Criminal Appeals ruled in 1966 that Jack Ruby did not receive a fair trial that sentenced him to the electric chair, while awaiting a retrial, Ruby makes a rare statement to the press as follows:

"Everything pertaining to what's happening has never come to the surface. The world will never know the true facts of what occurred – my motives. The people who had so much to gain, and had such an ulterior motive for putting me in the position I'm in, will never let the true facts come above board to the world."

Reporter – *"Are these people in very high positions, Jack?"*

Ruby – *"Yes."*

This is quite contrary to the Warren Commission finding that Ruby was so distraught by the killing of President Kennedy, he 'impulsively' shot Oswald to spare Jackie Kennedy the ordeal of having to appear at a trial.

Despite a newspaper article found in Ruby's apartment after the Oswald shooting that reported Mrs. Kennedy would be allowed to submit a video deposition as a witness rather than be compelled to return to Dallas, the Commission declared 'Case Closed' and essentially concluded:

> *Jack Ruby was an emotionally overcome lone nut who killed the lone nut who killed the President!*

Ruby's somewhat discombobulated statement above raises some provocative questions, such as:

1. What undisclosed motives for his actions is he talking about?

2. What people had *"ulterior motive for putting me in the position I'm in?"*

3. Who are the people *"who had so much to gain"* that *"will never let the true facts come above board to the world?"*

One such shady person that comes to mind is Carlos Marcello, the top crime boss of both Texas and Louisiana for almost 30 years.

The Warren Commission completely dismissed Marcello as anything but a person at personal feud with Attorney General Robert Kennedy.

G. Robert Blakey (center) with HSCA members declared a conspiracy to kill JFK, but couldn't name those involved.

The House Select Committee on Assassinations, I learned during my month of attending the hearings as a reporter, would name Marcello as a crime boss who "*Had the motive, the opportunity and the means in Lee Harvey Oswald to kill him* (JFK)."

MARCELLO – KENNEDY BAD BLOOD

Carlos Marcello hated the Kennedys, especially Attorney General Robert F. Kennedy, who first knocked heads with Marcello on March 24, 1959.

A.G. Bobby Kennedy's feud with Mafia led to JFK's death?

Marcello appeared before a Senate Committee investigating organized crime. With Senator John Kennedy sitting beside him, special council Robert Kennedy questioned Marcello about his mob history and associates.

To every question, Marcello invoked the fifth amendment because an honest answer might tend to incriminate him.

When JFK won the presidency the following year, he named Robert Kennedy as his Attorney General. On April 4, 1961, after less than three months in office, one of his first acts, without due process, was to have Marcello deported to Guatemala, Marcello's stated homeland.

Within months, Marcello was back in the United States. By this time, the Attorney General's office was really applying the heat to organized crime, especially Jimmy Hoffa and the Teamster's Union.

In an FBI wiretap, Marcello is heard threatening JFK. He tells Teamsters private investigator Edward Becker that while he hates Robert Kennedy...

"A dog will continue to bite you if you cut off its tail whereas if you cut off the dog's head, it would cease to cause you trouble."

Even with a motive clearly established, it is highly unlikely Carlos Marcello could have ordered and planned the 'hit' on the President on his own.

He didn't have to.

In hating the Kennedys, Marcello associated himself with other like-minded crime syndicate bosses who had their own agendas.

'GOOMBA' SANTO AND SAM

It was Meyer Lansky who partnered with Marcello to buy several casinos in the New Orleans area. Lansky was also near the top of Bobby Kennedy's most wanted list.

And it was Lansky who helped bring Florida mafia kingpin Santo Trafficante into the plan.

It is this connection that would eventually cause Jack Ruby to take his place in history. Are these the powerful people that Ruby was referencing in his strange comments to the press?

Florida mafia chief Santo Trafficante felt betrayed by the Kennedys.

Trafficante and Lansky had been casino partners with Cuban dictator Fulgencio Batista, who had allowed the mafia to build and operate a bustling Havana gambling empire, lining his own pockets quite nicely with the arrangement.

When Fidel Castro led the revolutionary overthrow of Batista, he turned the casinos into state-owned operations, deported Meyer Lansky and imprisoned Santo Trafficante.

Meyer Lansky unifies mafia bosses Marcello and Trafficante.

Curiously, researchers have uncovered reports that none other than Jack Ruby made several short trips to Havana, with prison guards reporting that they saw Ruby visit Trafficante in jail on numerous occasions.

During the early stages of the Kennedy presidency, Lansky and Trafficante were convinced they would soon be back in control of their confiscated casinos in Cuba. They believed this for two reasons:

1. The CIA had enlisted their support in helping to fund a coup against Castro to be led by Juan Almeida, a high-level Cuban army commander who was not pleased with Castro's broken promises once he assumed power.

Even though this plan had the blessing of JFK, government funding could not be tied to such an unofficial clandestine operation.

With millions of dollars being lost every passing month by the mafia casino stakeholders, funding the coup attempt seemed like a wise investment.

2. Trafficante and Lansky had a powerful ally in Chicago crime boss Sam Giancana, who believed he had the Kennedy boys in his back pocket.

It was Giancana who put the full force of his crime family to work in the 1960 election, conjuring up strong voting for Democratic candidate John F. Kennedy.

In winning the popular vote quite handily in Illinois, former Richard Nixon aide Pat Buchanan told CNN's Sixties docuseries that a post-election investigation noted a "particularly lively voting turnout in the cemetery districts."

Like Trafficante and Lansky, Sam Giancana thought his election 'favor' for patriarch Joe Kennedy would pave the way for prosperous times.

The Kennedy boys were now in the White House and not much fallout had come of the Organized Crime hearings.

ULTIMATE BETRAYAL

Chicago mob boss Sam Giancana betrayed by the Kennedy brothers?

When President Kennedy named brother Robert as Attorney General, he quipped "*I see nothing wrong with giving my brother*

Bobby some practical, legal experience as Attorney General before he goes out to practice law."

RFK nemesis James Hoffa, Teamsters head.

Many laughed at the President's light-hearted jab over the public outcry of nepotism, but it is safe to surmise that Carlos Marcello was not laughing the slightest bit.

Instead of looking the other way, Marcello, Lansky, Trafficante and Giancana became prime targets of a new Justice Department division created to go after organized crime.

Mafia friend Jimmy Hoffa became a primary target of the Attorney General's office and when the hot-tempered Teamsters boss engaged in a very public feud with the top lawman in the land, his mobster buddies became very nervous.

Although Hoffa also hated the Kennedy brothers, he was always considered too unstable to involve him directly in the eventual plot to kill the President.

Yet, Hoffa's access to union pension fund money would prove to be helpful in the secret CIA plots against Castro.

While the Castro attempts were in the works, the mafia quartet were between a rock and a hard place.

They didn't like the actions against organized crime by the Attorney General's office, but the pending removal of Castro would be highly lucrative and the illegal gambling goings on would be out of U.S. jurisdiction.

GAMBLE DOESN'T PAY OFF

Two historic events changed everything:

First, the Bay of Pigs invasion on April 17, 1961, not only failed to oust Fidel Castro, the CIA, working covertly with these organized crime leaders, laid the blame at the doorstep of JFK.

Fidel Castro survived several CIA-Mafia assassination attempts and died of natural causes at age 90 in late 2016, almost to the day 53 years after JFK died.

At the last moment, feeling misled by CIA intelligence, Kennedy ordered aerial plane support for the invading anti-Castro rebels to stand down.

Thus, hundreds of rebel freedom fighters, trained by the CIA and funded by mob money, were no match for Castro's forces. They were all either captured or killed without advancing beyond the beach.

Despite this public setback, other secretive operations were still underway, specifically targeted to assassinate Castro.

The Cuba-linked Mafioso's had little choice but to remain patient. That is until…

The Cuban Missile Crises of 1962 ended peacefully with President Kennedy publicly promising to never invade Cuba as part of his peace accord with Soviet Premier Nikita Khrushchev.

Imagine the anger of the mafia chieftains when they realized that their business interests in Cuba was formally gone.

CHANGE OF TARGET

Carlos Marcello and Santo Trafficante felt betrayed by the Kennedys, but by this time, Marcello was also personally feeling the heat of the Attorney General.

He decided there was only one way to fight back.

In that FBI surveillance recording, Marcello had mentioned to Ed Becker that "*A nut would have to be brought in to take the fall.*"

That lone nut would be a family member of one of Marcello's most successful bookmakers.

ENTER LEE HARVEY OSWALD

Admittedly, there is no beyond-a-doubt proof that Charles 'Dutz' Murret ever introduced his nephew Lee Oswald to Marcello. Murret was an underling to Marcello associate Sam Saia, a top Marcello lieutenant in New Orleans.

Yet, it is also a possibility that it happened, given the opportunity while Oswald lived in New Orleans.

When Oswald returned from living in the Soviet Union with his Russian bride, they moved in with the Murret family while Lee looked for a job.

It is certainly reasonable to assume that Oswald knew who his uncle worked for.

Marguerite Oswald's brother-in-law was Charles Murret, a New Orleans bookmaker linked to Carlos Marcello.

And it's also reasonable to surmise that Oswald would have known of the problems Marcello was having with the Kennedys.

Further, it's possible that Marcello knew that Murret's nephew Lee had lived in the Soviet Union and renounced his U.S. citizenship.

Perhaps for entirely different reasons, Oswald and Marcello were both displeased with the U.S. government, giving them a common adversary.

Much is subject to speculation, but if Marcello knew through Murret about Oswald's communist past, and perhaps even that Oswald had tried to murder ultra right-wing retired General Edwin A. Walker (See Chapter 2), what better way to take the heat off a possible organized crime connection when the named assassin can be labelled a 'Cold War' communist sympathizer?

We do know that Dutz Murret was unable or refused to help implicate his nephew Lee as the sole assassin, claiming that

Oswald's actions and behavior while living in the Murret home were uneventful.

Subsequently, the Warren Commission concluded that Oswald's time in New Orleans had little, if any bearing, in the assassination of President Kennedy.

PONDER THIS...

Carlos Marcello is heard on FBI surveillance tapes voicing his desire for JFK to be killed...

...And then the President is assassinated...

...The President's assassin, according to the government's investigation, turns out to be a family member related to a bookie in New Orleans working for none other than Carlos Marcello!

What are the odds of that merely being a coincidence?

ANOTHER OSWALD – MARCELLO LINK

New Orleans District Attorney Jim Garrison.

Jim Garrison, New Orleans District Attorney after the assassination and after the Warren Report was released, uncovered another link between Marcello and Oswald.

As verified by House Select Committee on Assassinations (HSCA) investigators, Oswald had links with a most unusual character named David Ferrie.

Ferrie was a private investigator for Carlos Marcello deportation lawyer W. Wray Gill. He was a former pilot for Eastern Airlines, who was dismissed for violations of the company's morality policies. He was a homosexual.

Several witnesses told the HSCA in 1978 that Oswald and Ferrie were both members of the New Orleans Civil Air Patrol going back to the mid 1950's.

By this time, both men were quite easy to identify. Oswald had become infamous as JFK's assassin and Ferrie was most unusual looking. He had no hair whatsoever, so he pasted on fake eyebrows and a red wig that hardly looked natural.

David Ferrie - Link to Marcello & Oswald?

It is believed that Oswald was in Ferrie's guerilla warfare boot camps in the Lake Pontchartrain area of Louisiana, sponsored by the CIA.

Oswald (far right) and Ferrie (far left) knew each other as far back as 1955.

As shown in the photo at left, a 15-year-old Lee Oswald (far right) is about to chow down with fellow Civil Air Patrol mates, led by David Ferrie (far left).

Ferrie took up the cause of recruiting and training anti-Castro rebels for a CIA-planned attack on the shores of the Bay of Pigs.

This was a splinter group called the Cuban Democratic Revolutionary Front of New Orleans. By this time, it is likely that Ferrie and Oswald were ideologically and geographically worlds apart.

Ferrie had become angry that Castro had chosen Communism's way of life for his people, so he took up the anti-Castro cause.

Oswald had defected to the Soviet Union and renounced his U.S. citizenship at the U.S. consulate in Moscow, but was somehow allowed to be reinstated as a U.S. citizen in good standing less than two years later and returned home.

Once back at home and living with his uncle Dutz Murret, Oswald took up the pro-Castro cause, helping to create the 'Fair Play for Cuba Committee' in New Orleans.

It is here that the link between David Ferrie and Lee Oswald gets cold, except for that one name that pops up – Carlos Marcello.

Conveniently hiding behind lawyer-client privilege, G. Wray Gill never spoke of Marcello's tie to David Ferrie, but one key possibility emerges.

Marcello was literally escorted to the airport and deported by Justice Department officials on orders from Robert Kennedy, but how did Marcello secretly get back into the country several months later?

Since all parties are now deceased, it is likely to remain a coincidence that Marcello's deportation lawyer just happened to have an investigator on the Marcello payroll who happened to be a skilled airline pilot – David Ferrie!

THE RUBY MOB CONNECTION

While Marcello's battle with Robert Kennedy was more personal in nature, to Florida mob boss Santo Trafficante, his hatred of JFK was mostly business based on betrayal.

Trafficante had much to lose when Castro deposed Batista in 1959. Similarly, he had much to gain with CIA plans to make Castro's reign on the island a short one.

When President Eisenhower and Vice-President Nixon hatched the planned Bay of Pigs invasion, Trafficante and his fellow mobsters held hopes of reclaiming their lucrative casino operations in Havana.

Newly elected President Kennedy green-lighted the plan to move forward, fanning Trafficante's hope, but as the date approached, JFK became skeptical of CIA intelligence based on what he believed to be an under-manned invasion.

Sensing that Castro's forces were much superior and better armed for a guerilla warfare attack, Kennedy pulled the promised air cover at the 11th hour, thereby condemning the anti-Castro rebels to a quick defeat.

Trafficante saw it as a betrayal since he was helping to fund and arm the anti-Fidel freedom fighters that were being trained at secretive CIA camps in Marcello territories.

Not only did Ruby establish ties via a few visits to the imprisoned Trafficante in Havana, the HSCA suspects Ruby of being a gun-runner between Dallas and New Orleans where much of the rebel training was taking place.

This gives Ruby a connection to both Trafficante and Marcello. Out of old-fashioned gangland respect and courtesy, Trafficante would never have conducted any kind of business in the two states under Marcello's control without his blessing.

Although Ruby was a low-level gangster, his top boss was Marcello. The HSCA found it unlikely that Ruby became a nightclub operator in Dallas by his own undertaking.

A carousel club operation, in strategic cities, was not only ideal fronts for bookmakers and pimps, food, alcohol and exotic dancers were routinely used assets to get in the good graces with police, judges and local lawmakers.

As discussed in chapter 3, there is no other way of explaining how Ruby avoided such intense police security at the cop station when he casually walked into the basement at the precise time that Oswald was being transferred.

Enter Ruby and exit Oswald!

SUSPICIOUS PHONE CALLS

There is no greater hint of Jack Ruby's ties to the key JFK assassination mafia kingpins than the unexplained upsurge in phone calls between Ruby and well-known mobsters leading up to the President's visit to Dallas.

While the Warren Report found no Ruby links to organized crime except long-severed boyhood activities in Al Capone's Chicago, the HSCA found that Ruby was a career mob thug with ties to Marcello, Trafficante, Jimmy Hoffa and even his old backyard, namely Sam Giancana and Johnny Roselli in Chicago.

Jack Ruby's phone records show a long history with some shady characters, but the volume of calls to fellow gangsters mysteriously surge in October and November of 1963.

From May to September of 1963, a total of approximately 35 calls were made to criminal types.

However, in the month of October alone, there were nearly 75 calls made. In the first 21 days of November, before JFK was killed on the 22nd, a total of 96 phone calls were made to or received from these notorious figures, among several others:

Hoffa tough guy Barney Baker had several pre-assassination phone calls with Jack Ruby.

• **Barney Baker** – An ex-boxer, ex-convict and close associate of Teamster's boss Jimmy Hoffa. A behemoth of a man at more than 350 pounds, he was Hoffa's 'muscle.'

RFK's justice department identified Baker as Hoffa's ears and mouth to sordid Mafia leaders.

Ruby's phone records show several lengthy phone discussions with Baker in the weeks leading up to the assassination, including back-to-back Chicago-Dallas exchanges on November 7 and 8.

When Ruby's apartment was searched after the Oswald shooting, Barney Baker's name and three associated phone numbers were found in a notebook. The handwriting was traced to Ruby.

• **Nofio Pecora** – A loyal Marcello associate, whose friend, Emile Bruneau, was the person who bailed Oswald out of jail in New Orleans after a publicized scuffle between Oswald (Fair Play for Cuba Committee) and anti-Castro activists.

• **Dave Yaras** – Started with Ruby as a petty criminal in Chicago, but rose to become a lethal 'contract' killer for Carlos Marcello. In 1962, Yaras is heard on FBI surveillance tapes bragging about his assorted 'hits' for Marcello.

- **Dusty Miller** – A top Hoffa confidante and head of the Teamster's southern conference. He was known as a 'ball buster' union boss who kept the troops rallied behind Hoffa despite the heat he was attracting from RFK's Justice Department.

- **Lewis McWillie** – A frequent associate of Jack Ruby, who moved from Dallas to Havana in 1958 to take care of the casinos owned by Santo Trafficante and Meyer Lansky. Ruby and McWillie are reported to have met oftentimes in both Dallas and Havana, where cash and guns often changed hands.

- **Lenny Patrick** – Justice Department files attribute more than 12 mob deaths at the hand of Lenny Patrick, who worked specifically for Sam Giancana in Chicago.

  He became a 'capo' in the family (Made Man in charge of a crew). Given Patrick's high standing, it's not likely that any significant phone or in-person business between Ruby and Patrick would have gone unknown to Giancana.

RUBY – MARCELLO LINK

It is highly unlikely that a low-level thug like Ruby had direct access to Marcello. There would have been one or more go-betweens, who were identified by Marcello biographer John H. Davis as these two Dallas crime family leaders:

Dallas top mobster Joe Campisi visited Ruby in jail after Oswald shooting.

- **Joe Campisi** – While operating Campisi's Egyptian Lounge in Dallas since 1946, Campisi grew in Dallas crime family stature until becoming top boss in 1973.

  He was one of Ruby's closest friends, with two direct get-togethers between November 21 and November 30, 1963.

On the night before JFK was assassinated, Ruby had dinner at Campisi's restaurant. And it was Campisi who visited Ruby in the Dallas County Jail within a week of him shooting Oswald.

- **Joe Civello** – Dallas crime syndicate from 1956 until his death in 1970, making him Marcello's top representative in Dallas. Civello was the 'boss' who would have had to OK Jack Ruby's nightclub in his territory.

RFK JR. STUNNER

Robert F. Kennedy Jr. has publicly confirmed that his father was not at all put at ease by the findings of the Warren Report,

RFK Jr. says his dad suspected mafia ties in JFK murder.

quoting his father as calling it a "Shoddy piece of craftsmanship."

RFK Jr. told Charlie Rose of ABC News in front of a live audience that neither he or his assassinated father believed the lone gunman theory.

Bobby Kennedy Jr. also confirmed that his father was somewhat intrigued by New Orleans District Attorney Jim Garrison's investigation, especially Oswald and Ruby links to the underworld.

Kennedy said his dad put investigators on it, per an ABC News report the next day.

"When they examined Jack Ruby and Lee Harvey Oswald's phone records, they saw what was essentially 'an inventory of the Mafia leaders that they had been investigating for the past two years' at the Justice Department," says Robert Kennedy Jr.

PHONE TAP CONFESSION

More than any other Mafia kingpin, the myriad of phone calls and other circumstantial evidence makes Louisiana and Texas godfather Carlos Marcello the primary force behind the assassination of President Kennedy.

Even he says so.

Lamar Waldron, author of Legacy of Secrecy, scoured through FBI files in the National Archives and found this most startling 1985 taped confession by Marcello:

"Yeah, I had the son-of-a-bitch killed. I'm glad I did. I'm sorry I couldn't have done it myself!"

Carlos Marcello died in 1993 without further known comment or ever having been brought to justice for the assassination of President Kennedy.

Interestingly, the Marcello-Trafficante link to the JFK assassination first came to the FBI's attention in 1975 when the government agency taped a conversation between the two mafia chieftains soon after Jimmy Hoffa went missing.

On that tape, Trafficante is heard to say, "*Now only two people are alive who know who killed Kennedy.*"

THE CUBA CONNECTION

The diverse Mafioso alliance that resulted in one of the darkest days in American history had one point of commonality – Early 1960's Cuba.

Let's connect the mafia dots at the highest possible level – the godfathers themselves:

Carlos Marcello

As a favorite target of Attorney General Robert Kennedy, Marcello felt double-crossed by the Kennedy brothers, who, at the very least, were turning a blind eye to CIA-Mafia efforts to assassinate Cuban dictator Fidel Castro.

If anything, Marcello felt that the Kennedy's were indebted to him. After all, Marcello had allowed anti-Castro militants to set up secretive CIA training camps on his territory near New Orleans.

And Marcello was allowing his underlings, like Jack Ruby in Dallas, to stockpile weapons for the planned attacks. This is a possible link between Ruby's many underground phone contacts in Dallas and New Orleans.

One of Marcello's closest kingpin allies was Santo Trafficante of Tampa, Florida, who had his casinos confiscated by Castro in 1959.

Once let out of prison and banished back to the U.S., Trafficante had no trouble calling in a favor from his long-time mafia friend, who shared an immense dislike of the Kennedys.

There is no evidence to support the notion that Marcello would also financially gain if the mafia regained control of the casinos in Havana, but both were equally motivated to work together in a plot to get rid of Bobby by first getting rid of Jack.

Meyer Lansky

Lansky was a mafia financial wizard who orchestrated the first mafia-owned casinos outside of Las Vegas. It was Meyer

Lansky who partnered with Cuban dictator Batista to build and co-own four casinos in Havana between 1955 and 1958.

As the Havana casino empire grew, Lansky brought in fellow mob boss Santo Trafficante to help operate the ventures while Lansky mostly oversaw the financial aspects, including the skimming of profits and payouts to Batista.

When Castro gained control of the island and nationalized the casino properties, Lansky was sent packing to Las Vegas. Like Trafficante, Lansky hoped to get his casinos back via the CIA assassination plots against Castro.

Strangely, there is little evidence that Lansky had a direct hand in the CIA assassination plots, or the subsequent plot to kill JFK.

Instead, being the financial mastermind, he seemed more interested in maintaining a close relationship with the deposed Batista, no doubt hoping to pick up where they left off once Batista was back in power.

It never happened.

An interesting footnote – In 2016, once the U.S. restored diplomatic relations with Cuba after more than 50 years, Lansky's children and estate filed a legal suit, claiming more than $70 million from the Cuban government as compensation for the casinos "illegally" taken from Meyer Lansky, the original and legitimate owner.

Santo Trafficante

Santo Trafficante and Carlos Marcello are directly linked together by Meyer Lansky, who owned and operated casinos in Louisiana with Marcello and casinos in Havana with Trafficante.

Once Batista had let Lansky and Trafficante into Cuba to develop and run all gambling operations, Trafficante, in particular, considered Cuba to be an extension of his mafia empire just 50 miles to the north, in Florida.

Needless to say, when it was all taken away from him literally overnight, he was not pleased.

Trafficante got to know Jack Ruby through fellow godfather Sam Giancana's associates Lenny Patrick and Dave Yaras in Chicago, as well as Marcello associate Lewis McWillie in Dallas.

When McWillie left Dallas to work for Trafficante and Lansky in Havana, it is believed that his old friend Ruby was brought in to help the flow of guns and cash to and from Cuba and mainland U.S.

In 1977, Trafficante was summoned to appear before the House Select Committee on Assassinations, which wanted to know these specific things:

Question – *"Prior to November 22, 1963, did you know Jack Ruby?"*

Question – *"While you were in prison in Cuba, were you visited by Jack Ruby?"*

Question – *"Did you ever discuss with any individual plans to assassinate President Kennedy?"*

Per his rights to not incriminate himself, Trafficante answered these questions by citing the First, Fourth, Fifth and Fourteenth Amendments to the U.S. Constitution.

At least Trafficante got to testify before the Committee hearings. Chicago mob boss Sam Giancana and his top lieutenant Johnny Roselli were not as fortunate.

1975 was not a good year for conspiracy theorists as three of four of the mafia alliance believed to have been involved both directly and indirectly were silenced forever.

In addition to the mob hits on Giancana and Roselli, Hoffa went missing with no signs of him to-date. Santo Trafficante was the benefactor of the removal of his three amigos, especially as Roselli started to talk to reporters like Jack Anderson of the Washington Post.

Sam Giancana & Johnny Roselli

The relationship between Sam Giancana and papa Joseph Kennedy is irrefutable. Many believe that without Giancana's help in Illinois, JFK would have lost the close 1960 election to Richard Nixon.

This mafia-political odd couple was no more important to anyone than Santo Trafficante, who had lost millions of dollars

Top Chicago mobster Johnny Roselli.

in the two years since being 'relieved' of his casinos and imprisoned by new dictator Fidel Castro.

And when Robert Kennedy's Justice Department went after Illinois 'capo' Johnny Roselli and his boss, Sam Giancana, the double-cross was set.

352

Giancana sought to remind JFK directly that he owed his presidency to him. He did that by sharing a lover named Judith Campbell Exner with the playboy President.

Campbell Exner (below) became a go-between, passing messages back and forth between her two powerful bedmates.

The plan did not work. Kennedy accepted Giancana's mistress gift, but would not call off his brother's pursuit of the Chicago gangsters.

Judith Campbell Exner shared a bed and messages with mobster Sam Giancana and President Kennedy.

Yet another betrayal occurred in the eyes of Giancana that may have sealed the fate of President Kennedy.

It is believed that in the early months of JFK's occupancy of the White House, patriarch Joe Kennedy had arranged for Giancana and Roselli to team up with Trafficante to help organize and fund clandestine CIA operatives planning to 'take out' Fidel Castro.

We can assume that JFK knew of his father's backroom arrangement with the head of the Chicago syndicate, but many Kennedy insiders deny it.

Regardless, this covert favor went either unknown or unappreciated by the Kennedy brothers. The heat of the Justice Department stayed on organized crime in Chicago.

And it is reported that after a couple of failed attempts to poison Castro, efforts continued until the Bay of Pigs fiasco and the Cuban Missile Crisis combined to change U.S. policy. Castro would be allowed to rule his rebel island, but suffer American isolationism as his punishment.

Coincidentally or not, after the President's assassination, Giancana and Roselli would avoid prosecution, but would not celebrate long lives like Carlos Marcello and Santo Trafficante.

Just before Giancana and Roselli were to testify about the Castro assassination attempts before the Senate Intelligence Committee in 1975, both were found murdered in classic gangland style, as noted previously.

CIA REBELS

For the record, it needs to be stated that the Central Intelligence Agency (CIA) was not formally involved in the assassination of President Kennedy.

That theory continues to have life because after the Bay of Pigs debacle, JFK felt so misinformed about the invasion that he fired CIA Director Allan Dulles and operations chief Richard Bissell.

Privately, Kennedy threatened to *"Shatter the CIA into a thousand pieces and scatter it into the winds."* It never happened.

In a twist of historic irony, the fired Allan Dulles would become one of the seven Warren Commission members that investigated the assassination of President Kennedy.

We now know that both the FBI and CIA were not forthcoming with any information to the Warren Commission that:

A) Would dispel any notion that both Lee Oswald and Jack Ruby acted alone.

B) Would implicate either agency in clandestine activities that could be related to the assassination.

Some historians believe that Dulles was assigned to the Warren Commission to act as a censure of information that would be

eventually submitted to the Commission.

As for the FBI, it was considered the chief investigative arm of the Warren Commission and therefore all its reports and findings went unquestioned.

THE HIDDEN CIA

Although CIA involvement in the Bay of Pigs is well established, a second clandestine operation was also underway.

This was not a CIA sanctioned 'black-op,' but rather it was undertaken by 'rebel' CIA operatives who privately trained Cuban exiles expressly to kill Fidel Castro.

While most of these 'operatives' have remained underground, a few interesting names have come to light, all of whom trained anti-Castro freedom

The 'tramp' on the right was arrested after JFK shooting and believed to be CIA agent E. Howard Hunt, also of Watergate fame.

fighters and took part in the Bay of Pigs, hence their anger toward JFK.

- **E. Howard Hunt** – A long-time CIA employee (1949-1970), Hunt appears to have been the CIA liaison with Vice-President Nixon during the planning stages of the Bay of Pigs.

Photographic experts have identified Hunt as one of the three 'tramps' arrested in Dealey Plaza after the assassination, only to be released without being booked. Hunt has also been closely aligned with former President George H.W. Bush when he was CIA Director.

Hunt was later charged with helping to plan the infamous Watergate break-in despite being retired. He served 33 months in prison for his crimes.

- **Frank Sturgis** – Not only was Frank Sturgis heavily involved in the anti-Castro movement, he was a notorious 'dark-ops' specialist in Latin American countries.

  Known as a guerilla warfare expert, Sturgis admitted to being involved in the Bay of Pigs invasion and the training of Cuban exiles.

  In 1975, the Rockefeller Commission concluded that Sturgis was never a CIA agent, yet served time in jail with CIA planner E. Howard Hunt after being caught as one of the five Watergate burglars.

  Sturgis has also been identified as the middle tramp shown on the page above, who was arrested with Hunt in

Dealey Plaza, only to be released with no record of detainment by Dallas police.

- **William Harvey** – A career CIA operative, Harvey is believed to be the man who initiated the Castro assassination plots and recruited friend Johnny Roselli into the plan, thus bringing the powerful Mafioso into play.

  E. Howard Hunt claims that 'outlaw' CIA associate Harvey was instrumental in the target being shifted from Castro to Kennedy in 1963.

  At around the same time, Harvey found himself 'promoted' to CIA station chief in Italy. There is no evidence that Harvey had any further personal involvement with his plan to assassinate Kennedy.

  Instead, Harvey left behind a unit of rebel CIA operatives and organized crime associates, all still fanatically opposed to the Castro regime in Cuba.

It should be noted that before his death in 2007, Hunt wrote 'American Spy – My Secret History in the CIA, Watergate & Beyond.' In his memoir, he names several former CIA agents as being involved in the JFK assassination, but says he only had a "peripheral" involvement himself.

IN SEARCH OF A CONCLUSION

The truth of what happened that awful day in Dallas has alluded us for decades. History may never reveal the truth.

Even more troublesome is the cover-up that ensued, especially if what is presented here is eventually accepted as the truth.

So why cover it up?

Can you imagine the fallout if it was discovered that the United States government was in the assassination business?

And even more alarming, what would the public think if they found out that the CIA was working in cahoots with organized crime in carrying out assassination attempts against Fidel Castro?

And most alarming of all, what would the repercussions be for the public to learn that this unwholly alliance changed targets from a foreign leader to the President of the United States?

From the JFK assassination in 1963, the Martin Luther King and Bobby Kennedy assassinations in 1968, Watergate in 1972, the Iran-Contra scandal of 1986 and beyond, Americans are no longer shocked to learn that their government officials lie, act illegally and try to cover it up.

If the above scenario is the shock that has been kept from us all these years, it's time for the U.S. government to come clean.

We can handle the truth.

Even more importantly, when we show that we can handle the truth, we will show future governments that we are always deserving of the truth.

Through the 'Oswald' Window

Sources and References

Note: To access live links for these reference materials, visit the author's website (www.ThroughTheOswaldWindow.com/resources).

Introduction – A History Changing 'Ah-Ha' Moment

- Time Magazine List of 10 Most Enduring Conspiracy Theories http://content.time.com/time/specials/packages/completelist/0, 29569,1860871,00.html
- JFK Researcher Mark Lane - https://www.amazon.ca/s/ref=nb_sb_noss?url=search-alias%3Dstripbooks&field-keywords=mark+lane+jfk+assassination
- JFK Researcher Penn Jones Jr. - https://www.amazon.com/Books-Penn-Jones-Jr/s?ie=UTF8&page=1&rh=n%3A283155%2Cp_27%3APenn%20Jones%20Jr
- JFK Researcher Mary Ferrell - https://www.maryferrell.org/pages/JFK_Assassination.html
- JFK Researcher Dr. Cyril Wecht - https://www.amazon.com/s?ie=UTF8&page=1&rh=n%3A2831 55%2Cp_27%3ACyril%20Wecht
- JFK Researcher Robert J. Groden - https://www.amazon.com/Robert-J.-Groden/e/B001IZ1CCG
- List of Warren Commission Witness Testimony - https://www.jfk-assassination.com/warren/wch/index.php

- New York District Attorney Re-Opens Dorothy Kilgallen Cold Case - http://nypost.com/2017/01/29/manhattan-das-office-probing-death-of-reporter-with-possible-jfk-ties/

Chapter 1 – The Day I Discovered that Oswald Nor Anyone Else Could Have Been JFK's Lone Assassin!

- The Sixth Floor Museum at Dealey Plaza - http://www.jfk.org/
- Robert J. Groden Website - http://www.jfkmurder.com/
- Mark Lane's 'Rush to Judgement' on Video - http://www.imdb.com/title/tt0060920/
- Oswald Did Not Act Alone – courtesy The Fedora Chronicles - http://thefedorachronicles.com/rants/2014/2014_11_22-oswald-did-not-act-alone.html
- 1964 CBS Documentary on the Warren Report – courtesy Hidden Passage YouTube Channel - https://www.youtube.com/watch?v=rQCgQsgCyMY
- House Select Committee on Assassinations Report - http://www.maryferrell.org/showDoc.html?docId=800

Chapter 2 - Oswald a Serial Killer?

Does Slain Cop J.D. Tippit and Targeted General Walker Point to Oswald as JFK's Assassin?

- Oswald in custody – "I'm just a patsy!" – courtesy Youxsearch Channel - https://www.youtube.com/watch?v=IQZ7W6ZeePA
- Deposition of Marina Oswald Porter before HSCA hearings – Wednesday, August 9, 1978, pages 382-384 - https://www.aarclibrary.org/publib/jfk/hsca/reportvols/vol12/pdf/HSCA_Vol12_MarinaOswald.pdf

- Did Oswald Kill J.D. Tippit? – courtesy of 22November1963.org -_http://22november1963.org.uk/did-lee-harvey-oswald-kill-officer-jd-tippit
- Oswald's Marine Rifle Training – Volume 13 of Warren Report - https://www.archives.gov/research/jfk/warren-commission-report/appendix-13.html#marines
- With Malice: Lee Harvey Oswald and the Murder of Officer J.D. Tippit - https://www.amazon.com/Malice-Harvey-Oswald-Murder-Officer/dp/0966270975
- Warren Commission Testimony of Officer Marrion Baker – Vol. III, page 242, Vol. VII, page 592
- Carolyn Arnold FBI Statement, March 1964 – Oswald on First Floor - http://22november1963.org.uk/carolyn-arnold-witness-oswald
- Johnny Brewer Testimony to Warren Commission About Oswald Arrest – April 2, 1964, Vol. VII, Page 1 - http://mcadams.posc.mu.edu/russ../testimony/brewer_j.htm

Chapter 3 – Jack Ruby:

From Goodfella's Kid to the Mafia's Most Notorious Hitman?

- https://www.youtube.com/watch?v=B_aNNQpgSS4 – courtesy of Saintly Oswald Channel
- Anthony Summers and Robbyn Swan Blog – Nov. 23, 2013 - https://anthonysummersandrobbynswan.wordpress.com/2013/11/23/the-claims-that-mafia-bosses-trafficante-and-marcello-admitted-involvement-in-assassinating-president-kennedy/
- Ruby Silences Oswald – courtesy of Mr. Kesselring's Video Channel -_https://www.youtube.com/watch?v=0xU7Lhd7Wwo
- G. Robert Blakey interview on ABC News - http://abcnews.go.com/WNT/story?id=131462&page=1

- Nov. 12, 2013 by Joseph A Palermo, historian, author & professor - http://www.huffingtonpost.com/joseph-a-palermo/the-50th-anniversary-of-t_3_b_4262826.html
- The Assassination - 35th Anniversary Edition – published by Texas Monthly - http://www.texasmonthly.com/issue/november-1998/
- Why Did Jack Ruby Kill Lee Harvey Oswald – courtesy of Quora.com - https://www.quora.com/JFK-Assassination-November-1963-Why-did-Jack-Ruby-kill-Lee-Harvey-Oswald
- Mafia-Cuba Gambling Connections - Carlos Rodrigues Martorell – New York Daily News staffer - http://www.nydailynews.com/latino/book-reveals-extent-mafia-cuban-empire-article-1.350649
- Marcello Confession - Jan. 06, 2009 Page Six Blog - http://pagesix.com/2009/01/06/jfk-assassination-confession/
- The Marcello-Hoffa Connection – courtesy of Spartacus-Educational.com -_http://spartacus-educational.com/JFKmarcello.htm
- Seth Kantor Testimony to Warren Commission about Seeing Jack Ruby at Parkland Hospital - http://aarclibrary.org/publib/jfk/wc/wcvols/wh15/pdf/WH15_Kantor.pdf
- The Ruby Cover-Up – By Seth Kantor, 1978 by Zebra Press - https://www.amazon.com/Ruby-Cover-Up-Who-Was-Jack/dp/0890836809
- Jack Ruby Testimony to Warren Commission, June 7, 1964, Appendix 17 – https://www.archives.gov/research/jfk/warren-commission-report/appendix-17.html

Chapter 4 – The Magic Bullet!

The Bullet They Say Acted Alone
so that History Could Say
Lee Harvey Oswald Acted Alone

- Interview with Dr. Cyril Wecht – January 8, 2017
- Warren Commission Findings of Shots Fired, Origin of Shots Fired and Results of Shots Fired - http://mcadams.posc.mu.edu/russ/infojfk/jfk6/timing.htm
- Sibert and O'Neill FBI Autopsy Report - http://22november1963.org.uk/sibert-and-oneill-report
- What is the Single Bullet Theory? – courtesy of LiveScience.com - http://www.livescience.com/41369-single-bullet-theory-jfk-assassination.html
- The Magic Bullet: Even More Magical Than We Knew? – courtesy of History-Matters.com - https://www.history-matters.com/essays/frameup/EvenMoreMagical/EvenMoreMagical.htm
- Dr. Malcolm O. Perry Testimony Before the Warren Commission - https://www.history-matters.com/archive/jfk/wc/wcvols/wh6/pdf/WH6_Perry.pdf
- No Proof for Arlen Specter's 'Magic Bullet' Theory – courtesy of WND.com - http://www.wnd.com/2013/09/no-proof-for-arlen-spectors-magic-bullet-theory/
- Dr. James J. Humes Testimony Before Warren Commission – Vol. 2, Page 348 – courtesy of jfk-assassination.com - https://www.jfk-assassination.com/warren/wch/vol2/page348.php
- The Killing of a President – The Complete Photographic Record of the Assassination, the Conspiracy and the Cover-Up – by Robert J. Groden - https://www.amazon.com/Killing-President-Photographic-Assassination-Conspiracy/dp/0140240039

- Governor John Connally Testimony Before the Warren Commission – Vol 4, Page 129 - http://mcadams.posc.mu.edu/russ/testimony/conn_j.htm
- Mrs. Nellie Connally Testimony Before the Warren Commission – Vol. 4, Page 146 - http://mcadams.posc.mu.edu/russ/testimony/conn_n.htm

Chapter 5 – The Bizarre JFK Autopsy that Failed History and the Truth

- Interview with Dr. Cyril Wecht – January 8, 2017
- Dr. Pierre A. Finck Testimony Before the Warren Commission – Vol. 2, Page 377 - http://www.history-matters.com/archive/jfk/wc/wcvols/wh2/pdf/WH2_Finck.pdf
- Commander Thornton J. Boswell Testimony Before the Warren Commission – Vol. 2, Page 376 - http://www.history-matters.com/archive/jfk/wc/wcvols/wh2/pdf/WH2_Boswell.pdf
- Dr. Malcolm O. Perry Testimony Before the Warren Commission - https://www.history-matters.com/archive/jfk/wc/wcvols/wh6/pdf/WH6_Perry.pdf
- Sibert and O'Neill FBI Autopsy Report - https://www.history-matters.com/archive/jfk/arrb/master_med_set/md44/html/Image1.htm
- Dr. Cyril Wecht Testimony Before House Select Committee Hearings on Assassinations – Vol. 1, Page 332 - https://www.history-matters.com/archive/jfk/hsca/reportvols/vol1/html/HSCA_Vol1_0168b.htm
- Warren Commission Report – Appendix IX – JFK Autopsy Report – courtesy of Archives.gov - https://www.archives.gov/files/research/jfk/warren-commission-report/appendix-09.pdf

- David W. Mantik, M.D. Ph.D. Review of JFK Autopsy Materials – courtesy of AssassinationResearch.com - https://assassinationresearch.com/v2n2/pittsburgh.pdf
- Attorney Mark Lane Denied Oswald Family Request for Representation Before the Warren Commission - http://spartacus-educational.com/JFKlaneM.htm
- Testimony of Secret Service Agent Clint Hill Before the Warren Commission – courtesy of JFKLancer.com - http://www.jfklancer.com/CHill.html

Chapter 6 – The Zapruder Film:

The Shocking 26-Second Home Movie that Won't Let History Be a Lie!

- Camelot's Court: Inside the Kennedy White House – by Robert Dallek - https://www.amazon.com/Camelots-Court-Inside-Kennedy-White/dp/006206584X
- Twenty-Six Seconds: A Personal History of the Zapruder Film – by Alexandra Zapruder - https://www.amazon.com/Twenty-Six-Seconds-Personal-History-Zapruder/dp/1455541699
- Dan Rather Describes His Viewing of the Zapruder Film – courtesy of the JFK Assassination Forum - https://www.youtube.com/watch?v=LuHdK-4M1Wc
- Zapruder Film Shown for First Time on Good Night America – Courtesy of David Von Pein's JFK Channel - https://www.youtube.com/watch?v=nxCH1yhGG3Q
- The Zapruder Film: Capturing When the World Changed in 26 Seconds – courtesy of CBS.News.com - http://www.cbsnews.com/news/the-zapruder-film-capturing-when-the-world-changed-in-26-seconds/
- The Zapruder Film – Played at Dave O'Brien JFK Assassination Seminars – Through the Oswald Window

YouTube Channel –
www.youtube.com/watch?v=UBKliGNC49c – With thanks to
Penn Jones Jr. and Robert J. Groden

- The Abraham Zapruder Film – courtesy of the Sixth Floor
  Museum at Dealey Plaza - http://www.jfk.org/the-
  collections/abraham-zapruder-film/
- Edward J. Epstein – First Journalist to Dispute Warren
  Commission -
  https://en.wikipedia.org/wiki/Edward_Jay_Epstein
- The Zapruder Film Digitally Remastered – courtesy of the
  World Public Union YouTube Channel -
  https://www.youtube.com/watch?v=P74Q2NUBmGk
- Dr. Malcolm Perry's Statement to the House Select Committee
  Hearings on Assassinations - https://www.history-
  matters.com/archive/jfk/hsca/reportvols/vol7/pdf/HSCA_Vol7_
  M59If_Perry.pdf
- Robert Groden Interview with WhoWhatWhy.org -
  http://whowhatwhy.org/2016/11/22/longtime-jfk-assassination-
  researcher-may-never-know-truth/
- Mary Ferrell Foundation Explains Single Bullet Theory -
  https://www.maryferrell.org/pages/Single_Bullet_Theory.html
- Governor John Connally Testimony Before House Select
  Committee Hearings on Assassinations – Vol. 1, Pages 11-29
  - https://www.history-
  matters.com/archive/jfk/hsca/reportvols/vol1/html/HSCA_Vol1_
  0008b.htm
- Secret Service Agent William Greer Testimony Before the
  Warren Commission – Vol II, Page 112 -
  http://mcadams.posc.mu.edu/russ/testimony/greer.htm
- Jacqueline Kennedy Testimony Before the Warren
  Commission – June 5, 1964 -
  http://www.jfklancer.com/jbk_wc.html

- Sworn Statement of Secret Service Agent Clint Hill – November 30, 1963 - https://www.history-matters.com/archive/jfk/wc/wcvols/wh2/html/WC_Vol2_0070b.htm
- Orville Nix Film – courtesy of JFK Assassination Truth Channel - https://www.youtube.com/watch?v=GU4mAVCprAU

Chapter 7 – The Top 8 Indicators That the Fatal Shot Did Come from the Grassy Knoll

- Interview with Dr. Cyril Wecht – January 8, 2017
- Sam Holland Testimony – Warren Commission Hearings, Vol. 7, page 243, April 8, 1964 - http://www.history-matters.com/archive/jfk/wc/wcvols/wh6/pdf/WH6_Holland.pdf
- 51 Witnesses – The Grassy Knoll, by Harold Feldman - http://www.jfk-online.com/jfk100knoll51.html
- Jay Watson Interview with Gayle and Bill Newman – Courtesy of JFK Assassination Forum - https://www.youtube.com/watch?v=e_MOc8mdNuE
- Why Didn't the Warren Commission Interview Billy Newman? – courtesy of JFK50d.blogspot.ca - http://jfk50d.blogspot.ca/2010/12/question-to-ponder9-why-did-warren.html
- Sworn Statement of Billy Newman – courtesy of McAdams.posc.mu.edu - http://mcadams.posc.mu.edu/russ../testimony/wnewman.htm
- Bobby Hargis testimony to Warren Commission – Vol. 6, page 294, April 8, 1964 - http://www.aarclibrary.org/publib/jfk/wc/wcvols/wh6/pdf/WH6_Hargis.pdf

- Robert J. Groden – The Killing of a President, pages 86 & 87 - http://www.barnesandnoble.com/w/the-killing-of-a-president-robert-j-groden/1114939523
- Lee Bowers Jr. Testimony Before the Warren Commission – April 2, 1964 – courtesy of Spartacus-Educational.com - http://spartacus-educational.com/JFKbowers.htm
- If JFK had Lived: 5 Ways History Would Change – by LiveScience.com -_http://www.livescience.com/41412-jfk-best-alternate-histories.html
- Crossfire: The Plot That Killed Kennedy – Ed Hoffman Interview with Author Jim Marrs, Pages 81-85 - https://www.youtube.com/watch?v=apMEs9xr-yo
- Acoustical Testimony of Dr. James Barger before the House Select Committee on Assassinations Hearings – September 11, 1978, Vol. 2, Pages 17-53 - http://www.history-matters.com/archive/jfk/hsca/reportvols/vol2/pdf/HSCA_Vol2_0911_4_Barger.pdf
- Dr. Cyril Wecht Testimony Before House Select Committee on Assassinations Hearings – September 7, 1978, Vol. 1, Page 332 - http://aarclibrary.org/publib/jfk/hsca/reportvols/vol1/pdf/HSCA_Vol1_0907_8_Wecht.pdf
- Dr. Robert McClelland on JFK Head Wound - by Philadelphia.cbslocal.com - http://philadelphia.cbslocal.com/2013/11/19/as-50th-anniversary-of-assassination-approaches-surgeon-who-treated-jfk-remembers/

Chapter 8 – The Three Arrested Tramps, the Disappearing Cop and Other Oddities of the JFK Assassination

- E. Howard Hunt's Deathbed Confession to His Son – courtesy of Anonews.com - http://www.anonews.co/jfk-murder-confession/
- The Last Confession of E. Howard Hunt – by Rolling Stone Magazine - http://www.rollingstone.com/culture/features/the-last-confession-of-e-howard-hunt-20070405
- Frank Sturgis Interview on Mary Ferrell Web site - http://www.maryferrell.org/wiki/index.php/Confession_of_Howard_Hunt
- Gaeton Fonzi – The Last Investigation - http://skyhorsepublishing.com/titles/11883-9781510713932-last-investigation
- James Leavelle Interview – www.mirror.co.uk/news/real-life-stories/james-leavelle-arrested-jfk-assassin-2711431
- Louie Steven Witt Testimony HSCA – The Umbrella Man – Vol. IV, Page 429 - http://www.history-matters.com/archive/jfk/hsca/reportvols/vol4/html/HSCA_Vol4_0217a.htm
- Who were the Three Tramps in Dealey Plaza? – by 22November1963.org. - http://22november1963.org.uk/three-tramps-in-dealey-plaza
- Affidavit of Howard Leslie Brennan – May 7, 1964 – courtesy of History-Matters.com - https://www.history-matters.com/archive/jfk/wc/wcvols/wh11/pdf/WH11_Brennan_aff.pdf
- Santo Trafficante Obituary in New York Times - http://www.nytimes.com/1987/03/19/obituaries/santo-trafficante-reputed-mafia-chief-dies-at-72.html

- Charles Harrelson Discusses JFK Assassination – by COPAorg YouTube Channel - https://www.youtube.com/watch?v=RpVlqh14WHY
- Oswald, the CIA and Mexico City – by PBS.org - http://www.pbs.org/wgbh/frontline/article/oswald-the-cia-and-mexico-city/

Chapter 9 – From Camelot to Cover-Up:

Ballistics Tests, Medical Findings & Photo Evidence Either Ignored or Altered to Suppress the Truth for 75 Years

- Entry Wounds Versus Exit Wounds Ballistic Test - http://www.aarclibrary.org/publib/jfk/wc/wcvols/wh17/html/WH_Vol17_0436b.htm
- AP Photographer James Altgens Photo - https://www.history-matters.com/archive/jfk/wc/wcvols/wh18/html/WH_Vol18_0054a.htm
- The Killing of a President by Robert J. Groden – Page 77 https://www.amazon.com/s/ref=nb_sb_noss?url=search-alias%3Daps&field-keywords=The+Killing+of+a+President+by+Robert+Groden
- Black and White Zapruder still frames published in Warren Report – https://www.historymatters.com/archive/jfk/wc/wcvols/ wh18/pdf/WH18_CE_885.pdf
- Dal-Tex Records Building Sniper Location - http://theconspiracyzone.podcastpeople.com/posts/60862
- The Robert Hughes Film - Courtesy JFK Assassination Truth YouTube Channel - https://www.youtube.com/watch?v=b9ZDVD-vq-w
- Physics and JFK Assassination: Final Evidence of a Second Sniper Behind the Stockade Fence – by Alberto Miatello –

GaryRevel.com -
http://garyrevel.com/jfk/PHYSICS_Proof_JFK_GrassyKnollSho
t.pdf

- The Case of JFK's Missing Brain – by theDailyBeast.com -
  http://www.thedailybeast.com/articles/2013/11/09/who-stole-
  jfk-s-brain.html
- Dr. Robert Shaw Testimony to the Warren Commission – Vol.
  VI, Page 83 -
  http://www.historymatters.com/archive/jfk/wc/wcvols/wh6/html/
  WC_Vol6_0047a.htm
- The Story of Dallas Motorcycle Cop Bobby Hargis – courtesy
  of the Welton Hartford YouTube Channel -
  https://www.youtube.com/watch?v=CfajL8aWMO8
- JFK and Governor Connally Bullet Fragments – by JFK-
  info.com - http://www.jfk-info.com/fragment.htm
- Nicholas deB Katzenbach Memo to Bill Moyers – Courtesy of
  22November1963.org -
  http://22november1963.org.uk/katzenbach-memo-moyers-
  warren-commission

Chapter 10 - The Mysterious Deaths of More than 100 People Linked to the JFK Assassination

- Hit List: An In-Depth Investigation into the Mysterious Deaths
  of Witnesses to the JFK Assassination – by Richard Belzer
  and David Wayne – https://www.amazon.com/Hit-List-Depth-
  Investigation-Assassination/dp/1634508521
- Jack Ruby's testimony before the Warren Commission June
  07, 1964 -
  http://mcadams.posc.mu.edu/russ/testimony/ruby_j1.htm
- Actuarial Study on JFK-linked Mysterious Deaths – by the
  Coalition on Political Assassinations -

https://politicalassassinations.net/2013/04/executive-action-jfk-witness-deaths-and-the-london-times-actuary/

- Robert F. Kennedy Jr. tells Charlie Rose that his father didn't believe Oswald acted alone - http://www.dallasnews.com/opinion/opinion/2013/01/12/what-to-make-of-rfk-jrs-conspiracy-view-of-the-jfk-assassination
- Carlos Marcello Discusses Killing the Tail of a Dog (Bobby) by Cutting Off the Head (the President) by Salon Magazine http://www.salon.com/2003/11/22/conspiracy_6/
- Witness Lee Bowers Jr. Murdered? – by AboveTopSecret.com - http://www.abovetopsecret.com/forum/thread710323/pg1
- Witness Hank Killam Murdered? – http://spartacus-educational.com/JFKjonesP.htm
- Warren Commission Member and Dissenter Hale Boggs Jr. – by Tripod.com - http://haleboggs.tripod.com/
- Chicago Mobsters Sam Giancana and Johnny Roselli Murders Linked to JFK Assassination Study – by JFK.Hood.edu - http://jfk.hood.edu/Collection/Weisberg%20Subject%20Index%20Files/R%20Disk/Roselli%20John/Item%2013.pdf
- New York District Attorney Re-Opens Dorothy Kilgallen Cold Case - http://nypost.com/2017/01/29/manhattan-das-office-probing-death-of-reporter-with-possible-jfk-ties/
- Dorothy Kilgallen Tried to Tell the Truth About JFK Assassination – courtesy of NYDailyNews.com - http://www.nydailynews.com/life-style/dorothy-kilgallen-expose-truth-jfk-assassination-article-1.2881474
- Witness Joseph Milteer Predicted JFK Death – by MaryFerrell.org - https://www.maryferrell.org/pages/Predictions_of_Joseph_Milteer.html
- Garrison Witness Eladio del Valle Murdered? – by Dick Russell – The Man Who Knew Too Much, Pages 292, 293 -

https://groups.google.com/forum/#!msg/alt.conspiracy.jfk/1PJA
2-ktrsM/cs4YRijp0KkJ

- Garrison Witness David Ferrie Link to Oswald and Marcello –
  by Nola.com -
  http://www.nola.com/politics/index.ssf/2013/11/jfk_assassinatio
  n_conspiracy_d_1.html
- The Guy Banister-Oswald-Ferrie Connection – by
  JFKonline.com - http://www.jfk-online.com/jfk100whoban.html

Chapter 11 - 12:30 p.m. CST:

What Happened in Those Six Seconds
That Changed American History Forever?

- HSCA Hearings – Sequence of Shots Fired -
  https://www.history-
  matters.com/archive/jfk/hsca/report/html/HSCA_Report_0055b
  .htm
- The Zapruder Film – Played at Dave O'Brien JFK
  Assassination Seminars – Through the Oswald Window
  YouTube Channel –
  www.youtube.com/watch?v=UBKliGNC49c – With thanks to
  Penn Jones Jr. and Robert J. Groden
- JFK's Plans for the War in Vietnam – by TheNation.com -
  https://www.thenation.com/article/jfks-vietnam-withdrawal-
  plan-fact-not-speculation/
- What if JFK Had Survived His Assassination? – by
  ConstitutionCenter.org -
  http://blog.constitutioncenter.org/2015/11/what-if-jfk-had-
  survived-his-assassination/
- Governor John B. Connally Testimony Before the Warren
  Commission – Vol. 4, Page 129 - https://www.jfk-
  assassination.com/warren/wch/vol4/page129.php

- Governor John Connally Never Believed the Warren Commission – courtesy of DemocraticUnderground.com - http://www.democraticunderground.com/discuss/duboard.php?az=view_all&address=125x302357
- Did Lee Harvey Oswald Get a Fair Trial? – by 22November1963.org - http://22november1963.org.uk/lee-harvey-oswald-fair-trial
- HSCA Concludes Elements of Organized Crime Involved in JFK Assassination – by Archives.gov - https://www.archives.gov/research/jfk/select-committee-report/part-1c.html#involvement4
- Did 3 Shooters Gun Down JFK? – by wnd.com - http://www.wnd.com/2014/09/did-3-shooters-gun-down-jfk/
- Lee Harvey Oswald – The Set-Up and Cover-Up – by MaryFerrell.org - https://www.maryferrell.org/pages/State_Secret_Chapter6.html
- Lee Harvey Oswald – "I'm Just a Patsy!" – by Reddit.com - https://www.reddit.com/r/conspiracy/comments/3glm7j/lee_harvey_oswald_im_just_a_patsy/
- Twenty-Six Seconds of the JFK Assassination – And a Lifetime of Family Anguish – courtesy of The Washington Post - https://www.washingtonpost.com/opinions/twenty-six-seconds-of-the-jfk-assassination--and-a-lifetime-of-family-anguish/2016/11/16/2b9f1c86-9547-11e6-bc79-af1cd3d2984b_story.html?utm_term=.7264a6ab615c
- Seth Kantor Testimony to Warren Commission about Seeing Jack Ruby at Parkland Hospital – Vol. XV, pages 80-82 - http://aarclibrary.org/publib/jfk/wc/wcvols/wh15/pdf/WH15_Kantor.pdf
- The Hitman and the Mobster: Jack Ruby and Santos Trafficante – by JFKfacts.org - http://jfkfacts.org/the-man-and-the-mobster-jack-ruby-and-santos-trafficante/

Chapter 12 - Oswald, Ruby and the Robert Kennedy Revenge Alliance that Assassinated JFK

- G. Robert Blakey Ties Mob to JFK Assassination in ABC News Interview -
  http://abcnews.go.com/WNT/story?id=131462&page=1
- Robert F. Kennedy Jr. tells Charlie Rose that his father didn't believe Oswald acted alone -
  http://www.dallasnews.com/opinion/opinion/2013/01/12/what-to-make-of-rfk-jrs-conspiracy-view-of-the-jfk-assassination
- Lamar Waldron – Legacy of Secrecy -
  http://www.legacyofsecrecy.com/
- Jack Ruby Phone Records – RFK Jr. Interview -
  http://jfkcountercoup.blogspot.ca/2013/01/oswald-and-ruby-phone-records-rfk-jr.html
- Essential Findings of the House Select Committee Hearings on Assassination of President Kennedy -
  https://www.archives.gov/research/jfk/select-committee-report/part-1c.html
- Deep Politics and the Death of JFK – by Peter Dale Scott -
  https://www.history-matters.com/pds/dp3.htm
- History Channel Series – JFK Declassified: Tracking Oswald – April 2017
  http://www.monstersandcritics.com/smallscreen/new-series-jfk-declassified-tracking-oswald-premieres-with-soviet-link-to-oswald/
- Oswald's Trip to Mexico City –
  www.throughtheoswaldwindow.com/articles/oswald-trip-to-mexico
- Oswald's Office of Naval Intelligence Records – by Coalition on Political Assassinations -
  http://archive.politicalassassinations.net/2013/02/oswalds-oni-records-revisited/

- Johnny Roselli Talks to Washington Post Reporter Jack Anderson - http://spartacus-educational.com/JFKroselli.htm
- Robert Kennedy Saw Conspiracy in JFK Assassination – courtesy of the BostonGlobe.com - https://www.bostonglobe.com/metro/2013/11/24/his-brother-keeper-robert-kennedy-saw-conspiracy-jfk-assassination/TmZ0nfKsB34p69LWUBgsEJ/story.html
- Robert F. Kennedy Believed JFK Was Killed Because of Him – courtesy of IrishCentral.com - http://www.irishcentral.com/roots/robert-f-kennedy-believed-jfk-was-killed-because-of-him
- RFK Struggled with JFK's Assassination – ABC News Report - http://abcnews.go.com/WNT/story?id=131457
- Attorney General Robert Kennedy's Feud with Teamster's Jimmy Hoffa – By KNKX.org - http://knkx.org/post/why-bobby-kennedy-went-after-teamsters-including-seattles-dave-beck
- CIA Connection with Juan Almeida and Jack Ruby – by FreeRepublic.com - http://www.freerepublic.com/focus/f-chat/1761442/posts
- Tina Sinatra Ties Father's Mob Connections to JFK Election – By ABC News - http://www.cbsnews.com/news/tina-sinatra-mob-ties-aided-jfk/
- The Marcello-Murret-Oswald Link – by TheMobMuseum.org - http://themobmuseum.org/notable_names/carlos-marcello/
- Did the Mob Do It? – By UPI.com - http://www.upi.com/The-Issue-The-Kennedy-assassination-did-the-mob-do-it/41021384680600/
- Did the Mob Kill Kennedy? – by The Washington Post - https://www.washingtonpost.com/archive/opinions/1979/02/25/did-the-mob-kill-kennedy/b684d171-36b7-474e-9f7d-40a619aede46/?utm_term=.192c4171bb11
- Jack Ruby's Link to the Mob – by ISGP-Studies.com - https://isgp-

studies.com/DL_1960s_70s_Jack_Ruby_Tom_Howard_Sam_
Giancana_Johnny_Roselli_Jim_Koethe_Bill_Hunter_deaths
- Mafia Kingfish – by John H. Davis -
http://www.goodreads.com/book/show/990184.Mafia_Kingfish
- Mob Connection to Havana Gambling – A History of the Year
1959 by Miles Bullough -
http://in1959.blogspot.ca/2010/02/downfall-of-havana-
mob.html
- Mob Hitman Confession – by Newsmax.com -
http://www.newsmax.com/Newsfront/john-kennedy-
assassination-confession-mafia/2014/11/20/id/608736/
- Revisiting Watergate – by The Washington Post -
http://www.washingtonpost.com/wp-
srv/onpolitics/watergate/howardhunt.html

Appendices

- Doctor Malcolm Perry Letters – Set of 3
- Dr. Perry Letters Donated by Dave O'Brien to the Sixth Floor
Museum at Dealey Plaza - http://www.jfk.org/
- The Mississauga News – February 21, 1979 – Black Day in
Dallas 15 Years Later

About the Author

- Consultant - Canadian Broadcasting Corporation 1983
Production – The Fifth Estate: Who Killed JFK? -
https://www.youtube.com/watch?v=h3xquKx4ttg
- The Mississauga Times – 14-part series on JFK assassination
– November 1972 – by Dave O'Brien
- The Mississauga News – February 21, 1979 – Black Day in
Dallas 15 Years Later – by Dave O'Brien

Appendices

Dr. Malcolm Perry Letters

Letter #1 of 3

Letter #2

15 Mar '72

Dear Mr. O'Brien,

I regret I can be of so little assistance to you, but as I noted, I have little information other than that already on record.

In many wounds the distinction between entrance and exit often turns on a change in the size, shape or axis orientation of the bullet. It is common in military situations, where full jacketed (and relatively undeformable) bullets are used) to note soft tissue tracts through which a pristine bullet, still oriented axially, can pass. In these cases the two skin wounds may be very similar. Also a fragment, at lower velocity, and smaller in shape, even cause confusion.

I have a rather wide range of experience with all types of bullet and knife wounds in humans, and considerable hunting experience. I also have hand-loaded my ammo for a variety of guns for 15 yrs or so, and have noted many interesting and

Letter #2 Page 2 of 3

occasionally confusing things about ballistics, and the vagaries of wounds and patients. It is easy to be misled, and difficult to be always right. I therefore clearly identified my opinions as exactly that, and not established fact. Dr. Carrico & I did not ever change any testimony, but the true autopsy findings (not the "unofficial" and speculative versions appearing in various magazines and papers) are not at variance with our observations. This does not confirm nor deny other theories, but only fails to preclude this explanation.

Had I taken the time to delay my vain effort at salvage, I could have carefully removed the blood from the wounds and measured them (I'm not even sure about actual size, only glancing at the wound), and I would have initially known of the posterior wound in the base of the neck. Since other things were more pressing, this data are not available, so I guess there will always be speculation, to what purpose I cannot imagine.

Letter #2, Page 3 of 3

It is of little importance to me what the motives of the sensationalist reporters are, but it would seem that each began with the initial premise that everyone was deliberately lying, and that the commission was seeking to obscure the real facts, and not trying to find the truth. I believe these assumptions to be unfounded, but I can't prove that either. It is always possible to assume a priori that someone is wrong or has ulterior motives, and then bias is introduced early. This often precludes objectivity, and as a scientist, I find these attitudes very disquieting.

I've really never understood why so many people want to believe that all official statements and opinions are base, and lies. It just might be that (like the blind man examining the elephant) each observer has stated his *opinion* (not fact) based on cursory exams in some cases, as honestly as possibly, and has not lied. It just might also be that the FBI, SS and commission were honest and tried to seek the truth. An exam of eyewitness testimony always disclosed discrepancies, even when the truth is known. I personally do not know exactly what happened, but have testified as to my observations and opinion, to add to the body of knowledge, and have not changed or falsified any facts.

Sincerely,
Malcolm Perry

Letter #3

MALCOLM O. PERRY, M. D.
5323 HARRY HINES BLVD.
DALLAS 35, TEXAS

16 Mar '72

Dear Mr. O'Brien

It seems almost redundant to point out that a bullet never travels exactly in a straight line, except at very high velocities. It is curved from its path by air, gravity, any obstruction. The passage of a bullet through tissue planes of varying toughness and hardness is obviously going to alter the trajectory, and in a three dimensional environment. It will be curved, perhaps more than once. This will be accentuated if the leading edge or part changes, enlarges, becomes deformed, and especially if the bullet tumples or fragments. Such capricious activity insures that any assumption of trajectory prediction in such situations is doomed to failure.

Perhaps these facts will also help your evaluation

MOPerry

Donation Acceptance Letter from Sixth Floor Museum at Dealey Plaza

December 14, 2010

Mr. Dave O'Brien

[address redacted]

Dear Mr. O'Brien,

Thank you very much for your recent donation of letters you received from Dr. Malcolm Perry regarding the assassination of President Kennedy. His replies to your inquiries, as a high school student, are certainly interesting and will likely be of help to future researchers and historians.

Thanks also for including a CD with scans of the letters, and also the envelope in which the last letter from Dr. Perry was sent. And the digital color photograph of you kneeling at the sniper's nest window in 1979 is especially interesting to me, for you were one of the relatively few who gained access to the building prior to it's opening as the Dallas County Administration Building.

Enclosed are two copies of our Gift Agreement form listing the items you donated. Please check them for accuracy, then sign and date both and return one to us in the enclosed envelope. That will complete your donation.

On behalf of The Sixth Floor Museum, thank you very much for your donation and your support!

Best regards,

Gary Mack
Curator

411 Elm Street • Dallas, Texas 75202 • 214-747-6660 • Fax 214-747-6662

Gift Agreement

411 Elm Street, Suite 120
Dallas, Texas 75202-3395
(214) 747-6660 (phone)
(214) 747-6662 (fax)

OFFICE USE ONLY	Approval Date:
Material:	Accession No.:
Donor:	No. of Items:
Collection Title:	Condition:
Copyright Owner:	Initialed:

GIFT AGREEMENT

Donor: Dave O'Brien

Address:

Phone:
Fax:
E-mail:

The Donor donates to The Sixth Floor Museum at Dealey Plaza (the "Museum") the following material (the "Material"): (See attached page if necessary)

Description	Condition
Three 1968 & 1972 laminated letters from Malcolm Perry to David O'Brien	Fair
One 1972 envelope to David O'Brien from the 1972 Perry letter	Fair
One photo CD of the Perry letters	Very good
One digital color photo of Dave O'Brien at sniper's nest window taken 2-11-79	Very good

1. The Donor hereby donates the Material to the Museum and assigns to the Museum all right, title, and interest that the Donor may possess in and to the Material, including, without limitation, all Copyright rights as enumerated in 17 United States Code §106, as well as any right to sue for past infringement thereof. These rights include, without limitation, the right to 1) reproduce, 2) make derivative works, 3) distribute the work by sale or other means, 4) perform the work publicly, 5) display the work publicly and 6) perform sound recordings by means of digital audio transmission. The Donor shall execute such further documents and perform such further acts as is reasonably necessary, useful or convenient to evidence or perfect the rights assigned herein.

2. The Donor warrants that they are the sole owner and have clear title to the Material. If this ownership is challenged in any way, the Donor will timely and diligently defend the title of the Material donated to the Museum.

3. The Donor wishes the gift to be acknowledged to the public as: The Dave O'Brien Collection.

4. The Museum acknowledges that the transfer of ownership will take place upon approval of the donation by the Museum's Executive Director.

5. The Museum is under no obligation to exhibit the donated Material either temporarily or permanently.

6. The Museum will have no obligation to retain any Material or the rights therein and may dispose of or modify any Material and the rights therein within the guidelines as approved by the Museum's Board of Directors.

411 Elm Street • Dallas, Texas 75202 • 214-747-6660 • Fax 214-747-6662

7. If this donation to the Museum is to be tax-deductible then it is the responsibility of the Donor to establish the value of the Material and to determine whether the gift complies with the applicable federal tax laws. The Museum does not make any representations regarding the value or deductibility of any Material.

8. This Agreement constitutes the entire agreement between parties and supersedes any previous written or oral agreements with regard to the subject matter hereof. No change, termination, waiver, amendment or modification of any of the provisions hereof shall be binding upon the parties, unless in writing signed by duly authorized representatives of the parties.

9. This Agreement shall be governed by and construed and enforced in accordance with the laws of the State of Texas, without regard to its principles of conflict of laws. Any suit or proceeding hereunder shall be brought **ONLY** in Dallas County, Texas, and each party consents to the personal jurisdiction of the courts, state and federal, located therein. Owner agrees to waive any objection that the state or federal courts of Dallas County, Texas, are an inconvenient forum.

X _____   X _____
Donor(s) Signature   Date

Print Name: _____

Acceptance of Gift Recommended By:

_____   Curator   11-2-10
Print Name: Gary Mack   Title   Date

Gift Accepted By:

_____   Executive Director   12/15/10
Nicola Longford   Title   Date

385

The Mississauga News:

Black Day in Dallas: 15 Years Later

Page 1 of 2

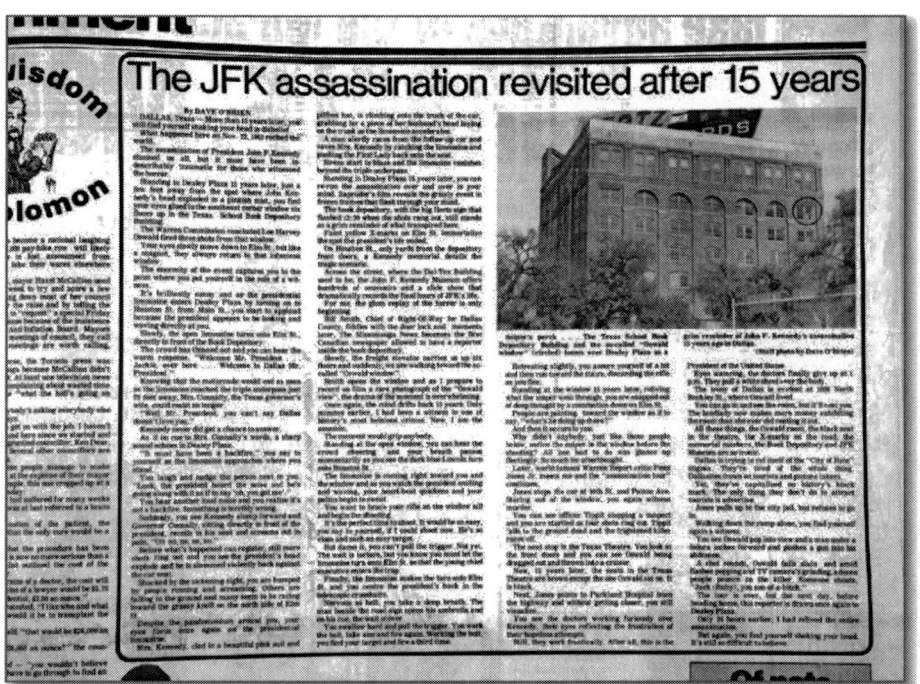

The JFK assassination revisited after 15 years

Page 2 of 2

About the Author

Dave O'Brien

JFK ASSASSINATION RESEARCHER

- Began studying the JFK assassination in 1965 at age 13.

- At age 13 and 14, read summary edition and 26 volumes of the Warren Commission Report.

- In grade 9, wrote a 100+ page history paper to establish reasonable doubt as would have been required at trial to find Lee Harvey Oswald not guilty as the assassin of President John F. Kennedy.

- Established a dialogue with Dr. Malcolm Perry between 1968 and 1972, the first doctor to tend to President

Kennedy at Parkland Hospital. The first letter is reproduced in Chapter 4 and all three letters are displayed in the Appendices section.

- The JFK assassination influences O'Brien to pursue a career in journalism.

- He spent most of his career as a journalist with the Metroland Group of Community Newspapers, which won several provincial, national and Suburban Newspapers of America (SNA) awards for excellence.

- 14-part series of articles – November 1972 in The Mississauga Times.

- Covered House Select Committee on Assassinations Hearings in Washington in 1978.

- February 11, 1979 – Granted rare access to the 'Oswald' window in the Texas School Book Depository Building.

- February 21, 1979 – 15th anniversary article in The Mississauga News featuring photos taken at the infamous 'Oswald' window (previous page). Full article in Appendices.

- Consultant to 1983 Canadian Broadcasting Corporation production – The Fifth Estate: Who Killed JFK? - https://www.youtube.com/watch?v=h3xquKx4ttg

- 1975 to 1999 – Presented JFK assassination seminars in Canada to audiences of eight to 1800 people.

- 2010 – Donated Dr. Malcolm Perry letters to Sixth Floor Museum at Dealey Plaza - http://www.jfk.org/ (Readable in Museum library).

- 2017 – Authored Through the 'Oswald' Window based on extraordinary observations from the assassin's position in the Book Depository Building, as well as more than 50 years of research, writings and seminars on the assassination of President John F. Kennedy.

O'Brien is also the author of a dating e-book for people over age 50. It is titled Over 50 Dating Secrets - https://www.amazon.com/Over-Dating-Secrets-Rediscover-Excitement-ebook/dp/B008MTE4MQ/

CPSIA information can be obtained
at www.ICGtesting.com
Printed in the USA
LVOW10s0955140717
541085LV00001B/3/P